COMPUTER STUDIES FOR YOU

Stephen Doyle

Hutchinson

London   Melbourne   Sydney   Auckland   Johannesburg

Acknowledgements

Thanks are due to the following for permission to reproduce photographs:

British Leyland pp.25, 131; British Telecom pp. 52, 165, 190, 191; Data General Ltd p.116; Digital Equipment Co. Ltd p.187; DS Ltd pp.99, 192, 193; Ferranti Computer Systems Ltd pp.57, 139, 184; Honeywell p.135; IBM pp.39, 40, 59, 60, 96, 97, 98, 100, 101, 102, 107, 109, 111, 112, 140, 156, 164, 174, 175, 176, 177, 178, 189; ICL pp.96, 110, 139, 155; Nottingham Building Society pp.159, 190; Philips p.56; Picker International p.186; Prestel pp.159, 160; Prism Consumer Products Ltd p.23; Rediffusion Computers Ltd p.136; Science Museum pp.91, 172, 173, 175, 176, 177; Tony Stone Associates pp.56, 98, 112; Richard Turpin p.103; Catherine Ursillo, SPL p.136; John Walsh, SPL p.60; Wayne Kerr Datum Ltd p.138; Willis Computer Supplies Ltd pp.101, 107, 111, 151.

Cover photo shows Omnibot Robot by Tomi.

Thanks are also due to the following for permission to reproduce past examination questions:

Associated Examining Board; Associated Lancashire Schools Examining Board; East Anglian Examinations Board; East Midlands Regional Examinations Board; Joint Matriculation Board; Liverpool Polytechnic Schools Education Centre; London Regional Examinations Board; North West Regional Examinations Board; Southern Regional Examinations Board; South Western Examination Board; University of Cambridge Local Examinations Syndicate; Welsh Joint Education Committee; West Midland Examinations Board.

Hutchinson Education

An imprint of Century Hutchinson Ltd
62-65 Chandos Place, London WC2N 4NW

Century Hutchinson Group Australia Pty Ltd
16-22 Church Street, Hawthorn, Victoria 3122, Australia

Century Hutchinson Group New Zealand Ltd
PO Box 40-086, Glenfield, Auckland 10, New Zealand

Century Hutchinson Group South Africa (Pty) Ltd
PO Box 337, Bergvlei 2012, South Africa

First published 1985
Reprinted (twice) 1986
© Stephen Doyle 1985

Designed and illustrated by
The Pen & Ink Book Co. Ltd

Cartoons drawn by Val Biro

Typeset in 11 on 13 pt Quorum by
The Pen & Ink Book Co. Ltd

Printed and bound in Great Britain by
Anchor Brendon Ltd, Tiptree, Essex

British Library Cataloguing in Publication Data

Doyle, Stephen
    Computer studies for you.
    1. Microcomputers
    I. Title
    001.64'04   QA76.5

ISBN 0 09 161261 6

Contents

1 Introduction _____ 7
Computers today
The uses of computers
Test yourself
Things to do

2 The computer itself _____ 10
What is a computer?
Information and computing
Hardware and software
Why use computers?
Input, process and output – the three stages of computing
Computers and memory
Test yourself
Things to do

3 Processing information _____ 14
Input, processing and output
Manual processing
Handling information
Test yourself
Things to do

4 Automatic processing _____ 18
What is automatic processing?
Some types of automatic processing
Complete control systems
Test yourself
Things to do

5 Robotics _____ 23
Robotics
Robots in the car industry
Test yourself
Things to do

6 Data sources _____ 26
Source documents
Form design
Coded information
Data created by equipment or machinery
Test yourself
Things to do

7 Flowcharts _____ 30
Flowcharts (or flow diagrams)
Computing flowcharts
Test yourself
Things to do

8 Data capture methods _____ 38
Indirect and direct methods of capture
Data capture methods which do not use any writing
Test yourself
Things to do

9 Data errors and source errors _____ 44
Transcription errors
Verification errors
Validation methods
Limitations of error checking
Test yourself
Things to do

10 Operating systems _____ 49
Simple program systems
Batch processing
Multiprogramming
Remote job entry
Multi-access
Real time operating systems
Remote access
Test yourself
Things to do

11 Output formats _____ 54
Printed output
Record storage using microfiche and microfilm
Screen output
Analogue to digital conversion
Test yourself
Things to do

12 The central processing unit (CPU) _____ 59
Inside the central processing unit
Large scale integration and chips
ROM and RAM
PROM and EPROM
The microprocessor
Test yourself
Things to do

13 Computer arithmetic _____ 63
Bistable systems
Storing information using a two state system
Number bases
Other number bases
Converting to and from binary

Binary arithmetic
Coding negative numbers
Test yourself
Things to do

14   Bits, bytes and words _____ **76**
Coding data
Bits, bytes and words
The computer and bits, bytes and words
Test yourself
Things to do

15   Computer logic _____ **79**
Electronic pulses
Logic gates
Chips
Logical elements
Logic diagrams
Other logic gates
Some other uses of logic diagrams
Test yourself
Things to do

16   Boolean expressions _____ **91**
Test yourself
Things to do

17   Computer peripherals _____ **96**
Peripheral devices
VDU and keyboard
Card readers
Punched tape readers (paper tape readers)
Document readers
Magnetic ink character readers (MICR)
Bar code readers
Printers
Graph plotters
Graphical display unit and light pen
Point of sale terminals (POS)
Test yourself
Things to do

18   Backing store _____ **107**
Magnetic tape
Magnetic disk
Floppy disks (diskettes)
Cassettes
Other backing store media
Test yourself
Things to do

19   Organization of data _____ **115**
How data is divided up
Key fields
Sorting and merging

Systems flowcharts
Updating
Some systems flowcharts
Test yourself
Things to do

20   Computer languages _____ **125**
Why we need computer languages
High level languages
Low level languages
Machine code
Test yourself
Things to do

21   Systems software _____ **128**
Translation software
Executive program or supervisor program
Test yourself
Things to do

22   Applications software _____ **131**
Applications packages from the manufacturer
who supplies the hardware
Employing programmers to write applications
packages
People in small businesses writing software
themselves
Documentation
Program libraries
Test yourself
Things to do

23   The people who work with computers _____ **134**
People who work inside the computer room
People who work with computers outside the
computer room
Test yourself
Things to do

24   Adopting a computer system _____ **144**
System analysis and problem identification
The feasibility study
Project approval
Designing a computer system
Training personnel
Writing instruction manuals and documenting
the system
Implementation
Monitoring the 'live' system
Test yourself
Things to do

25   Security and computer systems _____ **150**
Deliberate breaches of security
Accidental damage

The security of file data
Test yourself
Things to do

26 Wordprocessing _____ **154**
What is wordprocessing?
What are the advantages of wordprocessing?
Disadvantages of wordprocessing
The hardware of a wordprocessor
Software for wordprocessing (WP)
Test yourself
Things to do

27 Communication networks _____ **158**
Prestel (viewdata)
Ceefax and Oracle (teletext)
Prestel and the future
Test yourself
Things to do

28 Social implications _____ **163**
The impact on society of computers
The speed of change
Unemployment and computers
Improvement in working conditions
Trade union reactions to computers
Computers and privacy
Computers and crime
Test yourself
Things to do

29 The history of computers _____ **172**
The early calculator machines: cogs and levers
The beginning of data processing
Further developments in data processing with
punched cards
The development of electronics
The second generation of computers
1964 onwards: the third generation of
computers
Computers in the future
Test yourself
Things to do

30 Computer applications _____ **183**
Computers and the police force
Computers in medicine
Computers in dentistry
Computers in farming
Weather forecasting
Local authorities
Computers and banking
Computers in libraries
Computers in supermarkets

Test yourself
Things to do

31 Revision _____ **203**
Revising
Preparing for the exam
Project work
Careers in computing

32 Careers in computing _____ **213**

   Glossary _____ **214**

   Index _____ **218**

1
Introduction

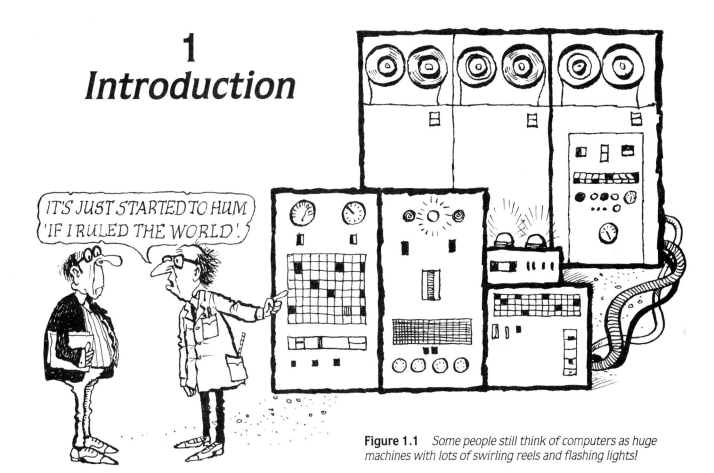

Figure 1.1 *Some people still think of computers as huge machines with lots of swirling reels and flashing lights!*

Computers today

If you think a computer is an unreliable beast that takes up a lot of space, has lots of flashing lights, swirling reels, and likes to live in an air-conditioned room, then you are out of date (Figure 1.1)!

Today, computers are compact systems – they don't take up much space. They are extremely efficient and reliable and are as much a part of our everyday life as washing machines and television sets.

Unfortunately, science fiction writers have given a lot of people the wrong impression about computers. Some people still think of them as electronic brains that can make things up and know what you are thinking. But this is not true. A computer is a machine. It can only do what it is told to do. It can only carry out instructions. It can't think up things for itself.

When people stop thinking of computers as mystery objects they can see how essential computers are. Now, most people don't see computers as a threat. Instead they realize that they are useful tools that can do many mundane tasks for them.

You may have heard computer studies being referred to as 'information technology'. Information is the key word. The world we live in is totally information based. Everything we do needs information whether we are applying for a driving licence or entering exams.

The human brain is an expert at collecting, storing and processing information. No computer can store as much information as our brain. Our brains can think intelligently – computers can't. Figure 1.2 shows some storage capacities. (A character is a letter of the alphabet, a number from 0 to 9, any punctuation mark or a space.) Computers are much faster than our brains, but as you can see from Figure 1.2, their storage capacity is much smaller.

Storage type	Capacity (millions of characters)
Human brain	125 000 000
USA National Archives	112 500 000
Encyclopaedia Britannica	12 500
Magnetic (hard) disk	313
Floppy disk	2.5
Book	1.3

Figure 1.2 *Types of information storage and their capacities*

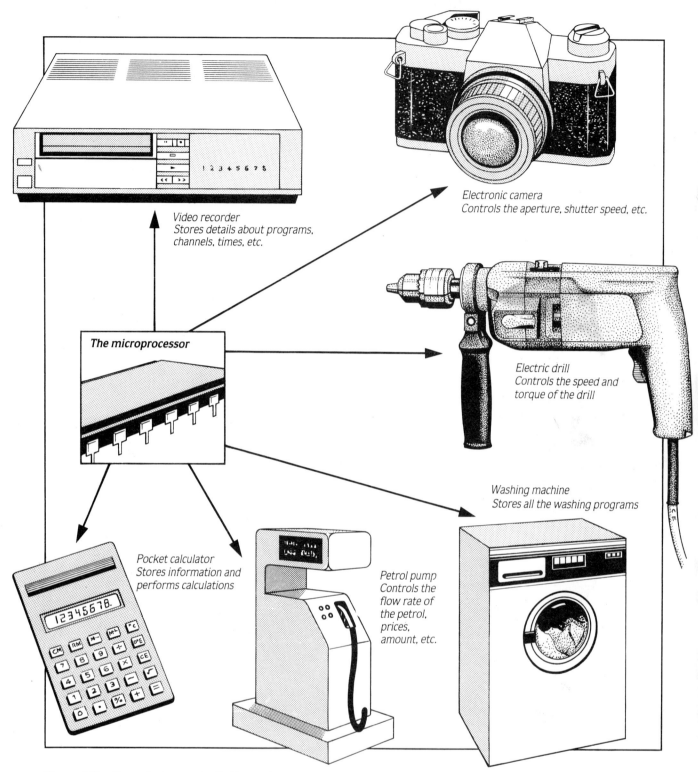

Figure 1.3 *Some devices controlled by a microprocessor*

The microprocessor

Video recorder
*Stores details about programs,
channels, times, etc.*

Electronic camera
Controls the aperture, shutter speed, etc.

Electric drill
*Controls the speed and
torque of the drill*

Washing machine
Stores all the washing programs

Pocket calculator
*Stores information and
performs calculations*

Petrol pump
*Controls the
flow rate of
the petrol,
prices,
amount, etc.*

The uses of computers

Today computers are used far more than they were
20 years ago. It would be hard now to imagine a
world without them. A lot of jobs that we take for
granted today would have been impossible without
computers. Two examples are travel in space and the
use of credit cards.

In the United Kingdom computer manufacture will
soon be a larger industry than car manufacture.
Computers are used for more and more tasks
because they have become smaller and cheaper over
the last 10 years. Computers are found in many
unlikely places such as cars, washing machines and
children's games.

None of this would have been dreamt of in the

1960s. The computer power in pocket calculators and small computers would have needed the space of a whole room then!

Computers have got smaller because of the silicon chip. All the components that are needed in a computer can now be etched onto a tiny piece of silicon. Every year the number of components we can put onto a chip doubles. Chip technology is responsible for all the things we now take for granted in computers: smaller size, larger storage capacity and reliability.

One type of chip is a **microprocessor**. This is a chip that contains all the electronic circuits for the **central processing unit** – the computer's 'brain'. The development of this chip has led to a lot of everyday things being controlled by computers. Microprocessors are used in cookers, video recorders, central heating timers, telephones, cars and many more (Figure 1.3). In fact, there is hardly any electrical device that couldn't have a microprocessor in it to make it run more efficiently.

Microprocessors can be used in industry too. For example, they can be used to control robots. Robots are already used in car manufacture. At British Leyland, side panels are welded together by a robot at a speed of 250 welds in 25 seconds. In the next few years industrial robots will be used in many of our factories.

Test yourself

Using the words in the list below, copy out and complete sentences A to F underlining the words you have inserted. The words may be used once, more than once or not at all.

larger   instructions   silicon   robots
information   smaller   microprocessor
machine

A A computer is only a ___machine___ that can carry out ___information___ ___instructions___
B ___ is the key word in computing.
C The storage capacity of a human brain is a lot ___small___ than the storage capacity of even the largest computers.
D Computers have become ___robu___ because of the invention of the ___silicon___ chip. ___micro___
E A type of chip called a ___silicon___ is used to control devices such as cookers and washing machines.
F Microprocessors are used in the car industry to control ___robot___

Things to do

1 Write down a short paragraph to explain what you think a computer is and what it can do.

2 The following list is a list of many different tasks. For each task say whether you think it could be performed using a computer. You should give your reasons for each one:
   a Flying an aeroplane
   b Making a cup of tea
   c Picking the winner of the Grand National
   d Writing a novel
   e Repairing a car
   f Painting a house

3 **a** Why do you think that science fiction writers have given the general public a false idea about computers? Think of two computers or robots in television programmes you have seen, or books you have read and say why you think the impression they gave was wrong.
   b One writer said that 'No-one will take any notice of computers until they are little and talking'. What do you think about this comment?

4 **a** Name two jobs it would be impossible to perform without computers.
   b For the two jobs you have named, give reasons why it would be impossible to perform them manually (by hand).

5 **a** Describe recent developments in the use of computers in everyday life.
   b Describe the extent to which you think these developments will have progressed in five years time.

6 The hand calculator and the digital watch are two examples of the use of microprocessors for a specific application. Name two other specific applications of the microprocessor with a brief description of the function of each device. Include in your description the particular properties of the microprocessor which are used in each case.

7 'The advent of chip technology and microprocessor systems has brought the world of computers nearer to the man in the street.' Discuss this statement with reference to size, availability and cost of computers, their usage and other relevant information.

2
The computer itself

What is a computer?

A computer is a machine that processes information. What we mean by 'processes' is that the information put into the computer has something done to it. Sometimes the computer is asked to do calculations with the information. Sometimes we ask the computer just to store the information so that it can be easily found when we need it.

Information and computing

Information is extremely important in our everyday lives. Our brains collect information all the time. They have to analyse it quickly so that we can make decisions depending on the information we have received. For example, supposing you are riding your bicycle along the road. Suddenly, the door of a parked car opens. Your brain receives this information from your eyes. Then it processes the information and decides what you should do. It will probably decide that you should either stop, or swerve out to avoid the door.

As the world about us gets more complicated, we have to process more and more information. This has become an enormous job. It is now not practical for people to do all the tasks and so computers are used instead. Today many of the jobs we take for granted such as weather forecasting, space travel, and clearing cheques would be almost impossible without computers. Without a computer these jobs would need so much paperwork and so many people that they would be very expensive and impractical.

Hardware and software

You have probably heard the words 'hardware' and 'software' used when people are talking about computers. **Hardware** is the part of the computer that you can touch and handle. It is the name given to all the devices that make up a computer system. These devices include the **input devices** (how we get

information into the computer) e.g. disk drives, tape drives and keyboards. They also include the **central processing unit (CPU)** and any extra storage, and the **output devices** (how we get information out of the computer) e.g. visual display units (VDUs) and printers. Figure 2.1 shows how these are linked in a simple computer system. Magnetic tapes and disks are also hardware.

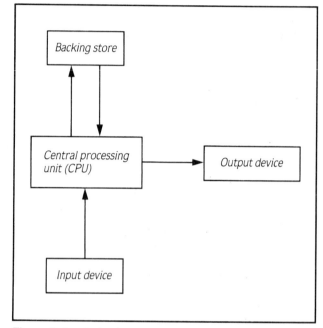

Figure 2.1 *A simple computer system*

Software is the name given to the actual programs that allow the hardware to do a useful job. Without software, hardware is useless. Software is programs made up of series of instructions that tell the computer what to do.

To understand the difference between hardware and software think of a tape recorder and a blank tape. The tape recorder and the tape would both be the 'hardware' because we can actually pick them up. But if we recorded some music onto the tape, then the music would be the 'software'.

Why use computers?

Computers are extremely fast

Computers can process information very fast. For example an IBM computer used at the weather forecasting centre at Bracknell can do 1 million calculations every second. Computers used by the electricity and gas boards work so fast that they can produce all the bills for their customers in a few days so that they all receive their bills at the same time.

2 Computers are very accurate

You may have read in the newspapers stories like: 'Computer sends housewife 1 million pound gas bill' or 'Computer pays headteacher her annual salary in monthly pay' (Figure 2.2)! Although these stories are true, they don't happen as often as they used to. Now most people realize that computers don't make mistakes — they only do what they are told to do. In computing there is a saying 'garbage in, garbage out' or GIGO for short: What it means is that if some information is put into the computer incorrectly the computer won't realize that it is incorrect so it will give out a strange answer. If the computer is given the right information, it will always come out with the right output.

Figure 2.2 *Computers don't make mistakes — they only do what they are told to do!*

3 Computers can keep large amounts of information in a very small space

Keeping all the information we need written on paper in files is an enormous task. Once you have gone through the tedious job of making up the files and cataloguing them, you then have the problem of finding the file you want — sometimes you may have millions of them to hunt through! But if you use computerized storage you can keep millions of files in a very small space and can get the information from them in seconds. You can also have a spare copy in case of accidents — imagine having duplicate written files!

4 Computers can work continuously for 24 hours a day

Computers don't become ill and they don't have to take time off. They don't take lunch breaks or tea breaks and they don't go on strike (Figure 2.3). Instead, if necessary, computers can work continuously, 24 hours a day. They also work at the same rate throughout the day — they don't have 'off days' like we do. So for some tasks computers are better than people. But there are of course many things that computers can't do, for example house painting, hairdressing and nursing (Figure 2.4).

Figure 2.3 *Computers don't have tea breaks and they don't go strike!*

Figure 2.4 *Some jobs are better done by people!*

5 Computers can do some jobs that would be impossible without them

A lot of services that we take for granted would not be possible without a computer. One example is Teletext. Another example is the use of cash dispensers and credit cards. These are only possible because computers can control how they work 24 hours a day. Space travel and successful weather forecasting would also be impossible without computers.

Input, process and output – the three stages of computing

All jobs can be split up into three stages whether they are being done by a computer or not. These stages are input, process and output. **Input** is all the information and materials you need to be able to do the job. What you do with the information or materials is the **process**. The **output** is the finished item of information. For example, suppose you want to make a cake. For the input you will need the ingredients and recipe. The process will be mixing the ingredients together in the correct way and then baking it. The output will be the finished cake.

In a computer the central processing unit (CPU) does the processing. Hardware can be connected to the CPU to input information. Some of the hardware devices can be used for output too. Figure 2.5 shows the three stages of computing.

Computers and memory

The central processing unit in a computer has a certain amount of memory. But the memory capacity is limited. Memory capacity is measured in K. The bigger the number of K a computer has, the more memory it has. So, for example, a Sinclair Spectrum microcomputer with 16K has less memory than one with 48K.

Usually the memory in the computer is used for the programs and the data that the computer is using at a particular time. But if more memory is needed then **backing storage** can be used. In most computers this is on magnetic tape or disk (Figure 2.6).

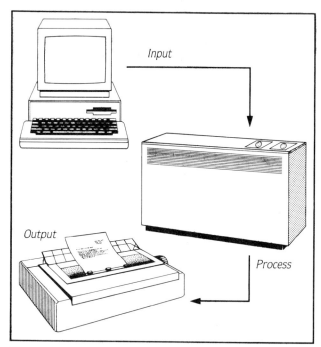

Figure 2.5 *The stages of computing*

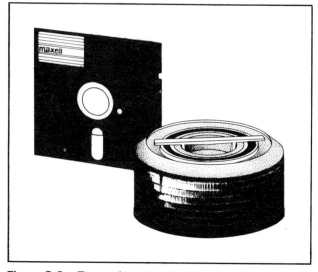

Figure 2.6 *Types of backing storage*

Test yourself

Using the words in the list below, copy out and complete sentences A to K underlining the words you have inserted. The words may be used once, more than once or not at all.

outside   input   space   software   backing
hardware   output   K   GIGO   processes
information   fast   programs   continuously

A A computer is a machine which _____ information.

B The computer consists of two parts: _____ and _____.

C The _____ is the _____ which allows the hardware to perform a useful task.

D A simple computer system usually consists of a CPU, input and output devices and some external storage called the _____ store.

E Gas boards use computers to produce bills because they are extremely _____.

F A computer will only give the right result if you feed it the correct information to start with. This is often referred to as _____.

G Computers can hold lots of _____ in a very small _____.

H Another advantage of using computers is that they can work _____.

I The three stages of computing are _____, process and _____.

J Memory size of the computer is measured in _____.

K Backing storage is used _____ the CPU.

Things to do

1 a What does 'computer' mean?
   b Give three examples of the sorts of jobs computers can do.
   c For the three examples above, say why you think computers are suited to doing the jobs.
   d Computers process information. What does 'process' mean?

2 a There are two parts to a useful computer system: hardware and software. Explain the difference between hardware and software.
   b Draw a diagram of a simple computer system showing the following devices: backing store, central processing unit, output device and input device.

3 Why are computers useful? Choose from these answers:
   a They can think for themselves
   b They can solve any problem
   c They can operate without a power supply
   d They never go wrong
   e They can make decisions when correctly programmed

4 Which of the following does computer hardware refer to?
   a The compiler
   b The program
   c The data
   d The electronics and casing
   e The output result

5 The diagram shows a typical computer system. Write down the missing names a to d.

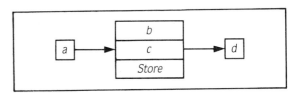

6 List **three** everyday sources of information with which you are familiar.

7 a What are the three stages of computing?
   b Think of a simple task and divide it up into those three stages.

8 The essential procedures in the use of a computer are: input – process – output. An example of this with a micro-electronic device in everyday use could be a pocket calculator. The input of numbers and instruction is via the key pad, the process is the internal calculation, the output is the answer display.
   Give two more examples of a device using microelectronics stating the input, process and output stages as in the example.

9 What is meant by the following terms which are commonly used in connection with computing?
   a CPU   **c** GIGO
   b VDU   **d** Backing store

10 Give four reasons for using computers and detail the advantages that they have over a corresponding manual methods.

11 How would you describe to a person not familiar with computers the difference between a simple pocket calculator and a computer?

3
Processing information

Input, processing and output

All tasks can be split up into three main stages: input, process and output. Figure 3.1 shows the order they are performed in.

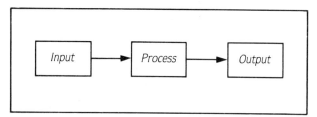

Figure 3.1 *Three stages of doing tasks*

Here are some examples of tasks and how they can be broken down into these stages.

Example 1 How much a man earns if he is paid by the hour

To calculate how much the man earns you need two pieces of information. The first is the amount of money the man gets paid per hour, and the second is the number of hours he works.

Input   This is the information you need before you start. Here this is the amount of pay per hour and the number of hours worked.

Process   This is what is done with the input. In this example the process is working out the answer by multiplying the amount of pay per hour by the number of hours worked. This will give us the amount of money the man earns. If we do the calculation manually, we can either work it out in our head, or we can do it on a piece of paper.

Output   When we have worked out the answer to our question we will probably want to write the answer down on a piece of paper. This written information (the amount the person earns) is the output.

One way of showing how we calculated the man's pay is to use a diagram like Figure 3.2.

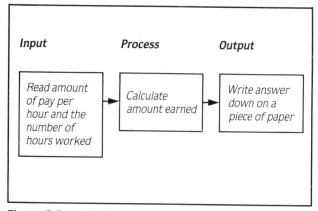

Figure 3.2 *Calculating pay*

Example 2 Producing an electricity bill by hand

To do this task we need to ask the three data processing questions.

1   Input – What information do we need?
To produce an electricity bill we would need this information:
Customer name
Customer address
Account number
Previous meter reading in units
New meter reading in units
Cost of electricity per unit

2   Process – What do we do with this information?
To work out the cost of the electricity we have to subtract the old meter reading from the new meter reading. This will give us the number of units used in the quarter. Then we have to multiply this by the cost of electricity per unit. This gives us the amount of money on the bill. Then we have to calculate VAT and add it to the bill.

3   Output – How are we going to present the answer?
The bill is printed out on paper. It has the following information on it:
Customer name
Customer address
Account number
Number of units used
Cost of electricity per unit
Total cost of electricity used
VAT amount payable
Cost of electricity and VAT

In Example 1, the process could be done manually or using a computer. If it had to be done in a company with only a few employees, then it would probably be done manually.

In Example 2, the process would in fact be done by a computer because a huge number of bills have to be produced in a short time.

Manual processing

Until computers became cheap, small and reliable, most tasks were done manually. Sometimes a machine such as a calculator was used for calculations, but most tasks were carried out manually with a pen and paper, (Figure 3.3).

As you can see in Figure 3.3, the information (input) would go into the 'in tray'. The clerk works out the calculation on a calculator and writes in the answer. This is the process. When he has finished he puts the paper in the 'out tray' which is the output. Wages and electricity bills could also be worked out in this way. The process in each task involves the person using brain power or the calculating power of the calculator and then writing in the information on paper.

Sometimes we may need some extra information that we can't keep in our head. If we are using a manual system we can keep this additional information in a filing cabinet. The information needs to be kept in some sort of order in the cabinet so that we can find the information we need as quickly as possible (Figure 3.4).

Handling information

People have processed and stored information for thousands of years. The earliest type of information storage system was clay tablets. The first calculating device was the abacus – a kind of counting frame.

We have seen that information is essential, but what information do we need? The answer depends on what we want to do. The following examples show the sort of questions we will need answers to.

Example 3   Preparing a payroll manually
Figure 3.5 shows how a clerk prepares a payroll manually. These are the questions she will ask:

1   What information do I need?
For this task the clerk will need to know:
a Whether people are paid hourly, weekly or monthly and the amount paid.
b Name and employee reference number.
c National insurance contribution.
d Tax code (this tells her how much tax to deduct).
e Any pension contribution.
f Any other deductions e.g. union dues.
g Saving schemes etc.

2   How can I get this information?
a and b Would come to the accounts department from the personnel department.
c Calculated from tables from the Department of Health and Social Security.
d Tax codes come from the Inland Revenue.
e From the pensions department.
f and g From the employee.

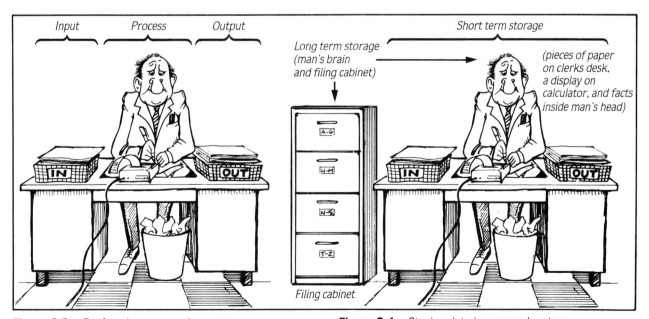

Figure 3.3   *Performing a manual process*   **Figure 3.4**   *Storing data in a manual system*

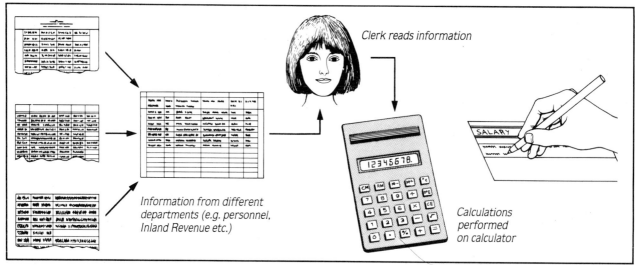

Figure 3.5 *Preparing a payroll manually*

3   How do I process the data?
Firstly the wages are calculated. Then the pension and insurance contributions are deducted. Then tax is calculated and deducted. Then any other deductions are made.

4   What results will I get and what updating must be done?
The result is a neatly printed out wage slip which shows the gross wage (how much is earned before deductions), the deductions themselves and the net wage. The slip also shows how much tax the employee has paid in the tax year and the total amount of national insurance paid. A card with these details on it will be updated ready for when the next payroll is performed.

5   How is the flow of data organized?
Before the clerk can process the information she has to get all the information from the different departments. Once she has the data she uses her brain or a calculator to work out all the different amounts. Then she writes them all out on paper.

Example 4   Preparing a payroll using a computer

Figure 3.6 shows how a clerk can use a computer to prepare a payroll. He will need the answers to the same questions as the clerk in Example 3.

1   What information do I need?
The clerk will need the same information as before. Some of the information will need typing into the computer and some of it will be stored in the computer.

2   How can I get this information?
This clerk too will have to get information from the same places as the other clerk.

3   How do I process the data?
This time the data is processed automatically by the central processing unit in the computer.

4   What results will I get and what updating must be done?
The line printer prints out the payslips very quickly. All the payslips are filled in correctly and neatly. Then the computer updates all its records ready for the next time the payroll is done.

5   How is the flow of data organized?
Most of the information will already be stored in the computer. This means that the clerk only has to type in information at the keyboard if something has changed. Originally the clerk would have received the information in the same way as the clerk doing the payroll manually.

Test yourself

Using the words in the list below, copy out and complete sentences A to F underlining the words you have added. The words in the list may be used once, more than once or not at all.

result   information   processed   process processing   cheap   manually

A   *The three stages that any task can be broken down into are input, _____ and output.*
B   *Input is the _____ you need before you start.*

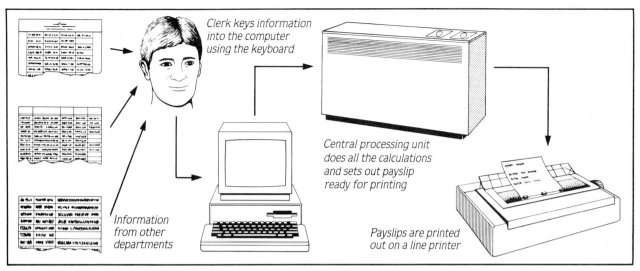

Figure 3.6 *Using a computer to prepare a pay roll*

Labels in figure:
- Clerk keys information into the computer using the keyboard
- Central processing unit does all the calculations and sets out payslip ready for printing
- Information from other departments
- Payslips are printed out on a line printer

C _____ is what is done with the information.

D The output is the final _____.

E People have _____ and stored information for thousands of years.

F Before computers became small, _____ and reliable, information was processed _____.

Things to do

1 Explain what each of the following means
   a Input
   b Process
   c Output

2 What are the input, output and process steps for each of the following tasks?
   a Writing a letter applying for a job you have seen advertised in a newspaper.
   b Working out some simple sums on an exam paper.
   c Making a pot of tea.
   d Servicing a car.
   e Preparing a telephone bill.
   f Filling in a crossword puzzle.

3 Read the paragraph below which describes how to produce an electricity bill. Then answer the questions as if you were going to do the task manually.

'Two meter readings are needed – the old one and the new one. If we subtract the old reading from the new reading we can find out how much electricity has been used. If we multiply the amount of electricity used by the cost of one unit of electricity, we can calculate the amount of the bill. Then we add a fixed charge to the bill and calculate VAT. This gives us the final amount. All these quantities are printed out. Other information printed out on the bill includes name, address and account number.'

   a What information is needed?
   b How can you get this information?
   c How will you process the data?
   d What will be your results and what updating will you need to do?
   e How is the flow of data organized?

4 a What information are you likely to find printed out on a payslip?
   b For each item of information you have mentioned, say where the information would come from.

4
Automatic processing

What is automatic processing?

For hundreds of years people have been inventing and developing machines to do jobs more quickly, and easily. In Chapter 3 we saw that tasks can be divided into three stages. The process stage is what we do with the information or materials used as input. Processes can be greatly speeded up using machines. When machines are used to do processes the processing is called **automatic processing**.

Some of the first machines that could do automatic processing were printing presses and weaving looms. These machines allowed the processing to be done much more quickly than before. They also allowed people to use their hands for other jobs. So by using the machines *and* the workers, more jobs could be done. Today, computer controlled robots on assembly lines can put together final products much more quickly and accurately than people can. So people can do other tasks. Computers can also be used to do lots of calculations very quickly. These computers allow us to use our brains for other things.

Some types of automatic processing

An **automatic machine** is a machine that goes through a whole process without human intervention. It is able to obey a series of instructions. These machines do not need to be supervised because all the processes are done, in order, by the machine itself. Here are some examples of automatic machines.

Automatic washing machines

Washing clothes manually can take a long time and needs constant supervision. So it is not surprising that an automatic washing machine was invented to get rid of the drudgery.

An automatic washing machine contains a series of **stored programs**. Each of these programs will carry out a series of processes in a particular order. Depending on the type of wash you want to do, you can select a suitable program to do the washing for

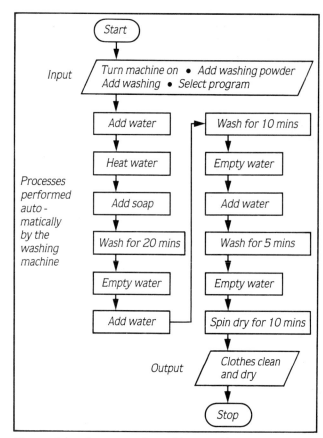

Figure 4.1 *An automatic washing machine wash*

you. Figure 4.1 shows a typical wash by an automatic washing machine.

Juke boxes

The input for a juke box has two parts – the money and the record selections. Money is part of the input because the juke box can't work without it and the amount of money you put in decides the number of records you can select. The processing is done automatically. Each record is picked out as it is selected. It is played and then it is put back into the storage area. The output is the music being played. Figure 4.2 shows all these stages. If you want more than one record, the sequence can be altered.

Video recorders

A video recorder usually contains a microprocessor. This is like a small computer. It can store all the instructions and can control the operations of the video recorder. The input is the starting time and length of each program you want to record and the channels. Once you have input this, the recorder will automatically go through the task of switching ON for recording and OFF at the program end and changing channel if necessary.

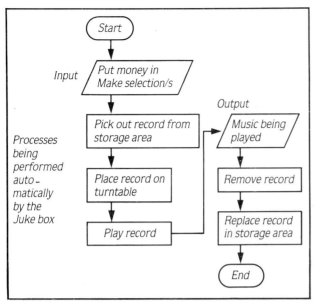

Figure 4.2 *Sequence of operations for a juke box playing a single record*

Other automatic machines in our homes

There are many other automatic devices in our homes, many of them much simpler than the ones we have looked at. They include alarm clocks, electric ovens, central heating thermostats, dishwashers, answering machines, programmable telephones and some children's games and toys.

Lifts and vending machines

Lifts are controlled automatically. In simple lifts the lifts only stop at the floors requested. But in very tall buildings the lifts are often controlled by computer so that they can take passengers to the floor they want in the quickest possible time.

Vending machines automatically do the process of making a particular drink depending on which buttons you press. The input is the buttons you press, because this decides what drink you get. The process is the actual making of the drink. The output is the drink itself.

Complete control systems

A **complete control system** is a system where the output is decided by the input and all the processes are automatic. These systems are in some of our factories. For example, in some modern steel works the customer's order is input into the computer and then the computer takes over completely. The computer controls the process of making the bars and cuts them to the correct size without human intervention (Figure 4.3). This is a very efficient process because it means that you don't need to hold enormous stocks that take up a lot of space and tie up

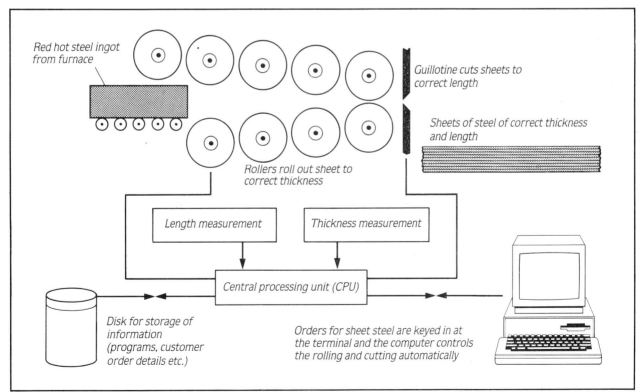

Figure 4.3 *In some modern steel works the computer makes steel bars and cuts them to the correct size according to the customer's order*

a lot of money. Instead you can 'tailor make' each customer's order. The computer deals with all the paperwork too, so the bills can be sent out with the goods. The disadvantage of this system is that it doesn't need many people, so it can cause a lot of unemployment.

Digital control systems

We can use a computer to control certain processes if we give it information. The computer prefers to get this information in the form of binary digits. Computers can also process information in ordinary numbers. Most ordinary computers are digital computers. The other type of control system is an analogue system. Analogue systems have a range of values. If we look at an ordinary radio we can see the difference between these two types of system. In a radio, the volume control has a infinite number of settings. It is an analogue device. On the other hand, the ON-OFF switch has a finite number of settings. It can only be ON or OFF. It is a digital device. Another example is a watch. A watch with hands is an analogue device because the hands keep moving – it has continuous values. But a digital watch gives the time in digits – it does not run continuously (Figure 4.4).

Digital devices are used for controlling some processes. For example, they can control machines by switching motors or pumps ON and OFF. If you input a number the computer converts it into binary. Then it transfers the binary coded information to a **port**. The process is controlled as the port switches various parts of the device ON or OFF via relays.

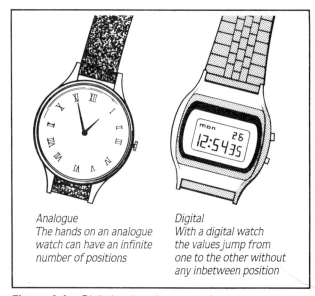

Analogue
The hands on an analogue watch can have an infinite number of positions

Digital
With a digital watch the values jump from one to the other without any inbetween position

Figure 4.4   *Digital and analogue watches*

Using a digital device to control a vending machine

We could use a microprocessor to control a vending machine. Depending on which buttons we push (the input), the machine would automatically prepare us the correct drink. It would work like this. We press a button. The microprocessor interprets this as a number. It converts this and sends a number in binary code to a port. An 8-bit port used in a vending machine would look something like Figure 4.5.

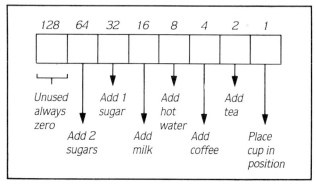

Figure 4.5

By outputting a number in binary to this port we can control what processes happen. For example, suppose the number 59 was output to the port. In 8-bit binary code this would be as in Figure 4.6.

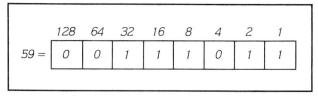

Figure 4.6

To see which processes are being carried out we have to look at the binary digits. In the example, the processes being performed are shown in Figure 4.7.

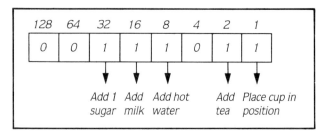

Figure 4.7

So for a cup of tea with milk and one sugar, the number 59 needs to be output to the port. To make different drinks we have to output different numbers to the port.

Analogue control

Analogue devices have a range of values. For example, a dimmer switch is an analogue device because it has an infinite number of positions between OFF on one side and ON at the other.

Information is fed into analogue computers as varying electrical voltages. The computer looks at this input and then decides on the output. For example, computers can control traffic flow in cities (Figure 4.8). The input is varying electrical voltages which the computer gets from pressure pads in the road. The computer can decide how long to keep traffic lights green depending on the flow of traffic.

Control box

Sensor pad in the road

To central computer

Figure 4.8 *In many large cities traffic lights are controlled by a central computer. Sensors in the road give the computer information about traffic flow*

Analogue computers can also be used to control processes. If a thermocouple (a device that converts temperatures to a varying voltage) is used, analogue computers can control chemical processes where temperature is important.

Analogue control devices are useful in situations that are continuously changing. So analogue computers are used for flight simulators, controlling traffic, process control, firing and controlling missiles and controlling hydraulic systems.

Digital computers can be used for analogue control if a device called an **analogue to digital converter** (**ADC**) is used. This device can convert analogue values to digital values.

Test yourself

Using the words in the list below, copy out and complete sentences A to J underlining the words you have inserted. The words may be used once, more than once, or not at all.

intervention   music   complete   infinite
control   input   digital   analogue
programs   automatic   physical

A *Processing performed by machines is called _____ processing.*

B *An automatic machine goes through a process without human _____.*

C *An automatic washing machine contains a series of stored _____.*

D *The output from a juke box is the _____.*

E *A _____ control system is a system where the output depends on the _____.*

F *Most ordinary computers are _____ computers.*

G *A watch with hands is an _____ device because the hands can have an _____ number of positions.*

H *Analogue devices work by representing data in the form of a continuous _____ quantity.*

I *Analogue computers can be used to _____ chemical processes.*

J *To operate analogue control with a digital computer you need an _____ to _____ converter.*

Things to do

1 **a** *What is meant by 'automatic processing'?*
   b *Give three examples of automatic machines.*
   c *For one of the examples you have given, describe the steps that are done automatically by the machine. Divide your steps into the three stages of computing: input, process and output.*

2 *What is meant by the following words?*
   a *Complete control systems*
   b *Digital control*
   c *Analogue control*

3 **a** *Explain the differences between an analogue device and a digital device.*
   b *Give two examples of*
      i An analogue device
      ii A digital device

4 An analogue computer represents data using which one of these?

   a Variables
   b Pulses
   c Variable voltages
   d Punched card
   e Magnetism

5 Complete the blank in this sentence:
In order to use a computer to control a robot arm, the output from the computer to the device would have to be converted from digital to _____ form.

6 For each of the following say whether it is an analogue or digital device:

   a A set of traffic lights
   b The gramaphone record
   c The data stored on a computer's magnetic disk
   d A magnetic compass

7 Here is a list of analogue and digital devices. Write them under the correct headings in the chart below.

finger   abacus   speedometer
thermometer   slide rule
calculating machine   cash register

Analogue device	Digital device

8 **a** Briefly explain the difference between analogue and digital data.
   b A car fuel injection system counts revolutions to measure the engine speed and uses an electronic sensor to measure the engine temperature.
     i Indicate why the engine speed is the digital signal
     ii What extra piece of equipment does the signal need and what does it do?

9 The process of steel rolling consists of compressing a hot bar of steel between rollers to produce a longer, but thinner bar. A computer controlled steel rolling mill automatically takes steel bars from the furnace, once they are sufficiently hot, and rolls them until they are of the required length. If the temperature falls below a pre-defined level before the rolling is complete, the bar is returned to the furnace for reheating.

   a Give two possible analogue inputs to the computer, saying briefly why each is an analogue quantity.
   b Give one possible output from the computer, stating whether it is analogue or digital.

10 An automatic record player uses an 8-bit store microprocessor to control it. The last two bits are unused by this system. The rightmost bits are called the port and they are connected to the controls of the record player.

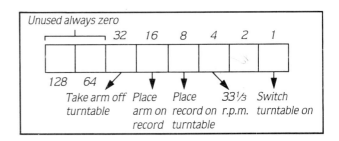

Using the 8-bit port shown above, answer the following questions:

   a What will happen when the number 13 is output to the port?
   b What are the conditions when the numbers output to the port are 00101000?
   c If you wanted to take the arm off the turntable and switch the turntable off, then what number would need to be output from the port?
     i in binary
     ii in base 10 (denary)

11 A particular microprocessor which uses 8-bit store locations is to be used to control the conditions in a greenhouse. Sensors for heat, light, draught and moisture are connected to the rightmost 4 bits of the store called port as shown below. The other 4 bits of the store port are unused and are always zero.

Unused – always zero				Moisture	Draught	Light	Heat
0	0	0	0				

Each sensor signals that it has detected a value that is too high by setting its bit in the store port to 1, otherwise the bit is set to zero. What are the conditions which result in the value of the store port being 00001001?

5
Robotics

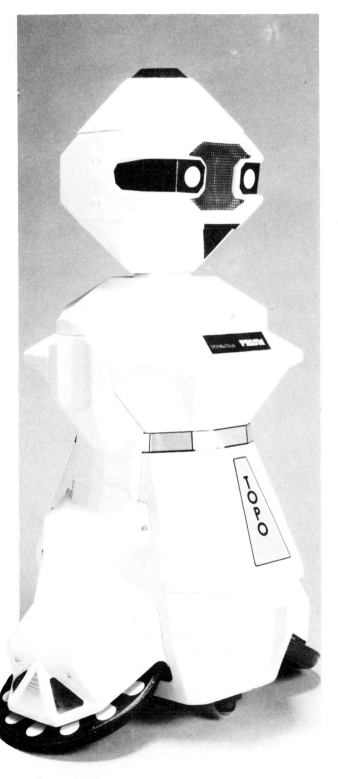

Robotics

Today robots are not science fiction, they are science fact! They are gradually being used in factories on assembly lines for doing repetitive jobs.

In a dictionary you will find a robot described as 'a mechanical man' or 'a more than humanly efficient automaton'. An **automaton** is something that moves by itself. It acts because of a routine rather than because it is 'intelligent'. This is what the robots in our factories do. They do repetitive jobs on assembly lines.

Science fiction writers have given people the wrong idea about robots as well as computers. Most people have the wrong idea about what a computer can and can't do. Television programmes have added to this. Robots such as K9 in Doctor Who and Metal Mickey don't give us a true picture of robots. In fact, the robots in factories just copy a series of instructions that they have been programmed to copy. Personal robots also just carry out instructions (Figure 5.1).

Using robots in factories means that work can be done quicker, cheaper and better than it could be done by people. Unfortunately though, it also means that people's jobs are taken over by machines. As more of these machines are used, more people may become unemployed. In Japan it is now possible to run a factory with almost no people at all — only 1% of the usual number of people are needed.

Robots can work in dangerous and unpleasant conditions. For example, the army uses robots to open car doors that might have been booby trapped. In the steel industry robots work in very hot and dirty conditions, which would be unbearable for people to work in. Usually robots are used for very boring jobs that are not suitable for people to do. This allows people to do the more interesting jobs.

Free standing robots

Most of the robots used in factories are free standing (Figure 5.2). This means that they don't move from place to place. Usually the robot is a flexible arm fixed to a stand. Sometimes the arm is controlled by a small computer built into the stand. Or sometimes the computer controls several robots through cables.

Many different tools can be attached to these arms,

Figure 5.1 *Topo the personal robot. He is operated by commands from a home computer. He can move from one room, to another and can even be made to talk!*

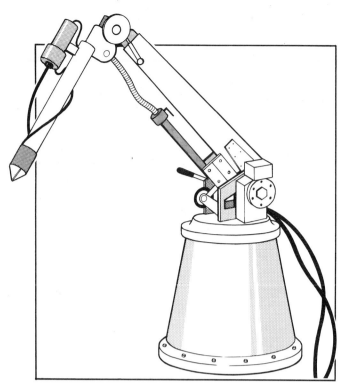

Figure 5.2 *A free standing industrial robot*

for example, paint sprayers, welding tips and soldering irons. To program these robots, an experienced human operator goes through a job using the tool attached to the flexible arm. The computer memorizes all the movements the operator makes. Next time the same job is given to the computer, it will be able to do all the movements itself. As long as the job is the same and all the materials are nearby, the computer controlled robot will be able to do the job quickly and accurately.

Many factories use robots to make their goods. Even the wiring of some computers is done by robots! Soon we will be able to see robots building robots (Figure 5.3)!

Figure 5.3 *One day robots will build other robots!*

Moving robots

Free standing robots need to be supplied with materials very quickly. Some factories use moving robots to do this. Moving robots are a bit like fork lift trucks. Instead of having arms like a free standing robot, they have wheels.

Usually these robots follow invisible lines set into the floor. To prevent collisions at crossroads, the computer gives one truck privilege. This means other trucks will stop and let it through. In some advanced systems using lots of these moving robots, if more materials are needed at a particular place, the computer will choose the robot nearest to the stores.

Moving and free standing robots in one

Now robots are being developed that have an arm and can also move around. For example, in one textile mill a robot moves around, cuts the yarn, starts a new spool, picks up a filled spool then returns to the store.

Robots in the car industry

You have probably seen adverts on television and in newspapers from car companies boasting that their cars are built by robots. Because the structure of cars is very complex and putting together all the parts is rather routine, robots are ideal for this job. In Britain nearly all the main car manufacturers use robots to some extent. Usually the newer car models are built by robots because of the expense of buying the necessary robots and production line equipment.

Building the Mini Metro by computer

The Mini Metro is built by computer at Longridge in the Midlands by British Leyland. Twenty-four computers are used in the production process.

One mini computer controls the whole system. It monitors (watches over) each stage in the production. It co-ordinates all the different activities together.

One of the most important factors in running a completely automated assembly line is making sure that all the necessary parts are quickly available. So, even in the stores at Longridge, mini computers are used to control cranes that pick up the various panels and store them or put them on a conveyor ready to be assembled. When the parts arrive at Longridge from other factories, a computer weighs them to check that they are not underweight.

At the start of each shift, the operators tell the

Figure 5.4   *Robots working on a Mini Metro*

Figure 5.5   *Putting a windscreen into a Montego*

computer how many car bodies it has to make. The computer then works out how frequently the parts will be needed. Computers can give priority to certain lines that may be running short of parts.

On the assembly line itself, the first robots put together the car frame. Side panels, roofs and floors are joined together by robots that can weld the parts together very quickly (Figure 5.4). Once assembled the bodies have to be painted, but not all the same colour, so the computer splits them up and sends them through automated spraying booths. After this, most of the work is done manually.

One of the latest developments in using robots in the car industry is automatic glazing. Figure 5.5 shows a robot putting a windscreen into a Montego car.

Test yourself

Using the words in the list below, copy out and complete sentences A to F underlining the words you have inserted. The words may be used once, more than once or not at all.

programmed   unemployment   free
motor   moving   quicker   copies

A   *A robot is a machine which _____ a series of movements which it has been _____ to perform.*
B   *Robots can perform tasks _____, cheaper and more efficiently than by manual methods.*
C   *Unfortunately, robots do cause _____.*
D   *A robot with a flexible arm attached to a metal base is called a _____ standing robot.*
E   *_____ robots transfer materials from the stores to the working positions ready for assembly by the robots.*
F   *Robots are used a lot in the _____ industry.*

Things to do

1   **a** *Look up the word 'robot' in the dictionary you use and write the definition down.*
    b *Think of two industries that use robots and write down the benefits you think that they have been to these industries.*
    c *What disadvantages are there in using robots in assembly lines?*

2   **a** *Explain what is meant by the word 'automaton'.*
    b *Many factories have or are in the process of installing robots. Explain why the workforce are likely to be sceptical about this.*

3   *You will have seen robots being used in films or television programmes. Explain why these programmes often show robots incorrectly and say what robots can and cannot do.*

4   *Using an example which you have read about or seen, describe how robots can be used to improve efficiency in certain industries. Explain how the various jobs were done before the robots were introduced.*

5   *Using **one** of the industries listed below, explain how the industry uses robots for the manufacture of its goods.*
    a *Car industry*
    b *Steel industry*
    c *Computer industry*
    d *Canned food industry*

6   *Some people say that in the very near future, our manufactured goods will be 'untouched by human hand'. Do you think they are right? Give reasons. Do you think that the unmanned factory is a reality or merely science fiction?*

6
Data sources

Source documents

Figure 6.1 shows some ways of representing data so that a machine can read it. The source of data is usually written information. Because of the wide variety of ways information comes into an office, it is usual for someone to transfer the information by hand onto a pre-printed standard form before it is put into the computer. The pre-printed form is called a **source document**. When it has been filled in, the form can be sent to the computer operator for inputting into the computer.

Many people try to use just one source document and to use this to input the information directly into the computer. In these systems, you don't need to type the information contained in the source documents into the computer. Unfortunately, however, information comes into organizations in many different ways and using source documents as direct input material for the computer is only possible in a few cases.

The electricity and gas boards use standard forms called **meter reading sheets** as source documents. When the meter is read, the person reading the meter shades in certain parts of the meter reading sheet. The meter reading sheet can then be used to feed the information into the computer using a mark reader.

The source of data for cheque clearing is on the cheques themselves (Figure 6.2). On cheques there are numbers at the bottom which are written in magnetic ink. Because the amount written on a cheque is not known at the time of printing, this number has to be added later, in magnetic ink, by the bank. A machine called a magnetic ink character reader is used to read the information from the cheque into the computer.

In the two examples we have just looked at, the source of information comes in a standard way. But in an office such as a sales office, the orders can arrive in a variety of ways. They may be telephoned in, telexed, typed on paper or even input direct from another computer. In many cases, the orders may come in with important details missing and this involves the

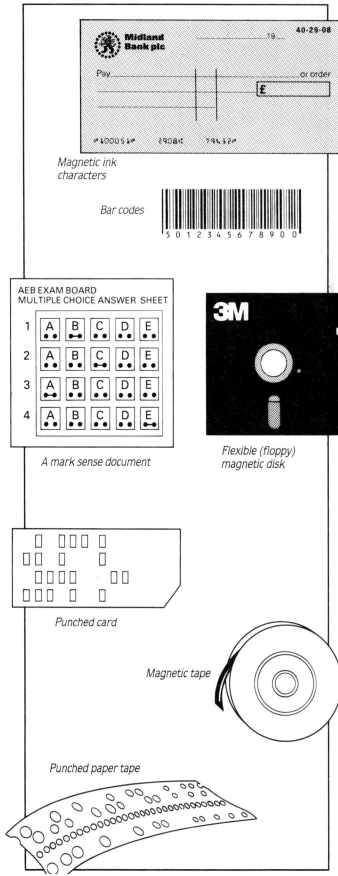

Magnetic ink characters

Bar codes

A mark sense document

Flexible (floppy) magnetic disk

Punched card

Magnetic tape

Punched paper tape

Figure 6.1 *Ways of representing data so that a machine can read it*

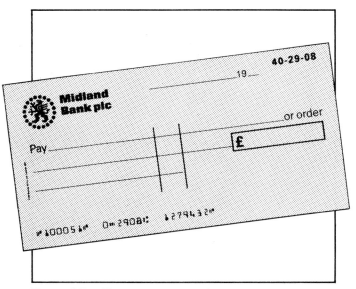

Figure 6.2 *Cheques are source documents*

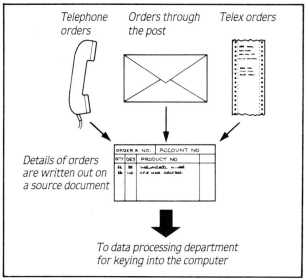

Figure 6.3 *Producing a source document*

sales clerk ringing up the customer to clarify the order. In situations like this, direct data entry is impossible.

In this sort of office, it is usual to transfer the information from a customer's order to a source document (Figure 6.3). This source document is then sent to the computer operator for keying into the computer. Source documents usually have a set format. This makes filling in and processing them a lot easier.

Form design

Data from various places is usually handwritten onto a standard form before being given to the operator for keying into the computer. The design of these forms is very important and they must be layed out so that they can be keyed into a computer easily.

Sometimes, the forms are filled in by the general public and these are used by the operator directly. Forms like this need to have clear, concise instructions, to tell the person who has never filled in such a form before what to do. You may have come across forms which never have enough boxes for your name and address. These are examples of badly thought out forms.

There are many examples of data being created by writing on standard forms. Application forms, tax returns, expense forms, car licences, order forms, requisitions, stock reports and questionnaires are all examples of forms that are used as source documents.

Questionnaires are often used in market research

surveys to find out why people vote for a particular political party, or why they use one toothpaste rather than another. Here, the information is usually in the form of a tick in a box and is put into the computer. The trouble with this sort of source document is that a lot of detail is lost and the questions cannot be answered by just yes or no. You may have seen questionnaires like this and you often find that among the alternatives there is not always one that you would choose.

Coded information

Sometimes, in order to get a large amount of information into a small space, information has to be coded. In a mail order catalogue, for example, each article has its own code number which you must include when ordering it. When this number is keyed into the computer, the computer automatically knows the name of the article because the computer has been told what each of the codes means. Although a lot less memory is taken up inside the computer, this method has the snag that the person writing out the order may write the code number down incorrectly since it has no meaning to them (Figure 6.4).

Each code is unique to a particular article, so there is no possibility of confusion over similar articles e.g. different sizes of the same make of washing powder. Another advantage is that a short code is much quicker for the operator to type in than a lengthy description of the article.

Codes can be **numeric** (just numbers) or **alphanumeric** (letters and numbers). Usually,

Figure 6.4 *Coded information is not obvious to humans!*

numeric codes are used in preference to alphanumeric codes because they are more straightforward. People are generally careful when writing down numbers but not so careful when they are writing letters.

Some of the codes we find around us are National Insurance numbers, employees reference numbers, car registration numbers, bank account numbers, bank code numbers, personal identification numbers, bar code numbers, and many more. The types of codes we use in everyday life are endless – you will probably be able to think of a lot more of your own.

Data created by equipment or machinery

Data for computers can be created by equipment or machinery. Data can be either **digital** or **analogue**. Analogue data includes temperature, pressure, flow rate, current, voltage and depth. These quantities are continuous. They have an infinite variety of values. They can be measured using special sensors. The data is usually fed to the computer via an analogue to digital converter which converts the analogue signals to digital ones. The computer then makes a decision according to how it has been programmed. It can then control the process by outputting signals which alter the conditions. Sometimes this is referred to as a **feedback loop**.

Suppose, in a chemical process, a container needs to be filled with water and heated up to 70°C. If we are using a computer to control the process, it will automatically turn the tap on to let the water into the container. Since water pressure depends on depth, a sensor will relay data about the depth back to the computer. When the depth reaches a certain value, the computer will switch the taps off. A temperature sensor will sense the temperature and relay the information back to the computer. The heater is switched on until the temperature reaches 70°C. The computer then switches the heater off. Any time the temperature drops below 70°C the heater is switched on again and so on to keep the temperature always at 70°C. Figure 6.5 shows how this works.

In some situations, data will be in a digital form, for example, the number of units produced by a machine. In situations such as these there is no need for an analogue to digital converter.

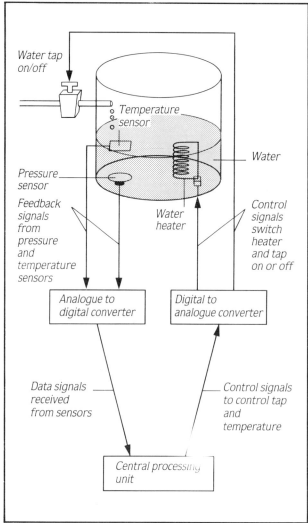

Figure 6.5 *Using a computer to control a chemical process*

Test yourself

Using the words in the list below, copy out and complete sentences A to I underlining the words you have inserted. The words may be used once, more than once or not at all.

digital   source   meter reading
magnetic ink   designed   coded   telexed
feedback loop   document   printed

A A _____ document is prepared before the information is keyed into the computer.

B Sometimes a source document can be used directly. Electricity _____ _____ sheets are used directly.

C With cheques, the _____ _____ characters are read directly and there is no need to write a source document.

D Often, information comes in a variety of different ways. It may be telephoned in, _____ or printed.

E In these cases a _____ _____ will need to be prepared.

F Source documents need to be _____ carefully, especially if they are to be filled in by the general public.

G Quite often, in order to save computer space, information is _____.

H Data created by equipment or machinery can be of two types: _____ or analogue.

I Computers can control processes by using a _____ _____.

Things to do

1 **a** Explain what is meant by a 'source document'.
   b Sometimes a computer can read what is on a source document directly. Give an application where this is done.
   c In a sales office, information comes in many ways. Name three ways in which the information can come into the office.

2 **a** Explain how
      i   meter reading sheets and
      ii bank cheques
   are used as source documents.
   b What advantages do these source documents have over the normal handwritten source documents?

3 **a** When source documents are designed, careful consideration is given to the design of the forms. Why is this necessary?
   b Questionnaires in market research surveys often have boxes where you put ticks for a YES or a NO. Why do you think the questions need to be worded carefully?

4 **a** Why do we sometimes code information?
   b What disadvantages does coding have?
   c Why are numeric codes (numbers) preferable to alphanumeric codes (letters and numbers)?

5 Explain the difference between
   a digital devices and
   b analogue devices.

7
Flowcharts

Flowcharts (or flow diagrams)

Flowcharts are used to break a task down into lots of different steps arranged into a logical order. The steps are written inside boxes. Some of the more common flowchart boxes are shown in Figure 7.1. There are others, but these will be dealt with later on in the book.

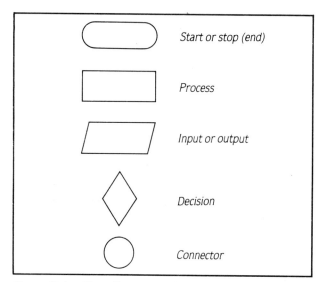

Figure 7.1 *Flow diagram symbols*

Stop or start boxes

These symbols are used at the start and end of the flow diagram (Figure 7.2). There is only ever one start symbol but there can be more than one stop or end box. The line with the arrow going into or out of the box shows whether it is stop or start box. There is always only one line of flow (line of arrow). The name of the box is placed inside the box (Figure 7.3).

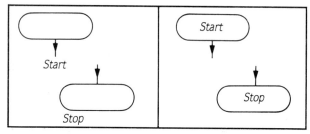

Figure 7.2   **Figure 7.3**

Process boxes

Process boxes have two arrows, one going in and the other going out. Sometimes they are called activity boxes, because something is done. A progress is something which is done with the information. Quite often, it will involve a calculation, but it could be just doing something e.g. hit a nail, pay some money etc. Anything that you have to do is put in a process box. The process is written inside the box. Figure 7.4 shows some typical process boxes. When we write flowcharts to write a program we usually put calculations in process boxes.

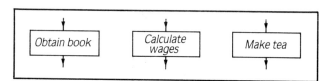

Figure 7.4

Input and output boxes

Input is what is required for the process to be done. If a calculation needs to be done, then the input will be some figures. If you are writing after a job, your input could be the job advertisement. The input box also has an arrow going in and one coming out. What the input is, is written inside the box. Figure 7.5 shows some typical input and output boxes.

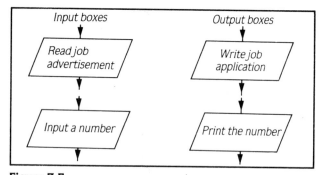

Figure 7.5

Decision boxes

These boxes are used to ask questions to which there are two answers: yes or no. The answer will always be either yes or no – never 'don't know'! Yes and no must be written by the paths to show which path is being taken (Figure 7.6).

One flow line goes into the decision box and two lines leave it once the decision inside the box has been made. The question inside the box must be one which has the answer yes or no. Some examples of decision boxes are shown in Figure 7.7.

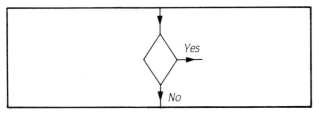

Figure 7.6

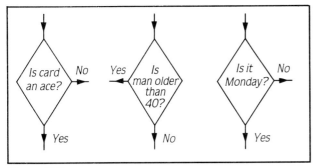

Figure 7.7

In decision boxes one of the flowlines can come out of the decision box to either the right or the left. This is useful in flowcharts where there are lots of decision boxes, because it stops the flowchart from becoming cluttered. The line coming out of the right or left of the flowchart eventually joins up at a place along the flowline going downwards. Figure 7.8 gives an example of this. This example forms what is known as a loop. If the answer to the question in the decision box is yes then one thing happens, if the answer is no then something else happens.

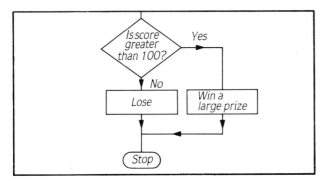

Figure 7.8

Connector boxes

These circular boxes are used to connect the flowlines when you have to turn over a page (Figure 7.9). They are usually numbered in case there is more than one flowline. When you first start drawing flow diagrams, it is best to start at the top of a clean page in order to avoid confusion.

Connectors can be useful in flow diagrams where

Figure 7.9

there are lots of loops, because they make the diagram look neater.

Example 1 Draw a flow diagram to apply for a job that you have seen in a newspaper

The steps involved are:
1   Deciding what input is required.
2   Deciding what needs to be done with the input material.
3   Deciding what output is required.

These can be summarized as:
1   Input
2   Process
3   Output

In the above example the input is the job advertisement. You need this for the description of the job and the address to write to. You need to read the advertisement. The process is deciding what to write, and the output is actually writing the job application. Figure 7.10 shows how the flowchart could be drawn.

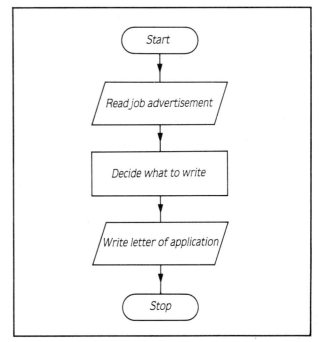

Figure 7.10   *Writing a job application*

Example 2 Draw a flowchart to show how you would play the following game

First you must answer a question. Then a coin is tossed. If it is heads you choose a number between 1 and 12. Each number wins a prize. If the number has been selected, then you must select again. If the number is 7 you win a booby prize. Figure 7.11 shows a flowchart for this. You could play a series of games by asking just before the stop sign if the player would like another game.

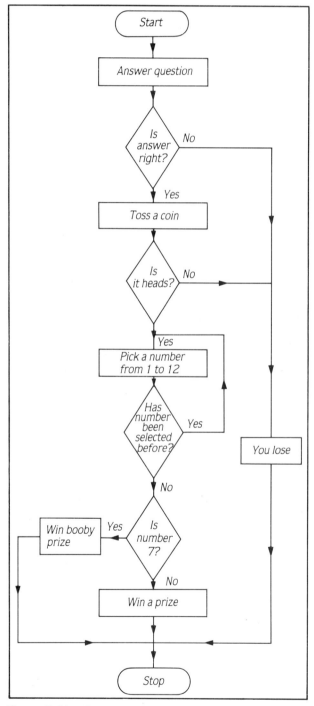

Figure 7.11 *Flowchart for a game*

Computing flowcharts

In the previous section we looked at non-computing flowcharts. These were flowcharts for doing various tasks that we have to do. It would be impossible for the computer to use them, but they show how a task can be broken down into a series of logical steps.

Now we will look at the way in which flowcharts can be used to help write computer programs. These computing flowcharts quite often involve numbers and the process boxes quite often contain arithmetic processes.

Steps for writing a computer flowchart

1   Deciding what output is required. It is very important to decide what output you require and the way it is set out. Also, you need to decide whether you require a hard copy (a printed copy).
2   Deciding on the method of solution. This involves deciding on the calculations you will use, headings, totals and loops.
3   Drawing a draft flowchart. This is just a brief sketch which shows the general flow of logic. You can tidy this up or alter it for the actual flowchart.
4   Drawing the final flowchart. You need to draw a neat and accurate flowchart.

Remember that a flowchart should be able to be used by other people. It must be easy to understand with clear statements inside the flowchart boxes.

Example 3 Draw a flowchart to work out the volume of any sphere with a radius, *r*

Include in the flowchart a step to end the process when required.

1   The output would be the radius of the sphere along with its volume. You need to include headings such as radius, area etc. so that the person using the flowchart can understand what the numbers mean.
2   You would solve the problem like this. This is a formula to work out the volume of a sphere. It is $V = \frac{4}{3}\pi r^3$. *V* is the volume and *r* is the radius. To work out the volume of any sphere, all we need to know apart from the formula is the radius. So the radius is the input. The calculation is carried out in the process box. We can print out the radius and volume. The decision box (diamond shaped) gives us the choice of either working out the new volume of a new sphere with a different radius or stopping.

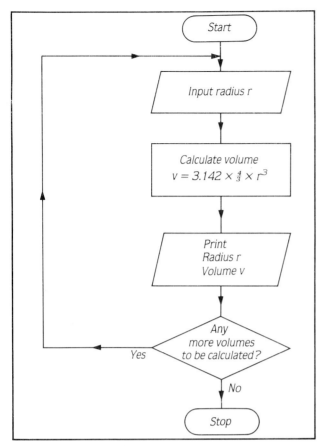

Figure 7.12 *Draft flowchart*

3 You would draw a draft flowchart, like the one in Figure 7.12, just to get the flow of logic right.
4 The flowchart in Figure 7.12 only has minimum information. It is very unclear to anyone except the person who wrote it. What is needed, are more details, headings and some explanation of what needs to be input. Figure 7.13 shows what the final flowchart looks like when this information has been added.

Dry runs

Once you have drawn a flowchart you need to check it for logical errors. You do this by performing what is called a **dry run**. A dry run is a check to make sure that the flowchart is correct. Test data is put into the flowchart and each instruction in the boxes is obeyed in turn. When the data has been processed by the flowchart, we make sure that the output is correct. If it is not correct, then a mistake has been made in the drawing of the flowchart.

Quite often, it is best to choose several numbers in turn and test each by doing a dry run. When performing a dry run, it is a good idea to keep track of what is happening by drawing a table.

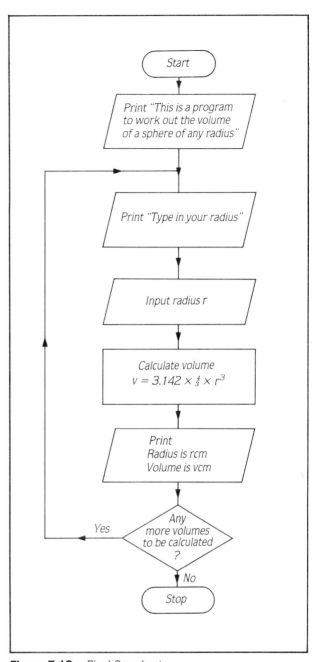

Figure 7.13 *Final flowchart*

Test yourself

Using the words in the list below, copy out and complete sentences A to G underlining the words you have inserted. The words may be used once, more than once, or not at all.

arithmetic   task   decision
dry run   steps   process
test   logical   table

A *Flowcharts are used to break a _____ down into a series of logical _____.*

B *A _____ box is used when something is done.*

C   The flowchart boxes which have questions to which there are either yes or no answers are called _____ boxes.

D   In computing flowcharts the process boxes often contain _____ processes.

E   After a flowchart has been drawn it should be checked for _____ errors.

F   A _____ _____ is performed to check the flowchart.

G   _____ data is put into the flowchart and the outputs are written in a _____.

Things to do

1   The flowchart symbol shown is used to represent which of the following?
   a   The input of data
   b   Decision making
   c   The start
   d   Assigning of a value to a variable
   e   A calculation

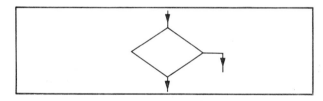

2   What is indicated by the following flowchart symbol?
   a   Input/output
   b   Process
   c   Repeated loop
   d   Decision
   e   Data from a backing store

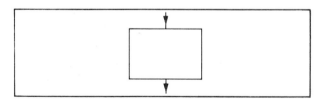

3   A 'dry run' is which one of these?
   a   A program to test that the computer is working correctly.
   b   The first time a program is processed on the computer
   c   A program RUN which produces no results
   d   A manual check of the program using test data
   e   A program RUN which produces incorrect results

4   Write a suitable statement in each of the following boxes:

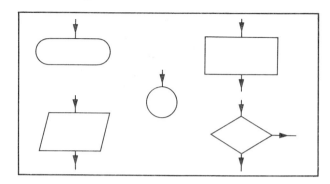

5   Give four reasons for using flowcharts.

6   Two boys play the game of marbles according to the following rules. The first player flicks his marble. The second player then has to hit the first player's marble. If he hits the marble, then he wins but if he misses, then the other player takes his turn to hit his opponent's marble. The game goes on until one of the players wins. Arrange the following flowchart symbols to produce a flowchart to play the above game until one of the players becomes bored and wants to stop playing.

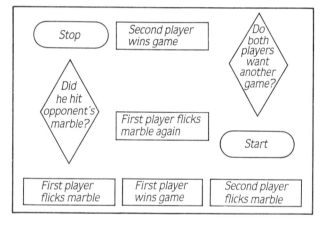

7   Draw a flowchart to make a pot of tea for four people.

8   Draw a flowchart to cross a road using the green cross code.

9   Mr Spock wishes to find himself a wife so he goes to the Perfect Partner Marriage Agency. His future wife must meet the following conditions:
   She must be 5 feet tall and if she is an Earth woman, she must not be older than 35 years. If, however, she is a Vulcan, she can be up to 400 years old.

34

Draw a suitable flow diagram to allow Mr Spock to see if a particular woman is suitable.

10 Draw a flowchart to show the start of a typical school day. From getting up to starting lessons.

11 The police wish to make up an identity parade. They must pick people with the following characteristics. They must be male, white, slim build and over 6 foot tall. They must not have blonde or red hair. Draw a flow diagram to show how the police could make their selections for this parade.

12 A singles tie-break in a tennis match is played in the following way. The starting player serves for one point. From then until the end of the game each player in turn serves for two points. The winner is the first player to reach seven points with a two point lead or to gain a two point lead after reaching seven points. Draw a flowchart to show this scoring method.

13 The flowchart below shows a simplified way to use a telephone. Put in the appropriate boxes and lines with YES or NO labels.
BEGIN

Lift up receiver and dial the number

Is it ringing?

Put down the receiver

Is it answered

END   Talk

Have you finished?

14 A shopkeeper normally sells pads at 6p each but if a customer buys more than 20 they will cost him 5p each. If he buys more than 50, then they will cost him only 4p each.

Draw up a flowchart to show how the shopkeeper does his calculations and outputs the total cost of the customer's order. Write down three items of data that would test all possible outcomes.

15 A family of four wish to go on a caravan holiday in Cornwall. They have a dog, so the site which they go to must be one which accepts dogs. They must go in the first two weeks of August and the site that they pick must have a private beach. The caravan must also have four berths. Draw a flowchart to show how the family could choose which caravan sites were suitable.

16 A game of darts is played by two players. The object of the game is to score 301 or over with as few darts as possible. The first person to reach 301 or over is the winner. Each player throws three darts in turn and the score at the end of each turn is added to the total for that player.
a Draw a flowchart to show the rules of the game.
b In a new diagram, draw a flowchart that has been altered, to include this condition:
   A player must score exactly 301 to win, otherwise he has to wait until his next turn if he scores over 301.
c Draw an extension to your flowchart to show which player has won. (Call them the first player and the second player.)

17 A dice game is played by two players. Each player, in turn, throws the two dice and adds together the two numbers showing. This is her score for that throw. The score is then added to her running total and the second player takes her turn. The first player to reach a running total of 41 or more is the winner. However, if a player throws a double, for example, two sixes or two fives, then her score is taken away from her running total. The running total can never be less than zero.
a Draw a flowchart to show the rules of the game.
b In a new diagram, draw a section of flowchart to show how your original flowchart would need to be altered to satisfy a new rule that a player must reach a running total of exactly 41 to win, and if that number is exceeded with a particular throw, than that throw's score is ignored.

c Draw an extension to your flowchart to indicate which player has won the game. (You should indicate the player by whether she threw first or second.)

18 Draw a flowchart to outline the scoring for one player in a new game of darts. The method of scoring is:

a A player starts with a total score of 650. The two players take it in turn to have a 'go'. (A 'go' involves throwing one dart.)

b The score for each 'go' is deducted from the current total.

c The game is over when a player's score for a 'go' reduces the total to exactly zero. (Note: if the score for a 'go' reduces the total below zero then that score is ignored.)

19 The total cost of renting a television depends on the type of set, the licence fee and the optional extras that go with it. One local firm calculates the cost for its customers from the following facts:

Colour television costs £90 per year
Black and white television costs £40 per year
Colour television licence costs £46 per year
Black and white television licence costs £15 per year

Optional extras

A remote control unit costs £8 for a colour television or £5 for black and white
A stand for either type of television is £8 extra
If the set is to be installed by the firm, then the installation cost is £10 for a colour television or £6 for a black and white television

Using the above information, draw a flowchart that would enable the dealer to calculate easily the total cost of renting a television, in order that he may advise his customers.

20 Draw a flowchart to grade eggs by weight using the following information:
Less than weight W1 grams, graded '4'
Less than weight W2 grams, graded '3'
Less than weight W3 grams, graded '2'
Less than weight W4 grams, graded '1'
If the eggs are cracked they are discarded

21 The flowchart shows the rules of a game of darts.
a Using the numbers printed below, which

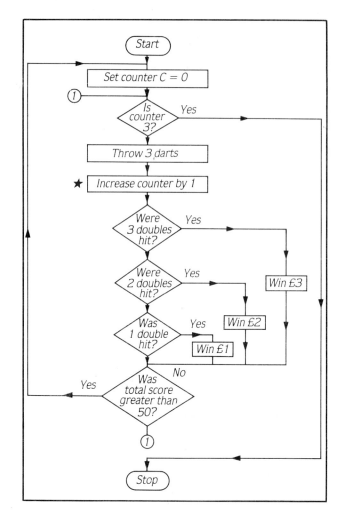

represent the scores on the 3 darts, give the expected results.
  i 1st three darts (double 4, double 6, double 4)
  ii 2nd three darts (double 1, 5, 8)
  iii 3rd three darts (double 10, double 20, double 3)
b List the rules of this game.
c If the box marked with the star (★) is removed, what effect does this have on the game?

22 You are given a list of numbers which are not arranged in order of their size. Draw a flowchart to show how you would find the largest number in the list.

23 The flowchart shown in the diagram is used for producing a list of candidates who have passed or failed an examination, and their respective marks. The candidate's name and mark are input into the computer. The computer must know the pass mark to be able to determine whether the candidate has passed or failed.

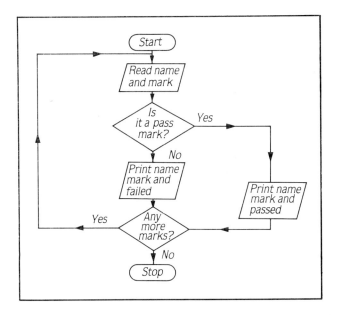

Redraw the flow diagram to show which pupils
have obtained an extremely high mark which
warrants a distinction. Also include some steps
which can be used to output the total number of
candidates who took part in the examination.

24 Read the following:

Situation
On a long train journey to Marseilles, Michael
Oldpound had become closely acquainted with a
French girl, Susanne Brun, who lived in
Marseilles. On his next visit to the city, he
decided to call on Susanne, but he had neither
her address nor her telephone number.

Problem
To contact Susanne Brun by telephone.

Analysis
Michael remembered the following facts:
  i Susanne lived by a lake
  ii She lived in a street named after a flower

Michael also had the following aids available:
  i Street map of Marseilles
  ii A telephone directory
  iii Coins to make any number of calls
  a Design an algorithm to help solve this
    problem, writing down the critical steps.
  b Draw the flowchart for your algorithm.

25 Draw a flowchart to represent an algorithm
which does the following:
Accepts numbers intended to be in the range 0
– 10 but terminated by a rogue value of 999

Checks each input number to see if it is in this
range or is the rogue value. (Numbers failing
this check procedure produce an error message
'INVALID DATA' and are not otherwise
processed apart from in part 4 below.)
Outputs the following:
  1 The average of the valid numbers input
  2 The largest valid number input
  3 The smallest valid number input
  4 The number of invalid numbers detected in
the output

26 Rearrange the boxes and draw in connecting
lines with arrows to form a flowchart which
describes how to process an electricity bill
according to the following rules. Read the
records in turn from the customer file and find
out how many units each customer has used by
subtracting the previous meter reading P from
the present meter reading Q.
Check to find out whether the meter readings
are sensible. If the readings are sensible, print
the details from the customer record and print
the charge. If they are not sensible, print the
details from the customer record and print an
error message.
The charge is 3.00p per unit for the first 50
units, and 2.00p per unit for extra units after
the first 50.

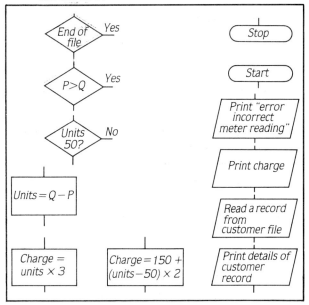

27 Draw a flowchart, for use before writing a
program, which will input a class list with seven
test results for each pupil and output the list
with each pupil's average mark and highest
mark with appropriate headings.

8
Data capture methods

Data capture is getting information together for the computer to process (Figure 8.1).

Figure 8.1 *Data capture!*

Indirect and direct methods of capture

Indirect methods

Indirect methods of data capture involve preparing data into a form which the machine can read before feeding the data into the computer. Paper tape or punched cards can be used as input mediums. First they have to be punched and verified (checked). These methods involve a lot of extra work and lots of errors can be introduced. Because of this, this method is not used as much as it used to be.

Key to disk

Most computers use this method of data capture. It usually involves typing in information contained on a previously filled in form. This form is called a **source document**. Source documents are specially designed forms which are filled in by clerical staff. Sometimes orders for goods etc. can be typed straight into the computer without writing any forms. This method is better as it reduces the number of mistakes made. A system where the information is keyed in via the keyboard and then stored on disk is called a **key-to-disk** system.

Direct methods

Because of human errors in the handling of data, methods have been developed so that the computer can read the information directly without needing any keying in. This means there are no typing errors. These methods are also better because input is a lot quicker.

Data capture methods which do not use any writing

The central processing unit of a computer works extremely fast. If the system is to work efficiently data should also be input fast. Typing is a fairly slow process so quicker methods of putting information into the computer have been explored.

MICR (magnetic ink character recognition)

In this form of data capture the computer can read certain numbers which are written in magnetic ink. You can see these numbers written on the bottom of bank cheques. Millions of cheques are handled by the banks each day and the clearing process only takes about three days. Without MICR cheques would take much longer to clear. Someone would have to key all the information contained on the cheque into the computer. You can imagine how long it would take to do this with the 7 million cheques that are handled every day.

When a cheque arrives at the bank there is only one figure that needs to be typed in. This is the amount of the cheque, since this is not known during the printing of the cheques (Figure 8.2). When the cheques reach the clearing house where all the cheques are sorted for all the banks the magnetic numbers are read by a magnetic ink character reader (Figure 8.3). This reader can read cheques at a rate of about 2500 per minute.

Figure 8.2 *Cheques use MICR for data capture*

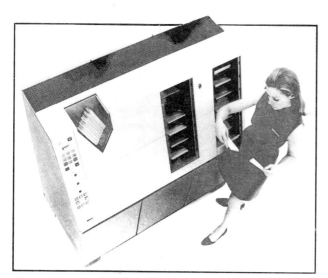

Figure 8.3 *An MICR reader/sorter*

OCR (optical character recognition)

Optical character readers can read characters that are printed in ordinary ink by the amount of light they reflect. Usually, the reader can only be used with characters that are of a particular style or font.

Machines are now available which can read people's handwriting directly. This is quite an achievement because people's handwriting styles are very different. Naturally, the handwriting must be neat so that the computer can understand it.

Optical character readers are very expensive devices because they are very complex. Before long we will see many more of these machines in use.

Bar codes

You will probably have seen the bar codes printed on the labels of goods in shops (Figure 8.4). Bar codes are made up of a series of light and dark bands. To feed the information into the computer either the bar coded item is passed over the reader, or a wand shaped reader is passed over the bar code. Usually the first method is used, because it is much quicker.

The bar code reader sends out a laser beam of light

Figure 8.4 *Bar codes are found on labels*

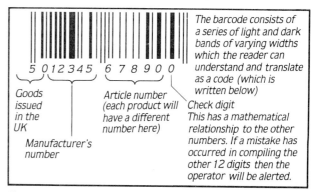

Figure 8.5 *What the bars mean on a bar code*

across the bar code. It detects the width of the lines and the computer can understand the information contained in them such as price, manufacturer and size (Figure 8.5). Some libraries also use bar codes for recording information about which books have been lent and when they should be returned.

Mark sensing

Mark sensing involves detecting pencil or ink marks made on a document. Usually, this involves drawing a line or marking in a certain area on the document. You might have seen these forms if you have ever done a multiple choice exam (Figure 8.6).

Mark sensing is used mainly for marking multiple choice examination papers, questionnaires and making up information after electricity or gas meters have been read so that it can be input directly into the computer. Football pools coupons are also read using mark sensing.

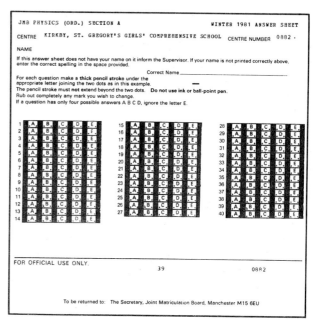

Figure 8.6 *Multiple choice answer sheets*

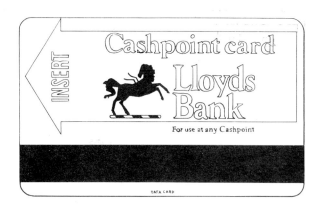

Figure 8.7 *Cash dispenser cards use magnetic encoding*

Figure 8.8 *Using a wand reader to read the price from a magnetic stripe on a price tag. The information is fed into the computer automatically via the till.*

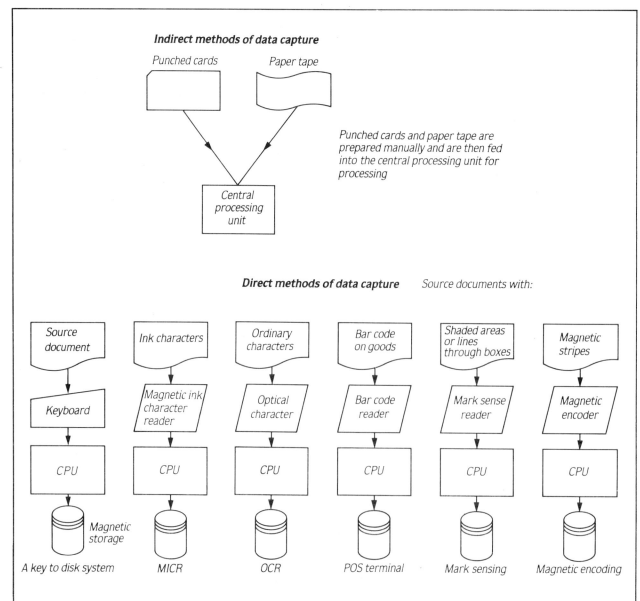

Indirect methods of data capture

Punched cards   Paper tape

Punched cards and paper tape are prepared manually and are then fed into the central processing unit for processing

Central processing unit

Direct methods of data capture   *Source documents with:*

Source document	Ink characters	Ordinary characters	Bar code on goods	Shaded areas or lines through boxes	Magnetic stripes
Keyboard	Magnetic ink character reader	Optical character	Bar code reader	Mark sense reader	Magnetic encoder
CPU	CPU	CPU	CPU	CPU	CPU
Magnetic storage					
A key to disk system	MICR	OCR	POS terminal	Mark sensing	Magnetic encoding

Figure 8.9 *The different types of data capture*

Magnetic encoding

If you look at a bank credit card or a card that can be used in a cash dispenser you will notice that it has a dark band on the front (Figure 8.7). The stripe on the cash card consists of a magnetic material which can be used to hold information. When the card is inserted into the cash dispenser the bank's computer can read the information in the magnetic stripe. This is called **magnetic encoding**.

Magnetic encoding is sometimes used on price labels on goods in certain shops. The information contained on the price ticket is read directly into the computer using a wand reader (Figure 8.8).

Figure 8.9 gives a summary of the data capture methods.

Test yourself

Using the words in the list below, copy out and complete sentences A to J underlining the words you have inserted. The words may be used once, more than once or not at all.

magnetic	indirect	key-to-disk
direct	credit	MICR	cheque clearing
sensor	readable	source	bar code
sale terminals	errors	OCR

A There are two methods of data capture. They are direct and _____.

B Using the indirect method the data is prepared into a machine _____ form before it is fed into the computer.

C The _____ method involves fewer data _____.

D When information is keyed via the keyboard, the method of data capture is called _____ - _____ - _____.

E Usually, the information to be keyed in is written out on a form called a _____ document.

F Banks use the direct system for ____ ____ _____.

G _____ involves reading characters printed in ordinary ink.

H A _____ _____ reader can often be seen in supermarkets. The special tills are called points of _____ _____.

I A _____ sensor can detect marks made on a document such as a multiple choice answer sheet or a meter reading sheet.

J Sometimes, information can be held on a magnetic stripe. This is called _____ encoding. It can often be seen on _____ cards.

Things to do

1 Write down four different methods of inputting data into a computer. In each case, state an application which would be suitable for the given method of input.

2 MICR script looks like this:

⑈ ⑈ 196517⑈⑈ 22⑈⑈30221⑈

OCR script looks like this:

25 2320 0550 10   684000006800

Give **one** reason why banks prefer to use MICR script rather than OCR script on cheques. Give **one** reason why a company might prefer to use an OCR system rather than MICR.

3 a What are magnetic ink characters?
b Where might they be used?

4 Data capture can be divided into two: **indirect methods** and **direct methods**. Explain what is meant by each of these terms. Indirect methods of data capture are not used very often nowadays. Why not? Explain your answer.

5 Explain what is meant by the following words:
a Source data
b Data capture
c Key-to-disk system

6 a Why are people who are employed by the computer companies constantly looking for new methods of data capture?
b Why is it desirable to input data at high speed into the CPU?

7 a Briefly describe a key-to-disk system.
b Why is the use of key-to-disk systems in business increasing?
c Give an advantage of key-to-disk system.

8 Write down the meanings of the following abbreviations:
a CPU
b MICR
c OCR
d POS
e VDU

9 Magnetic ink character recognition, optical character recognition, bar codes, mark sensing and magnetic encoding are all methods of data capture. Write down with reasons which method (or methods) would be most suitable for the following applications.

a Recording the sale of goods at a large multiple store such as Tescos

b Clearing cheques at the main clearing house in London

c Automatically marking a GCE O Level paper which consists of multiple choice questions

d Obtaining cash from a cash dispenser with a cash or credit card

10 Below is a bar code as found on products sold in supermarkets.

a Explain how the data from the bar code is input into the computer.

b Say how this method of data input is beneficial
   i to the customer,
   ii to the supermarket.

5 000136 999709

11 a Name one type of document on which magnetic ink character recognition (MICR) is used.

b Name one type of document on which optical character recognition (OCR) is used.

c Name one type of document on which mark reading is used.

d i How is magnetic ink character recognized?
   ii What must be done to a magnetic ink character before it can be read by a machine?

e How is a character like the one shown here recognized?

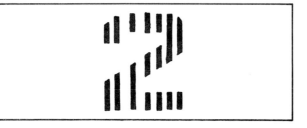

f Give one advantage and one disadvantage of each of the following:
   i magnetic ink character recognition,
   ii optical character recognition,
   iii mark reading.

g These numbers are copied from the bottom of a cheque. What do they tell you?

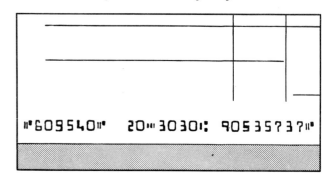

12 Why is it so important to eliminate errors at the data preparation/input stage of processing? Describe what happens after a possible error is found during a load and validation run.

13 The following are special methods of entering information into a computer system. Briefly describe an application of each.

a Magnetic ink character recognition
b Optical mark recognition
c Bar codes
d Kimball tags

14 'The ideal data capture method would not involve the handling of the information by humans.'

Explain what is meant by this statement. Explain how a bar code reader in a supermarket can avoid all the errors of the conventional methods used to record sales.

15 a Name **four** ways in which data can be input into a computer. Name the device you would use in each case.

b List any advantages and disadvantages of each method.

16 Outline some methods of data capture and explain for each one the sort of errors that could occur.

17 Diagrams a, b and c illustrate three ways of representing data in machine-readable form. What input device would be required to read the data?

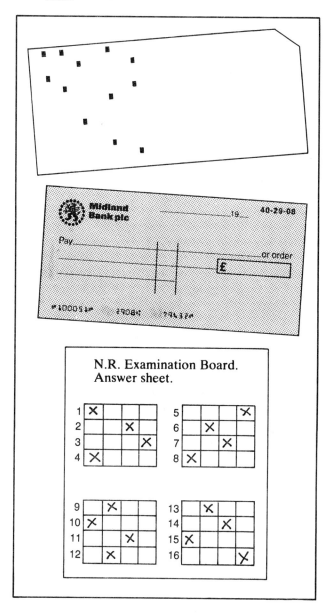

18 In many computer applications the collection of data is an error-prone and time-consuming activity.

a Describe **three** possible causes of errors when data is collected and prepared manually for input.

b Name **three** ways of collecting data without the need for data preparation. In each case describe how the data is represented in machine-readable form and how it is read.

c Describe **two** different applications where automatic collection of data is an important feature. In each case, explain the advantages gained by automatic data collection.

9
Data errors and source errors

Figure 9.1 *Computers need to be accurate as well as fast*

As well as being fast, computers must also be accurate (Figure 9.1). The problem of accuracy usually lies with the person who inputs the data into the computer. There are many types of possible errors and there are many ways of avoiding them. Usually it is best to avoid human handling of the data as much as possible. If this can't be avoided then other methods must be used. Of course some errors are unavoidable. Modern methods of data capture such as bar code readers and magnetic ink character readers are less prone to errors.

Transcription errors

Transcription errors are errors which happen when the source data is input into the computer. Transcription errors include the misreading of the source documents by the operator, entering the wrong values and the transposition of digits (putting numbers in the wrong order) e.g. 1021503 instead of 0121503 (Figure 9.2).

The usual method of data capture is key-to-disk so all these errors are likely to occur. But now there is a move towards more direct data capture methods such as bar code readers and optical character readers. If these methods are used then transcription errors can be avoided.

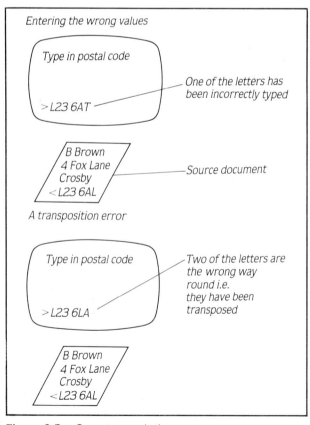

Figure 9.2 *Some transcription errors*

Verification methods

Verification is a pre-input check on data before it is accepted into the computer. It involves typing the information into the computer twice. Usually in key-to-disk systems two different operators type in the information. The computer only accepts the information for processing when the two type in exactly the same information. Any discrepancies are pointed out to each operator for correction.

One of the disadvantages of verification is that it is time consuming. A lot of companies prefer to trust the operator's accuracy and type the information only once.

Validation methods

Validation checks are made on the data to make sure that the data is valid i.e. allowable (Figure 9.3). The validation is performed by a computer program. It looks at the data to see if it is of a certain type or of a certain range. If the data is not valid the program stops and lets the operator know why it is not acceptable so that it can be checked again. Here are some of the validation checks normally performed by the program.

Range checks

Range checks make sure the data is within a certain range. In other words they check that the data is not too large or too small. For example, if an average person's age was input it would be unlikely to be above 110 and never less than 0. So a range check could be carried out to make sure that the data was within this range (Figure 9.4).

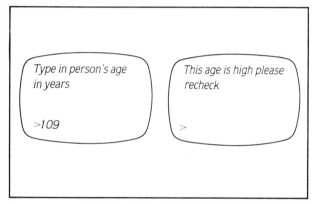

Figure 9.4   *A range check*

Figure 9.3   *Bad program validation!*

Field checks or data type checks

Field checks or **data type checks** are used to see if the data is of a certain type. For example, they detect numbers where letters should have been and vice versa.

Check digits

Check digits are used to detect errors in data after it has gone through the verification stage. The check digit is placed at the end of a series of numbers or characters and is used to check them.

This system is used in the International Standard Book Number (ISBN) which can be seen on the cover of any book published, including this one. This is how the check digit works. Suppose a book has the ISBN 0 7195 2844 5. The check digit is the 5 at the right hand side. Working from the far left hand side and ignoring the check digit, the first number we come to is zero. This is multiplied by 10. The second number is a 7. This is multiplied by 9. The third number is multiplied by 8 and so on.

$$
\begin{array}{rcl}
0 \times 10 & = & 0 \\
7 \times 9 & = & 63 \\
1 \times 8 & = & 8 \\
9 \times 7 & = & 63 \\
5 \times 6 & = & 30 \\
2 \times 5 & = & 10 \\
8 \times 4 & = & 32 \\
4 \times 3 & = & 12 \\
4 \times 2 & = & 8 \\
\textbf{Total} & = & \textbf{226}
\end{array}
$$

The results of the multiplication are added up and then divided by 11. The remainder of this division is subtracted from 11 and if the ISBN is correct the result gives the check digit.

$226 \div 11 = 20$ remainder 6
$11 - 6 = 5$ which is the check digit

When the ISBN number is typed into the computer, the computer performs these calculations and checks the calculation result against the check digit. If there is any discrepancy, then the computer will ask for the number to be keyed in again. The ISBN check digit system uses weighted modulus 11. 'Weighted modulus' means that each digit in the ISBN, excluding the check digit, has a certain weight depending on its position. This is a bit like place values in number bases. Each number is multiplied by its weight – the value of its position. So the left hand number has a weight of 10, and is multiplied by 10, and so on. Then the total is divided by the modulus, 11. Finally, the remainder is subtracted from the modulus, 11.

Another application using weighted modulus 11 as a method of checking is the accounts codes on cheques. Have a look at an account number on a cheque (it is the number over to the right hand side on the bottom of a cheque). Ignore the check digit and work out what it should be for yourself.

Hash totals

Hash totals are the totals of numbers input into the computer. This is how it works. Suppose we want to input the numbers 6 and 7 into the computer. Using this check we would also input the number 13 which is the hash total. The computer will automatically check the input numbers with the hash total. If the two numbers are different then they must be rechecked.

Batch totals

If a large number of data numbers are input it is easy to make a mistake. To try to avoid these mistakes the numbers can be added up and the total input as well. If the computer adds up the numbers and doesn't get the same total as the input one, then one of the input numbers must be incorrect.

Limitations of error checking

Despite all these checks some errors will occur. it is very easy for example, for a typist to type letters or numbers in the wrong order, especially is she is working at high speed. Most computers cannot distinguish between correctly and incorrectly spelt words although some wordprocessors can do this. Probably the best way of ensuring that as few mistakes occur as possible, is to type in the data twice.

Test yourself

Using the words in the list below, copy out and complete sentences A to J underlining the words you have inserted. The words may be used once, more than once or not at all.

verification   transcription   range
program   batches   field   hash
check   source   valid

A _____ errors happen when the source data is input into the computer. They involve the operator misreading _____ documents, entering the wrong values and putting the digits the wrong way round.

B _____ is a pre-input check on data. It involves typing the information into the computer twice.

C Validation means checking the data to see if it is _____.

D Validation is performed by the computer _____.

E _____ checks make sure that the data is in a certain range.

F A check which could detect numbers where letters should be is called a _____ check.

G _____ digits are used to detect errors after the verification stage.

H In an International Standard Book Number (ISBN) the last number is a _____ digit.

I _____ totals are totals of numbers input into the computer.

J Batch totals are totals of _____ of numbers that are input into the computer.

Things to do

1 Explain in detail what is meant by verification and validation. Suggest appropriate checks to ensure correct input of:
  a Dates of birth of pupils in your school
  b Surnames
  c Bank account numbers

2 Explain how the following are used as data validation methods to check data:
  a Batch totals
  b Range checks
  c Field checks
  d Check digits

3 a What is meant by a 'check digit'? Give two circumstances in which check digits are used.
  b Briefly outline some of the limitations of error checking.

4 a Below is an ISBN (International Standard Book Number).
ISBN 0 903 885 19 0
Explain how a check digit may be used to detect a transcription error in the above code number.
  b Explain what a hash total is and how it is used.

5 The flowchart gives a simple method for calculating a check digit for a given account number.
  a Use the method in the flowchart to calculate a check digit for this account number: 4629
  b Why are check digits used?
  c Name an application which would make use of check digits.

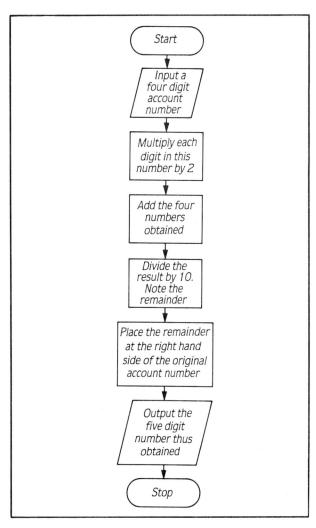

Start

Input a four digit account number

Multiply each digit in this number by 2

Add the four numbers obtained

Divide the result by 10. Note the remainder

Place the remainder at the right hand side of the original account number

Output the five digit number thus obtained

Stop

6 'Computer sends housewife a £1 million gas bill.'

We would probably all agree that this statement is misleading because the computer cannot make a mistake. However, in the preparation of a gas bill, errors occur at any of the following stages:

1   Meter reading
2   Data preparation
3   Data transmission
4   Production of gas bill

State the types of error which could occur at each stage, and explain how such errors are detected and corrected.

Indicate any error which may not be detected. Give reasons for your answer.

7 A company manufacturing parts uses a six digit reference number for each type of item produced. The sixth digit of the reference number is a check digit.

a For the number 13378, devise a check digit, showing your working.

b Using an appropriate example, briefly explain two errors which may be detected by the use of a check digit.

8 The following number is an ISBN (International Standard Book Number) which is found on all books. The last number which we will call X is the check digit.

ISBN 0 09129931 X

a Draw a flowchart to show how you could work out a check digit for the above number.

b Use your flowchart to find the value of the check digit X.

9 Data is entered into a computer from the document below.

For each of the following validation techniques, choose two fields in which the technique could be used to check the data.

a Format check
b Range check
c Check digit
d Data type check

Name	S	M	I	T	H	M	A	R	K		
Form										5	A

Date of birth	2	1	0	6	6	9

School no.	1	2	3	4	3

Candidate no.	4	2	0	7	2

10 Operating systems

Two terms often used in connection with computers are **on-line** and **off-line**. On-line means that the equipment is directly under the control of the central processing unit (CPU). This means that any device which is on-line, for example, a line printer, can be used by the computer at any time. Off-line means that the equipment is not controlled by the CPU. Paper tape and card punches are off-line devices.

All computers have **operating systems**. An operating system is a collection of computer programs. Operating systems are sometimes referred to as **executive** or **supervisor programs**. The operating system controls the overall operation of the computer. It performs tasks such as giving programs and data places in the memory, scheduling jobs and controlling the overall input and output of the computer. The CPU can work at extremely high speeds but other devices are much slower. So the operating system co-ordinates the activities of the other parts of the system so that the CPU is used as efficiently as possible.

There are many types of operating systems used by computers. Let's look at a few of them.

Single program systems

This is the type of operating system used by microcomputers. Only one program can be processed at a time.

Batch processing

Most of the larger computers can carry out **batch processing** (Figure 10.1). Batch processing is the system of collecting all the different inputs or programs together and putting them into a computer in one set or a 'batch'. The computer operator only has to do one loading and running operation, no matter how many programs are in a batch. The programs are processed as a single unit. This avoids wasting a lot of time loading programs. Nowadays batch processing is not used so much for running a series of programs. Instead, input data is usually batched.

Batch processing is used when a particular job needs to be done in one go rather than by doing parts of the job now and again. All the relevant data is collected and put through the computer in one go. Preparing a company's payroll would be a good example of batch processing. All the information such as hours of work, pay per hour, tax and national insurance contributions would be collected for each employee and put into the computer. Batch processing can be used for payrolls because they are performed in one go (once a week or once a month). Electricity, gas and telephone bills are all prepared in one go so batch processing is used. Using batch processing means that bills can be produced quickly and cheaply and they can all be sent out at the same time. Very high speed laser printers are used to print out the bills. Cheque clearing also uses batch processing. This makes the job cheap and very quick.

Multiprogramming

The central processing unit is a very fast device. It is much faster than the peripherals used to input or output information. So the CPU spends a lot of time doing nothing. Rather than waste this valuable time on the CPU we can use the CPU to process other programs. So many programs can be processed, apparently at the same time, by a single CPU. A system like this has a **multiprogramming**

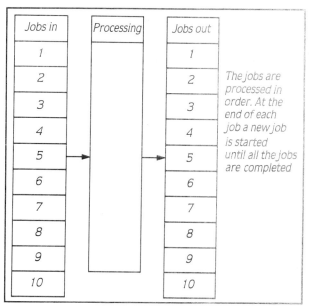

Jobs in	Processing	Jobs out	
1		1	
2		2	*The jobs are processed in order. At the end of each job a new job is started until all the jobs are completed*
3		3	
4		4	
5		5	
6		6	
7		7	
8		8	
9		9	
10		10	

Figure 10.1 *Batch processing*

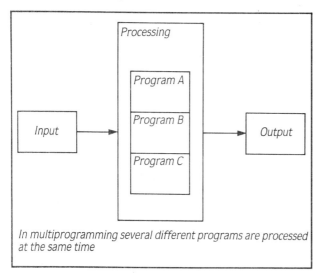

In multiprogramming several different programs are processed at the same time

Figure 10.2 *Multiprogramming*

operating system (Figure 10.2). The operating system decides what order the programs are carried out. Some of the programs are given priority and it is possible for the computer operator to change the order.

Sometimes multiprogramming systems are called **multitasking** systems because they can perform many different tasks 'at the same time'. They don't have to complete one task before starting another. Although computers can only perform one task at a time, a computer works so fast that it seems as if several tasks are being performed simultaneously.

Remote job entry

Remote job entry is when jobs are entered at a terminal away from the computer and cards or paper tape are punched at a distant site. The terminal would be connected via telephone lines to the CPU. Cards and paper tape would probably be sent by post for processing. The terminal would operate under a multiprogramming system and the cards or paper tape would use the batch processing system.

Multi-access

Multi-access allows many terminals to gain access to the CPU at the same time. A device called a **multiplexer** controls the amount of time that each terminal has allocated to it. The multiplexer is connected between the CPU and the terminals. The amount of time is controlled by the operating system. So are the memory requirements of each terminal.

Multi-access can be used for airline reservation systems. Many terminals situated in travel agents and booking offices use just one CPU to book airline tickets.

Most multi-access systems give the user the impression that she is the only one using the computer. The computer serves other people during the time she takes to press the keys. This principle is often called **time sharing** (Figures 10.3 and 10.4).

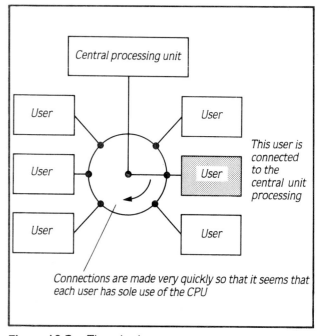

Connections are made very quickly so that it seems that each user has sole use of the CPU

Figure 10.3 *Time sharing*

Real time operating systems

Real time operating systems perform real time processing. This means the computer is constantly kept up-to-date with information supplied by the operator. The computer actually communicates with the operator. The information in the computer is constantly being changed and updated.

Airline companies and travel agents were the first people to use real time processing. Now, hospitals, shops, robots in factories and banks all use real time processing.

Remote access

Large companies tend to have branches or offices all over the country or even the world. Quite often, the CPU will be in the Head Office and terminals and other peripherals such as line printers will be dispersed over large distances (Figure 10.5). Data

Figure 10.4   *Time sharing!*

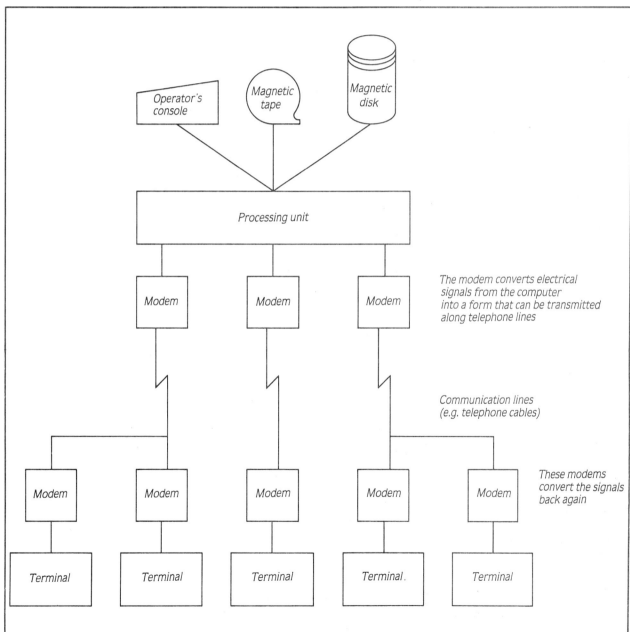

Figure 10.5   *A data processing network with terminals far away from the computer*

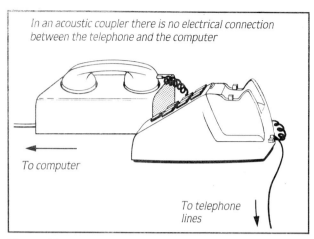

Figure 10.6 *An acoustic coupler*

Figure 10.7 *A modem connects a telephone and a computer. It converts the signals from the computer so that they can be passed along telephone lines. Then it converts them back again*

and information is passed between the devices using telephone cables. Either an acoustic coupler or a modem is used to convert the data into a form that can be passed along telephone cables (Figures 10.6 and 10.7).

Test yourself

Using the words in the list below, copy out and complete sentences A to J underlining the words you have inserted. The words may be used once, more than once or not at all.

off   programs   multi-access   multiplexer timesharing   executive   on   microcomputers multiprogramming   batch   single   real time

A _____-line means that a device is under the control of the CPU.

B _____-line means that the device is not under the control of the CPU.

C *Operating systems, sometimes called _____ or supervisor programs, are a collection of computer _____.*

D *An operating system only allowing one program to be processed at a time is called a _____ program system. This system is mainly used by _____.*

E _____ *processing is used where a job is done in one go rather than in bits now and again.*

F _____ _____ *allows the computer to work on several programs at the same time.*

G *A _____ system allows many terminals to gain access to the CPU.*

H *Each terminal has a certain amount of time allocated to it and this is controlled by a _____.*

I *The principle of giving each terminal a certain amount of time is called _____.*

J _____ *processing is where the computer is constantly being kept up-to-date by the operator.*

Things to do

1 *For the following applications, place a tick in the correct column to show whether it would be a batch processing or a real time application. The first application has been ticked for you.*

Application	Batch	Real time
Airline reservations		✓
Payroll		
Computer aided instruction		
Traffic sight control		
Electricity billing		

2 *An airline seat booking system is an example of which system?*
   a *An off-line system*
   b *A batch processing system*
   c *A time sharing system*
   d *A real time system*
   e *A microcomputer system*

3 *Explain the meaning of the words*
   a *Batch processing and*
   b *Real time processing*
   Which of the two methods above would be used for the following?
   i *Reserving theatre tickets*

    ii   *Cheque clearing*
   iii *Doing a payroll at the end of the month*
   iv *Controlling some of the equipment in an intensive care unit*
    v *Producing electricity or gas bills at the end of a quarter*
   vi *Booking airline tickets*

4 *Choose **one** of the following fields: medicine, industry, commerce. From your chosen field, suggest a job which is most suited for each of the following given systems. Give reasons for each suggestion.*
  a *On-line*
  b *Batch*
  c *Real time*

5 *For each of the applications given below, state whether the method of data processing would be off-line, on-line, real time or batch. In each case, give **one** reason for your choice.*
  a *A bank cash dispenser which can also give a report of the current balance in a customer's account*
  b *An examination board system for collecting marks from examiners using mark sense forms*
  c *An automatic device in a car which can set and maintain a given speed on a motorway*

6 *An interactive processing system must **always** be which one of the following?*
  a *On-line*
  b *Multi-access*
  c *Batch*
  d *Time sharing*

7 **a** i *What is multi-access computing?*
      ii *Name an application which uses multi-access computing.*
  b i *Explain the meaning of real time computing.*
      ii *Name an application which uses real time computing.*

8 **a** *Describe the essential features of a real time system.*
  b *Describe what is meant by batch processing.*
  c *Name **one** example of each of the above.*
  d *Choose either a real time or a batch processing application you have studied and describe it. Give details of the equipment used, the information input and output, and the people involved.*

9 *Explain what is meant by the following words:*
  a *Remote access*
  b *Multiprogramming*
  c *Multi-access*

10 *Real time processing is being used increasingly because the information is always up-to-date. Batch processing still has advantages for doing certain types of jobs.*
  a *What types of job are these?*
  b *What advantages does batch processing have over real time processing?*
  c *What is meant by the term 'up-to-date'?*

11 **a** *What is meant by the term 'time sharing'?*
  b *Several terminals can be connected to a single central processing unit. Why does each terminal appear to have sole use of the computer?*

12 *Some computers are able to run several programs on several terminals at the same time. This is called multiprogramming.*
  a *Explain how the computer can do this.*
  b *In order to do multiprogramming, the computer will need an operating system. What is meant by 'an operating system'?*

13 *Multiprogramming is one method of improving the efficiency of the use of the CPU. How does multiprogramming improve the efficiency of the use of the CPU?*

11
Output formats

Figure 11.1 *Sometimes a computer user needs to take away a hard copy!*

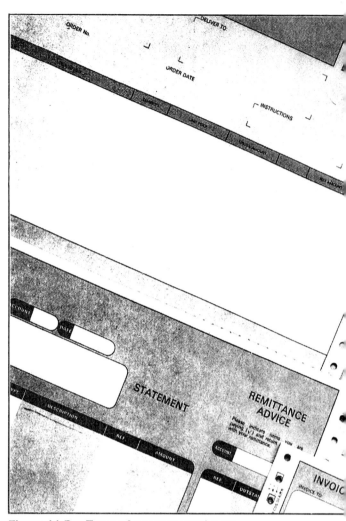

Figure 11.2 *Types of computer stationary*

The **output format** is the way the output from the computer is presented to the user. Sometimes the information presented on a visual display unit (VDU) may be sufficient, but if the user needs to take the output away and study it, then she will need a hard copy from a printer (Figure 11.1).

In chapter 6 we saw that input has to be in a standard format. Output also needs to be presented in a standard way. For printed output, the layout is very important. Bills, cheques, accounts, payslips, sales figures etc. will all be printed on pre-printed continuous stationery and the figures and words must go in the various spaces on these documents.

Printed output

In most office uses of computers the output from the computer is printed on paper. When the output is printed out like this, it is sometimes called a **hard copy**. It is called a hard copy because, like hardware,

it can be picked up and moved around. A lot of documents used in the day to day running of a company need to be in writing for legal reasons. Also, if the documents need to be sent out by post, then they must be printed out. There is now a system for electronic mail, where documents can be sent through the telephone lines and can appear hundreds, or even thousands, of miles away on a VDU screen, but this is not very common yet because of the expense.

Invoices, cheques, payslips, accounts, financial reports and sales analysis reports are all examples of documents which need to be printed out. All of these could be printed out on pre-printed continuous stationery (Figure 11.2). For invoices, the company's headings and terms and conditions of contract would all be pre-printed on the continuous stationery before it is put into the computer. The computer line printer then fills in all the variable information in the right places for each invoice. To make sure the line printer places its output in the correct places, careful

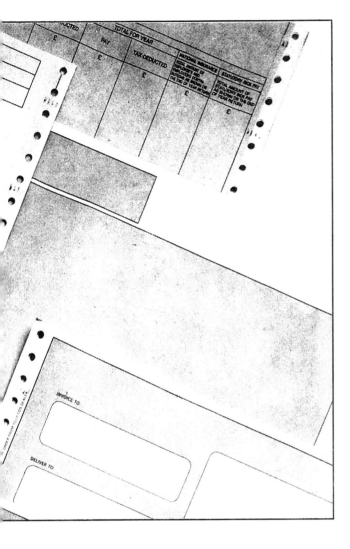

planning is needed when the computer is programmed. Some computer printers can print company headings etc. in different size types and even different colours. These printers are called ink jet printers because they spray ink onto the paper. There are some advantages in this method. Pre-printed continuous stationery is very expensive, and although ink jet printers are expensive, they soon work out cheaper because of the saving on stationery.

Wordprocessors produce their output on single sheets of paper, rather like a typewriter. They are also able to print out sticky labels containing names and addresses so that they may be stuck on the envelopes ready for posting (Figure 11.3).

Invoices, cheques, payslips, receipts etc. that are printed out with headings and boxes on continuous stationery are referred to as **standard forms** (Figure 11.4). The computer fills in the relevant details of the output in the spaces provided.

```
       ***      VICTOR VALUE      ***

            CARRIER BAG            .03
            VAL ALSORTS            .59
            OVENCLEANER            .59
            CHICKEN CURR           .68½
            POTATOES               .29½
            IRISH STEW             .39
            POTATOES               .20
            WHOLE MUSHRM           .38
            AMER GINGER            .23
            PASTE                  .24½
            NOODLES                .39½
            CRNISH PASTY           .36
            WHOLE MUSHRM           .38
            BALANCE DUE            4.77

            CASH                   5.00

            CHANGE DUE             .23

      23/10/84 15:52 1208 0001   2      1006
          **  THANK YOU - COME AGAIN  **
```

Figure 11.4   *A receipt from a point of sale terminal*

Record storage using microfiche and microfilm

As well as outputting information from the computer onto paper, we can also photograph the information

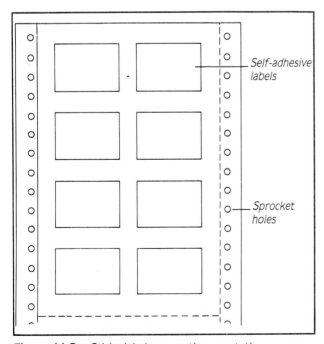

Figure 11.3   *Sticky labels on continuous stationery*

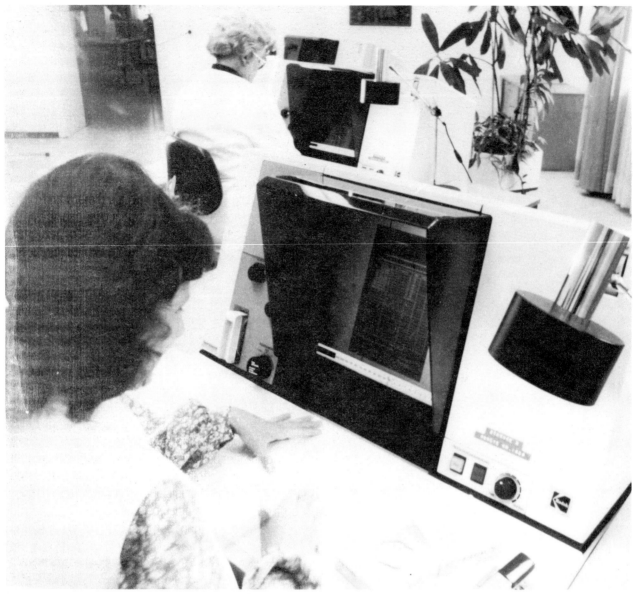

Figure 11.5 *Microfilm viewer*

on the screen and then reduce it in size. The obvious advantage in doing this is that a large amount of printed material can be held in a very small space. The process is often referred to as COM (**Computer Output on Microfilm/Microfiche**).

Information is held on film in two ways. If it is held on a reel, the film is called **microfilm**. If it is contained on small sheets, it is called **microfiche**. Both ways need a machine called a viewer to find and magnify the information held on the film (Figure 11.5).

Microfilm and microfiche are best used for information that stays fairly constant and doesn't need updating very often. There are output devices which can record the data held on magnetic tape and turn it directly into microfilm or microfiche.

Figure 11.6 *The screen output from a Philips viewdata system. Garages can use this system to find any unsold British Leyland car which is needed by a customer*

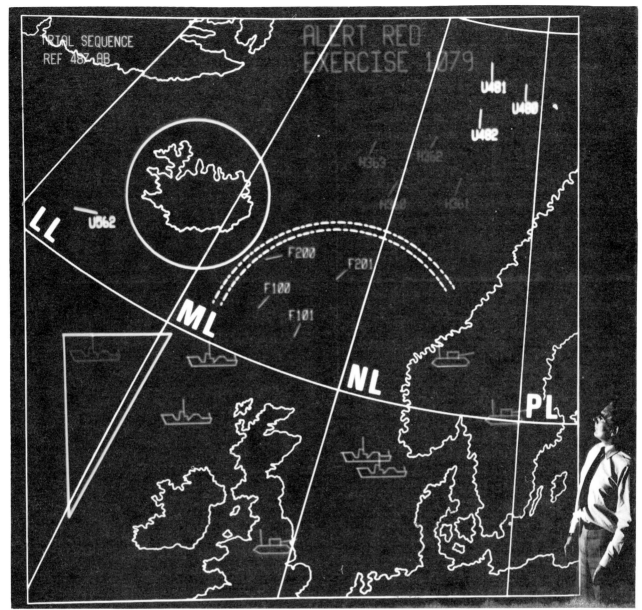

Figure 11.7 *Outputting data on a much larger screen. The screen can be up to 4 metres square. This means as many as 10 people can look at it at once.*

Screen output

There are many situations where the output from the computer does not need to be output on paper. Examples include computer games, advertisements and information retrieval systems such as Ceefax, Oracle and Prestel (Figure 11.6). In these systems, the computer displays (outputs) the information on a **visual display unit** (**VDU**).

When information is output on a screen, the same care needs to be taken about its presentation as if it were to be printed out (Figure 11.7).

Analogue to digital conversion

Sometimes, output from the computer is not required either in the form of a display on a VDU or as a hard copy from a line printer.

In process control, the computer receives data in the form of analogue signals and has to process these signals and decide on the output. In order to process the information by a digital computer, the computer has to change the analogue readings to digital ones. The device that does the conversion is known as an **analogue/digital converter**. When the digital computer produces the output signal, it needs to convert it back into an analogue form so that it can control the machine or process. This situation is called a **feedback loop**.

Test yourself

Using the words in the list below, copy out and complete sentences A to M. Underline the words you put in. The words can be used once, more than once or not at all.

hard copy	legal	stationery	ink jet
regularly	single	control	pre-printed
output	format	microfilm	continuous
reduce	retrieval	Oracle	Prestel
hardware	VDU	labels	photograph
microfilm	signals	microfiche	

A The output _____ is the way the output is set out.

B When the output is printed out on paper it is often called a _____ _____ because it can be picked up and moved around like _____.

C Often, output is printed out on paper for _____ reasons.

D Quite often _____ continuous _____ is used and the information which varies is printed out in the spaces.

E There are now line printers called _____ _____ printers that can produce company headings in different colours on plain paper.

F Wordprocessors produce their output on _____ sheets of paper rather than using _____ stationery.

G They are also able to print sticky _____ which can be used to stick on envelopes or parcels.

H In order to obtain a permanent copy without using paper it is possible to _____ the information on the _____ screen and reduce it in size.

I This process is referred to as COM which means Computer _____ on _____.

J The film is either held in the form of sheets or reels of film. Film on a reel is called _____ and film on a sheet is called _____.

K COM is used mainly when the information does not need to be changed _____ such as books in libraries.

L Information _____ systems do not need to be printed out on paper. The information can be set out neatly on a __ _____ Such systems include _____, Ceefax and _____.

M In process control, the computer produces _____ which are fed back to _____ an industrial process.

Things to do

1 Explain what the following words mean:
  a Output format
  b Hard copy
  c Continuous stationery
  d Microfilm
  e Microfiche

2 Below is a list of types of computer output. Which of them would require a hard copy? Give reasons for your choices.
  a Production of an electricity bill
  b Signals to control an automatic paint sprayer
  c Production of a company's accounts
  d Producing an employee's wage slip
  e Screen output for a game such as space invaders

3 **a** What is meant by the abbreviation COM?
  b What advantages does COM have over other output formats such as hard copy?
  c There are two types of COM, microfilm and microfiche. What is the difference between them?

4 **a** Name **four** documents that are produced on a line printer using pre-printed stationery.
  b Give **two** reasons why hard copies are needed of certain documents.
  c Name **two** applications where a hard copy would not be required. Give reasons for your choices.

5 **a** What is an analogue/digital converter?
  b What is its purpose in computerized process control?
  c What is a feedback loop?

12
The central processing unit (CPU)

Figure 12.2 *A typical computer system. In the centre are the VDU and keyboard (input devices). The central processing unit is on the right and the line printer (the output device) is on the left*

Inside the central processing unit

The **central processing unit** can be divided into three main parts. These are the **control unit**, the **arithmetic and logic unit** (**ALU**) and the **main memory** (**immediate access store**) (Figure12.1). Each part has a particular task.

The central unit controls the step-by-step running of the computer system. It sends the electrical signals to the various parts of the system. The arithmetic and logic unit (ALU) does all the calculating and performs all the logical operations. The main memory or immediate access store stores all the programs and data that are being used. As the data or programs are needed immediately, the memory is immediately accessible.

To get information into the CPU, you need an input device. To get information out you need an output device. The input and output **buffers** are part of the CPU where the data is stored temporarily to cope with the difference in speeds of the various peripheral (input and output) devices.

Figure 12.2 shows a typical computer system.

Large scale integration and chips

Semiconductors are special types of materials that are used for making transistors. In older computers, the transistors, along with all the other electrical components needed, could be connected together with wires to form a circuit. Nowadays, it is possible to produce all these circuits inside a single crystal of semiconductor. This is called an **integrated circuit**.

Because the circuits can be made as single electrical components, they are extremely small, cheap to make and extremely reliable. The semiconductor material used is silicon. The very thin wafer of silicon crystal that these circuits are made on is called a chip (Figure 12.3). Silicon chips are responsible for the big increase in computers and microprocessor controlled devices.

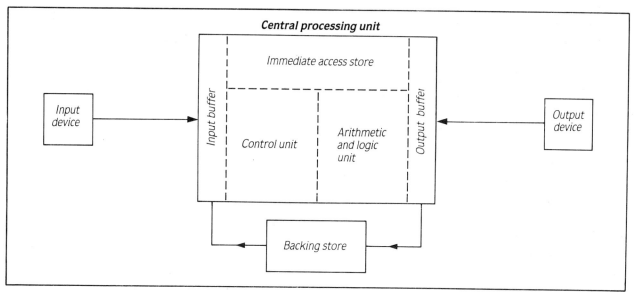

Figure 12.1 *Inside the CPU*

Figure 12.3 *Silicon chips. The threaded needle at the bottom of the photo gives some idea of how small the chips are*

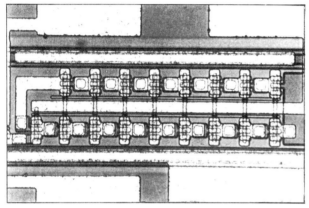

Figure 12.4 *A transistor circuit for a very large scale integrated (VLSI) circuit*

If more than 1000 electronic components are on one chip it is called a **large-scale integrated circuit** (**LSI**) (Figure 12.4). Scientists think it will be possible in the near future to get as many as one million electronic components on a silicon chip.

ROM and RAM

ROM and **RAM** are the two types of memories inside the central processing unit. RAM is the abbreviation for **random access memory** and ROM is the abbreviation for **read only memory**.

RAM is a temporary memory. Anything stored in RAM is lost when the computer is switched off. RAM is sometimes referred to as **volatile** memory because stored data disappears when the computer is switched off. Data and instructions which are currently being processed by the computer are stored in the RAM. Because the access is random the data and stored instructions can be accessed immediately.

Information and data can be put into the RAM using input devices such as keyboards, light pens, wand readers etc. After the data has been processed, it can be output using an output device such as a line printer, VDU etc. Information and data contained in RAM can easily be changed.

ROM can only be read from. It cannot be changed. Programs which need to be kept permanently are stored in ROM. Programs kept in ROM include the operating system and sometimes the language the computer uses, such as BASIC.

ROM is a permanent memory and is often referred to as being **non-volatile**. ROM is put in a silicon chip when it is manufactured and this is why it is impossible to change its contents.

PROM and EPROM

PROM stands for **programmable read only memory**. It is possible, using a special hardware device, to record information that is needed regularly, on a chip. Once this information has been recorded onto the chip, it cannot be altered by reprogramming.

EPROM stands for **erasable programmable read only memory**. This memory chip can have its contents erased and it may be reprogrammed (Figure 12.5). To erase the information contained on the chip, the chip is exposed to ultra violet light.

Both PROM and EPROM can only be read when they are in the computer.

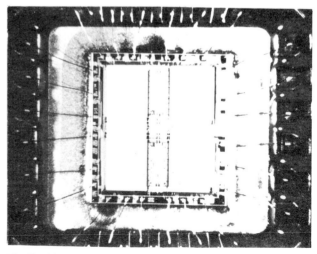

Figure 12.5 *An EPROM chip*

The microprocessor

A **microprocessor** is an LSI chip which is used to produce the CPU of a computer. The various parts that make up the CPU, i.e. the ALU, the control unit and sometimes the memory, are all in one chip.

Microprocessors are not just inside computers. They are found in childrens toys, washing machines, cookers, video recorders and many other places. In fact any device which needs to be controlled could have a microprocessor inside it. Soon, every type of device will be controlled by microprocessors.

Test yourself

Using the words in the list below, copy out and complete sentences A to J. Underline the words you have inserted. The words may be used once, more than once or not at all.

output   peripheral   control unit   silicon
integrated   RAM   input   buffer   ROM
changed   chip   random   microprocessor
erasable

A The central processing unit may be split into three parts. They are the arithmetic and logic unit, the _____ _____ and the main memory.

B To put information into the CPU and take it out you need an _____ and _____ device.

C A _____ is a temporary store which holds data to cope with the different speeds of the _____ devices.

D A crystal of a semiconductor can be used to make a complete circuit. This is called an _____ circuit.

E The semiconductor used most often is _____. It is sometimes called a silicon _____.

F There are two types of memory ROM and _____. ROM means read only memory and _____ means _____ access memory.

G _____ is a volatile memory whereas _____ is a non-volatile memory.

H PROM stands for programmable read only memory. Its contents cannot be _____.

I EPROM stands for _____ programmable read only memory and its contents may be changed.

J A _____ is a chip which contains all the circuits used to produce the CPU of a computer.

Things to do

1 The letters CPU usually refer to which of the following?
   a The control panel unit
   b The central programming unit
   c The computer printing unit
   d The central processing unit
   e The current program used

2 The part of a computer used for calculating and comparing is which of these?
   a Console
   b Arithmetic logic unit
   c Tape or disk unit
   d Acoustic coupler

3 A buffer allows which of these?
   a Peripherals to work at different speeds from the CPU
   b Programs to crash gently without damage to the computer
   c A computer to operate when the power is switched off
   d One program to run into another

4 ROM stands for which of these?
   a Round off multiples
   b Read onto microprocessor
   c Repeat of monitor
   d Read only memory

5 The store that forms part of the CPU has which type of access?
   a Serial access
   b Sequential access
   c Random/direct access
   d Immediate access

6 What is the arithmetic and logic unit? Choose from:
   a A peripheral device
   b A type of input unit
   c A type of output unit
   d A section of the full adder
   e Part of the central processing unit

7 Integrated circuits are part of one of these. Which?
   a Transistors
   b Capacitors
   c Valves
   d Microprocessors
   e Resistors

8 Explain why a buffer is used in the output of data to a line printer.

9 What is the name of the technique which made possible the assembly of a large number of components on a 'chip'.

10 Describe briefly the difference between a microprocessor and a microcomputer.

11 The diagram below shows a basic computer system. Choose one name from the list of words to put inside each of the five rectangles.

store   output device   algorithm
control unit   input device   assembler
arithmetic unit   abacus

What name is given to the dotted rectangle?

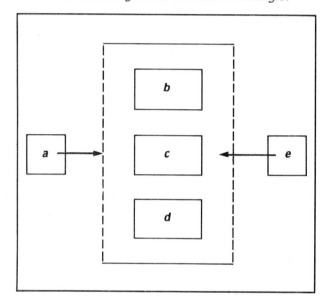

12 Within the next few years, the microprocessor may revolutionize small and medium sized computers. A single integrated circuit will form the CPU and, with the addition of some memory and suitable peripheral devices, it will be the basis of the future microcomputer system. This will mean that the microcomputer will cost considerably less than the computers that exist today. At the same time, this micro system will have the same powers as existing main frame computers.

a What do the initials CPU stand for?
b What is meant by peripheral device?
c What is meant by an integrated circuit?
d Give **one** reason, other than cost, why we may expect to see more use made of microcomputers in the future.

13 A particular popular computer is advertised as having 16K ROM and 16K RAM, expandable to 48K.
a What decimal value is represented by K?
b ROM stands for 'read only memory' and RAM stands for 'random access memory'. Describe the differences between these two types of memory.
c For what purposes might these two types of memory be used?
  i   ROM
  ii RAM

14 The central processing unit of a computer has been compared with the human brain. However, apart from technical details, there is a single fundamental difference between the two. Explain what this difference is.

15 **a** What is a microprocessor?
b Name **three** devices in which you would be likely to find a microprocessor.
c For each of the devices you have named, give the reason why a microprocessor is used.

16 The CPU of a computer can be divided into three parts.
a Name each of these parts.
b Give a description of the function of each part you have named.
c The input and output devices are connected to the CPU through a buffer. What is a buffer and what is its use?

17 There are two types of memory inside the CPU of a computer: ROM and RAM.
a Explain the differences between ROM and RAM
b RAM is often referred to as being 'volatile' and ROM as 'non-volatile'. What does this mean?

13
Computer arithmetic

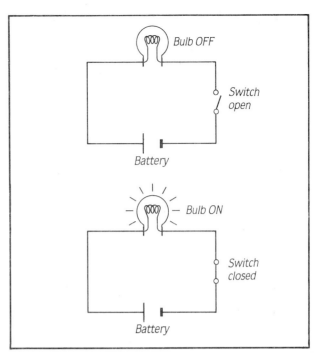

Figure 13.1 A two-state system

Bistable systems

Figure 13.1 shows a two state system. Depending on whether the switch is on or off, the bulb can be in two states only: OFF or ON. There is no in-between state. Systems which only have two states are called **bistable systems**. Figure 13.1 shows a typical bistable system. Figure 13.2 shows some other examples.

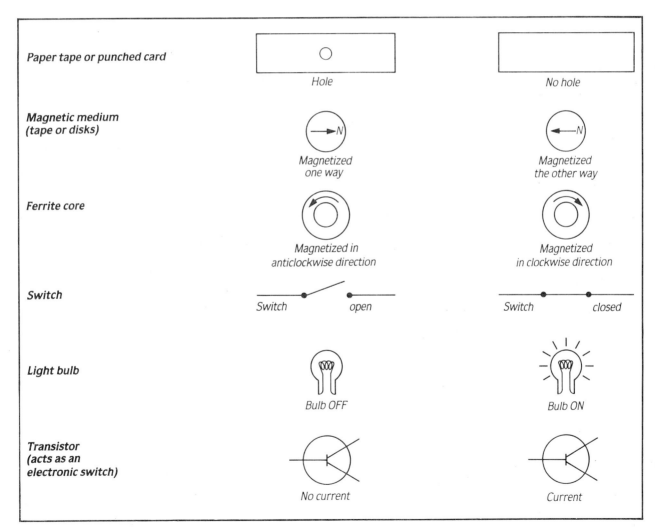

Figure 13.2 Some two-state systems

Storing information using a two state system

We can use a two state system to store information. Figure 13.3 shows a circuit that could be used to store information. Using this circuit we could use:

Bulb OFF   number is 0
Bulb ON   number is 1

In this way we could use a series of bulbs to represent information. What we need is a number system which only uses two digits. The binary system is ideal for this because it only uses two digits, 0 and 1. Binary (base 2) digits are called **bits**. All computers use binary codes for storing information.

Number bases

Denary numbers (base 10)

You are probably used to using base 10 (ordinary numbers) so we will first have a look to see how this base works. When we count from 1 to 10 we use the digits 0, 1, 2, 3, 4, 5, 6, 7, 8, 9. All other numbers are made up from these digits.

The position of each number within a series of numbers is very important. The position of the number determines how large it is, or its value. The number 123 is one hundred and twenty-three. The 1 is not one but one hundred. The 2 represents twenty and the 3 is just three. If we were to mix these digits up we could have a completely different number. In all number bases we have **place values**. These tell us what the number is.

In base 10, the place values are as follows:

1 000 000   100 000   10 000   1000   100   10   1

Suppose you want to work out what the number 7256 is. First write it out under the place values:

Place values	1000	100	10	1
Digits	7	2	5	6

Then multiply each digit by its place value and add all the numbers up. So, to work out the value of 7256:

$$
\begin{aligned}
7 \times 1000 &= 7000 \\
2 \times 100 &= 200 \\
5 \times 10 &= 50 \\
6 \times 1 &= 6 \\
\hline
&\ 7256
\end{aligned}
$$

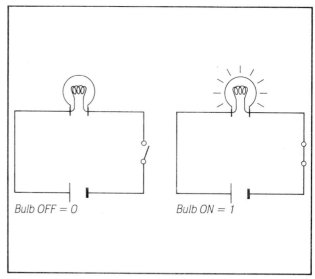

Figure 13.3   *Two state systems like this one can be used to store information*

You may think this is obvious, but when you come to use other number bases which you are not familiar with, you will have to use this method.

If you look at the place values in base 10 carefully, you will see that they go up in powers of 10:

$$10^6 \quad 10^5 \quad 10^4 \quad 10^3 \quad 10^2 \quad 10^1 \quad 10^0$$
1 000 000 100 000 10 000 1000   100   10   1

Notice that any number to the power zero is always one. $10^0 = 1$, $2^0 = 1$, $X^0 = 1$ etc.

Binary numbers (base 2)

The binary number system just uses two numbers, the binary digits 0 and 1. All other numbers can be made up from a series of these two numbers. The place values in the binary number system go up in powers of two.

$2^6 = 64$ $2^5 = 32$ $2^4 = 16$ $2^3 = 8$
$2^2 = 4$ $2^1 = 2$ $2^0 = 1$

Sometimes these are written:

64   32   16   8   4   2   U   (units)

The binary digits 0 or 1 can then be written below the place values.

Converting binary numbers to decimal is easy:
1   First write out the place values, starting from the right hand side.
2   Write each binary digit under its place value.
3   Multiply each binary digit by its place value.
4   Add up the total number. This is the number in base 10.

Example 1 Convert the binary number 101101 to a base 10 number

First write out the place values with each binary digit below its place value:

Place values	64	32	16	8	4	2	U
Binary digits		1	0	1	1	0	1

Then multiply each binary digit in turn by its place value and add up the total:

$$
\begin{array}{rcl}
1 \times 32 &=& 32 \\
0 \times 16 &=& 0 \\
1 \times 8 &=& 8 \\
1 \times 4 &=& 4 \\
0 \times 2 &=& 0 \\
1 \times 1 &=& 1 \\
\hline
&& 45
\end{array}
$$

So the number 101101 in binary is the number 45 in base 10.

Example 2 Convert the base 2 number 100100 to a base 10 number

Place values	64	32	16	8	4	2	U
Binary digits		1	0	0	1	0	0

To save time you only need to multiply the binary digits by the place values when they are one.

$$
\begin{array}{rcl}
1 \times 32 &=& 32 \\
1 \times 4 &=& 4 \\
\hline
&& 36
\end{array}
$$

So the base 2 number 100100 is the base 10 number 36. We can write this like this:

$$100100_2 = 36_{10}$$

The small numbers tell us what the bases are. If the base used is base 10, we usually leave out the base. So, a number without a base written at the bottom is regarded as a base 10 number.

Other number bases

All computers use binary numbers to store and process data. Because lots of binary digits are needed to store large numbers in base 10, it is often convenient to work in other number bases that store large numbers using fewer digits (Figure 13.4). Two bases often used in this way are base 8 (**octal**) and base 16 (**hexadecimal**). It is quite easy to change from base 8 and base 16 to base 2, so this is why these two number bases were chosen.

Base 8 (octal) numbers

The place values in base 8 are:

512   64   8   1

You can see that fewer numbers are needed to store large numbers in base 8.

We can work out base 8 octal numbers in the same way as we did with base 2. Remember that you cannot write an 8 under a place value. The maximum allowed is 7.

Example 3 Convert the octal number 521_8 into a base 10 (denary) number

Place values	512	64	8	1
Base 8 number		5	2	1

$$
\begin{array}{rcl}
5 \times 64 &=& 320 \\
2 \times 8 &=& 16 \\
1 \times 1 &=& 1 \\
\hline
&& 337
\end{array}
$$

Therefore $521_8 = 337_{10}$

Figure 13.4

Example 4 Convert the base 8 number 1111_8 into a base 10 number

Place values	512	64	8	1
Base 8 number	1	1	1	1

$$1 \times 512 = 512$$
$$1 \times 64 = 64$$
$$1 \times 8 = 8$$
$$1 \times 1 = 1$$
$$\overline{585}$$

Therefore $1111_8 = 585_{10}$

Base 16 (hexadecimal) numbers

In base 16 (hexadecimal) the place values are:

Place Values   256   16   1

Under each place value we write either a number or a letter. Numbers are used from 0 to 9, but instead of writing 10, 11, 12, 13, 14, 15, we write A, B, C, D, E and F.

Base 10	0	1	2	3	4	5	6	7	8	9	10	11	12	13	14	15
Base 16	0	1	2	3	4	5	6	7	8	9	A	B	C	D	E	F

Example 5 Convert the hexadecimal number 111_{16} to base 10

Place values	256	16	1
Hexadecimal number	1	1	1

$$256 \times 1 = 256$$
$$16 \times 1 = 16$$
$$1 \times 1 = 1$$
$$\overline{273}$$

Therefore $111_{16} = 273_{10}$

Example 6 Convert the base 16 number A9 to a number in base 10

Place value	256	16	1
Hexadecimal number		A	9

Since A = 10:
$$16 \times 10 = 160$$
$$9 \times 1 = 9$$
$$\overline{169}$$

Therefore $A9_{16} = 169_{10}$

Example 7 Convert the hexadecimal number 1A1 to a base 10 number

Place values	256	16	1
Hexadecimal number	1	A	1

$$256 \times 1 = 256$$
$$10 \times 16 = 160$$
$$1 \times 1 = 1$$
$$\overline{417}$$

Therefore $1A1_{16} = 417_{10}$

Example 8 Convert the base 16 number D9 to base 10

Place values	256	16	1
Hexadecimal number		D	9

D = 13 so:
$$13 \times 16 = 208$$
$$9 \times 1 = 9$$
$$\overline{217}$$

Therefore $D9_{16} = 217_{10}$

Converting to and from binary

Conversion from denary (base 10) to binary (base 2)

Suppose we had the number 247 in base 10 and wanted to write it in base 2. To convert the number we would need to follow these steps:

1 First write out the place values up to the place value which is just greater than the base 10 number that you wish to convert.

For the number 247, we would write the place values up to 256.

256   128   64   32   16   8   4   2   1

2 Now work through the place values deciding on whether to place a 1 or a 0 under the place value.

Since the number is 247 we do not write anything under the 256.

256   128   64   32   16   8   4   2   1
          1

We would need a 128 which would leave us with $247 - 128 = 119$. We now have 119 to distribute under the other place values. We need a 64. This leaves $119 - 64 = 55$.

256   128   64   32   16   8   4   2   1
          1   1

We can now place a 1 under the 32. This leaves 23.

256	128	64	32	16	8	4	2	1
	1	1	1					

A 1 is placed under the 16 which leaves $23 - 16 = 7$.

256	128	64	32	16	8	4	2	1
	1	1	1	1				

We can't subtract an 8 from a 7 so we place a 0 under the 8 and move to the next place value which is a 4.

256	128	64	32	16	8	4	2	1
	1	1	1	1	0			

The 7 remaining can be made up from a 4, a 2, and a 1. So, the number becomes:

256	128	64	32	16	8	4	2	1
	1	1	1	1	0	1	1	1

Example 9   Convert the base 10 number 107 to binary
We only need to write place values up to 128.

128	64	32	16	8	4	2	1
1	1	0	1	0	1	1	

Therefore $107_{10} = 1101011_2$

Conversion from octal (base 8) to binary (base 2)

7 is the maximum number we can have under any place value in the octal number system. In binary this is 111 so we can make up any number between 0 and 7 using a group of three binary digits (or **bits**). For example, the octal number 5 can be represented by the three binary digits 101 (Figure 13.5). We can write down the octal numbers (up to 7) and their corresponding binary equivalents in a table:

Octal	Binary
0	000
1	001
2	010
3	011
4	100
5	101
6	110
7	111

Working from the right hand side of the number to the left each octal number can be made up of three binary digits. Then the groups of three binary digits are joined together to give the final binary number. Suppose we want to convert the octal number 321 to base 2. This is what we would do:

1   Work from the right of the octal number looking at each number in turn.
    In this example we look at the number 1 first. From the table we can see that the number 1 is represented by the three binary digits 001. The next number in the octal number is 2. This is represented by the binary number 010. The final number is 3 and this is represented by 011.

Figure 13.5

67

2 Now put all the binary numbers together under the octal number.

Octal number   3   2   1
Binary equivalent   011   010   001

So 321 in octal is the number 011010001 in binary.

When you do questions on conversions from octal to binary or vice versa, it is best to start off by writing down the conversion table. With practice, it is possible to do these conversions very quickly by looking at the table.

Example 10   Convert the octal number 526 to binary

First, write down the conversion table for converting the numbers from 0 to 7 to three digit binary numbers.

Octal	Binary
0	000
1	001
2	010
3	011
4	100
5	101
6	110
7	111

From the table, look up each octal number and write down the binary equivalent.

    5   2   6
101   010   110

So 526 in octal is 101010110 in binary.

Conversion from binary to octal

To convert a binary number to octal, we do the opposite to the process we have just looked at. The binary number is split up into groups of three digits (or bits) working from the right hand side of the number. For example,

100   111   101

If the binary number can't exactly be divided into groups of three, you go as far as you can and then add zeros at the left hand end until you have a group of three. So in this number

11   011   010

we would need to add an extra zero at the left hand

side. Adding an extra zero does not alter the number in any way. It is still exactly the same number. The number now becomes

011   011   010

Now we use the conversion table, but the other way round. So this time we look up the three bit binary number to find its octal equivalent. Starting from the right hand side of the binary number, from the table we get

010 = 2
011 = 3
011 = 3

Now we can write the octal equivalent under the binary number:

   011   011   010
    3   3   2

Therefore, 011 011 010 in binary is the number 332 in octal.

It is often best to copy out the octal to binary conversion table before starting a question.

Example 11   Convert the number 1010000101001 in base 2 to base 8

First write the conversion table:

Octal	Binary
0	000
1	001
2	010
3	011
4	100
5	101
6	110
7	111

Then divide the base 2 number into groups of three adding zero's if required. So

001   010   000   101   001
Two extra zero's added.

Now convert each group of three bits to their octal equivalent using the conversion table.

Binary   001   010   000   101   001
Octal   1   2   0   5   1

So, the binary number 1010000101001 is equivalent to the octal number 12051.

Conversion from hexadecimal (base 16) numbers to binary (base 2) numbers

In the hexadecimal number system, we have to go from 0 to 15. Three binary numbers would not be sufficient to do this so we have to use four. So each hexadecimal digit is equivalent to a four digit (or 4 bit) binary number.

When we write out the conversion table from base 16 to base 2 we have to remember that we can't write 10 – 15 in hexadecimal. Instead, we use the letters A, B, C, D, E, F for the numbers 10, 11, 12, 13, 14 and 15. This gives us this conversion table:

Hexadecimal	Base 10	Binary
0	0	0000
1	1	0001
2	2	0010
3	3	0011
4	4	0100
5	5	0101
6	6	0110
7	7	0111
8	8	1000
9	9	1001
A	10	1010
B	11	1011
C	12	1100
D	13	1101
E	14	1110
F	15	1111

The base 10 number column can be left out with practise, as long as you realize that you are trying to make the numbers 10 to 15 into their binary equivalents.

Example 12   Convert the number 410 in hexadecimal to a binary number
Looking up each number in the conversion table in turn, we get:

Hexadecimal	4	1	0
Binary	0100	0001	0000

So 410 in hexadecimal is equivalent to 010000010000 in binary.

Example 13   Convert the number A2D in hexadecimal to a binary number

Hexadecimal	A	2	D
Binary	1010	0010	1101

So A2D in hexadecimal is 101000101101 in binary.

Example 14   Convert the base 16 number EF to a base 2 number

Hexadecimal	E	F
Binary	1110	1111

So EF in base 16 is 11101111 in base 2.

Conversion from binary (base 2) numbers to hexadecimal (base 16) numbers

This is very similar to converting binary numbers to octal ones, but instead of grouping the binary digits in groups of three, we group them in groups of four.

To convert base 2 to base 16, you divide up the binary number, starting from the right hand side, into groups of four bits (digits). As before, it may be necessary to add noughts onto the left of the number if the last group does not have four digits. When you have done this, use the binary to hexadecimal table, but in reverse.

Example 15   Convert the number 1010011010 in base 2 to base 16
First divide up the number from the right, into groups of four:

10   1001   1010

We need to add two noughts to make this group up to four digits. So the binary number now becomes:

0010   1001   1010

Now look up each group of four binary digits in the table to find their hexadecimal equivalent.

0010   1001   1010
  2   9   4

So, 001010011010 in binary is the equivalent of 294 in hexadecimal.

Example 16   Convert the binary number 10111110101 to base 16
Divide the number into groups of four:

101   1111   0101

Add an extra nought, then look up each group of digits in the conversion table.

Binary	0101	1111	0101
Hexadecimal	5	F	5

The binary number 10111110101 is 5F5 in base 16.

Binary arithmetic

The four main arithmetic operations in base 2 are addition, subtraction, multiplication and division, just like in base 10.

Binary addition

When you add binary numbers, you must remember that you can only have the binary digits 0 and 1 in binary number systems. The number 2 and above are not allowed.

There are five possible additions in binary. We can show them like this:

```
   0        0        1        1        1
 + 0      + 1      + 0      + 1      + 1
 ___      ___      ___      ____     ____
   0        1        1       10       11
 ___      ___      ___      ____     ____
```

carry from previous stage in addition ➤ 1

Using these rules, we can add any number of binary numbers together.

Example 17 Add the following binary numbers together

```
   1  0  1  1
 +    1  0  0
 _____
   1  1  1  1
 _____
```

Example 18 Add the following binary numbers together

```
      1  1  1  0
 +       1  1  0
 _____
   1  0  1  0  0
 _____
```

Example 19 Add the following three binary numbers together

```
   1  1  0  1
      1  0  1
 +       1  1
 _____
```

To do this sum, it is best to add the first two rows together and then add this result to the third row. Adding the first two rows gives

```
      1  1  0  1
 +       1  0  1
 _____
   1  0  0  1  0
 _____
```

Adding the result to the third row gives

```
   1  0  0  1  0
 +          1  1
 _____
   1  0  1  0  1
 _____
```

When adding base 2 numbers together, it is often a good idea to check your answer. You can do this by turning the numbers to the base 10 equivalent and then adding them up in base 10 and changing them back to binary. If the two answers agree then you have probably worked them out correctly. If we check the previous example by converting to base 10 we get

Binary

```
      1  1  0  1
         1  0  1
 +          1  1
 _____
   1  0  1  0  1
 _____
```

Base 10

```
   13
    5
 +  3
 ____
   21
 ____
```

The two results are the same, so the answer is probably correct.

Binary subtraction

For binary subtraction, there are only a few sums to remember. They are

```
   0        1        1        0
 - 0      - 0      - 1      - 1
 ___      ___      ___      ___
   0        1        0        1
 ___      ___      ___      ___
```

In the last subtraction a 1 is borrowed from the next more significant (higher value) digit.

Example 20 Work out the following binary subtraction

```
   1  0  1  1
 - 1  1  1  1
 _____
```

To do this you will have to borrow a 2 in the third column from the right (in base 10 you would borrow a 10). The answer is 0100.

Example 21   Work out this binary subtraction

```
  10101
-   110
  ─────

  ─────
```

The answer is 01110.

Coding negative numbers

Negative numbers are coded because we need to use them when we do subtraction (Figure 13.6). There are three ways of coding negative numbers. They are sign and magnitude, two's complement and one's complement. We will look at two of these.

Figure 13.6   *Decoding negative numbers*

Sign and magnitude coding

In sign and magnitude coding we use one bit to represent the sign of the number and the other bits to represent the size or magnitude. The bit used to represent the sign of the number is called the sign bit. It can be at either end of the number. If the sign bit is 1 then it means that the number is negative. If it is 0, then the number is positive. We underline the sign bit so that it doesn't get confused with the rest of the number. Some examples of sign and magnitude coded numbers are:

```
 1 0 1 0 0   =   +10
 1 1 1 0 1   =   −13
1 0 0 0 0 0   =   +16
1 1 0 1 0 1 0   =   −42
```

Two's complement coding

The most significant bit (highest value bit) in two's complement coding represents a negative number. The number is represented in binary with the same place values. For example,

Place values	−32	16	8	4	2	1
	1	0	0	0	0	0

In this example the two's complement number would represent −32.

If we wanted to store a smaller negative number, we could put ones where required, under the other place values. For example, suppose we wanted to store the negative number −10. We could represent it like this:

−32	16	8	4	2	1
1	1	0	1	1	0

This gives us −32 + 16 + 4 + 2 = −10. So using a six bit, two's complement number, we could represent −10 as 1 1 0 1 1 0.

Using six bits like this the largest negative number that we could store is −32. If we want to store negative numbers larger than this, we need more binary digits (or bits). Suppose we wanted to store −58 using two's complement. We could use seven bits as this would make the most significant bit −64. But usually when numbers are represented using two's complement, we use either six or eight bits, so here we would use eight bits.

Using eight bits, the most significant bit would be −128.

−128	64	32	16	8	4	2	1
1							

To get −58 we need to add 70 to −128. To make 70 we could use 64+4+2. So −58 can be represented as

−128	64	32	16	8	4	2	1
1	1	0	0	0	1	1	0

In two's complement a positive binary number is related to its negative counterpart in a simple way. We can compare the two numbers using six bits. For example, look at − 13 and + 13

		−32	16	8	4	2	1
−13	=	1	1	0	0	1	1
+13	=	0	0	1	1	0	1

To convert a positive number to its corresponding negative number in two's complement you change the 0s to 1s and the 1s to 0s and then add 1.

Example 22   Change -20 to a number using two's complement coding using six bits

First write down the place values for six bits making the most significant (largest) bit negative.

$$-32 \quad 16 \quad 8 \quad 4 \quad 2 \quad 1$$

Now store the positive number.

-32	16	8	4	2	1
0	1	0	1	0	0

Now place a zero below the negative place value because the number is positive. Reverse all the bits.

-32	16	8	4	2	1
1	0	1	0	1	1

Now add one to this number.

-32	16	8	4	2	1
1	0	1	0	1	1
$+$					1
1	0	1	1	0	0

So in two's complement coding -20 is 101100.

Subtraction using two's complement coding

We have just seen how negative numbers can be obtained using two's complement. Now we can look at how they are used to do subtraction.

We can do subtraction by adding a positive number to a negative number. For example, $15 - 8$ would be the same as $15 + (-8)$. We can find what -8 is by using two's complement. We can then find 15 and add the two resulting numbers together. To work out $15 - 8$ we need to work through these steps:

1 Work out the negative number first in two's complement by writing the positive number, reversing the bits and adding one.
2 Write down the positive number in two's complement.
3 Add the two two's complement numbers together.

We can write this out like this:

	-16	8	4	2	1
Store $+8$	0	1	0	0	0
Reverse bits	1	0	1	1	1
Add 1	$+$				1
Gives -8	1	1	0	0	0
Store 15	0	1	1	1	1
Adding gives $15 - 8$	(1) 0	0	1	1	1

overflow bit

The bit in brackets is carried over from the -16 column. This bit is called the **overflow** bit. We ignore this overflow bit so $15 - 8 = 0\,0\,1\,1\,1$ in two's complement, when converted back to denary this is 7.

Example 23   Calculate $31 - 17$ using two's complement

	-32	16	8	4	2	1
Store $+17$	0	1	0	0	0	1
Reverse bits	1	0	1	1	1	0
Add 1	$+$					1
Gives -17	1	0	1	1	1	1
Store 31	0	1	1	1	1	1
Adding gives $31 - 17$	(1) 0	0	1	1	1	0

Converting back to denary the answer is 14.

An important note on storing numbers in two's complement

When you answer questions involving writing numbers in two's complement, you must know how many bits the number should occupy. It should always tell you the number of bits in the question you are answering. As the most significant bit (the one over to the left) is always negative in two's complement, this will affect the number of different bit lengths used.

Example 24   Store -20 using a six bit two's complement number

	32	16	8	4	2	U
Store 20	0	1	0	1	0	0
Reverse bits	1	0	1	0	1	1
Add 1	$+$					1
Gives -20	1	0	1	1	0	0

If we wanted the two's complement using eight bits rather than six we would work it out like this. The most significant bit using eight bits would now represent -128.

	-128	64	32	16	8	4	2	U
Store 20	0	0	0	1	0	1	0	0
Reverse bits	1	1	1	0	1	0	1	1
Add 1	$+$							1
Gives -20	1	1	1	0	1	1	0	0

As you can see the two bit patterns are different because different bit lengths have been used. So it is essential that you know the bit length before you answer the question. The usual bit length is either six or eight but other bit lengths could be asked for.

Test yourself

Using the words in the list below, copy out and complete sentences A to K, underlining the words you have inserted. The words may be used once, more than once or not at all.

least significant   hexadecimal   zero
2   binary   bistable   store   ferrite
cores   negative   most significant
positive   bits   two's complement
place value   16   octal

A   A system which has only two states is called a
_____ system.

B   Bistable devices include paper tape, punched cards, magnetic devices and _____ _____.

C   Bistable systems can be used to _____ information.

D   The _____ number system only uses two digits 0 and 1. These are called _____.

E   A number has a value which depends on its position. This is called its _____ _____.

F   Computers all use base _____, but sometimes it is cumbersome for making up large numbers.

G   It is easier to use base 8 or base _____ and let the computer convert it to binary.

H   Base 8 is often called _____ and base 16
_____.

I   There are two main ways of storing negative numbers. One is by sign and magnitude coding and the other is by _____ _____ coding.

J   In two's complement coding the _____
_____ bit is made _____.

K   If a printed number is stored using two's complement coding, the most significant bit will be _____.

Things to do

1   Convert the following base 10 numbers to binary (base 2):
   a 10   **e** 254
   b 43   **f** 365
   c 126   **g** 412
   d 143   **h** 512

2   Convert the following base 2 numbers to base 10 (denary):
   a 0101   **e** 111111
   b 1111   **f** 10101010
   c 10100   **g** 10111111
   d 101011   **h** 10101111

3   Convert the following base 10 numbers to hexadecimal (base 16):
   a 9   **e** 144
   b 16   **f** 256
   c 33   **g** 536
   d 61   **h** 600

4   Convert the following hexadecimal numbers to base 10:
   a 2   **e** 10A
   b 16   **f** CCD
   c 15   **g** EFE
   d 36   **h** AOB

5   Convert the following base 10 numbers to base 8 (octal):
   a 32   **e** 365
   b 45   **f** 1002
   c 100   **g** 5320
   d 107   **h** 1010

6   Convert the following base 8 (octal) numbers to base 10:
   a 77   **e** 1000
   b 64   **f** 1200
   c 102   **g** 132
   d 365

7   Work out the following additions in binary:

   a   101   **e**   11101
         + 111   + 10111
         ─────   ─────

   b   1010   **f**   101010
         + 111   + 1111
         ─────   ─────

   c   1111   **g**   101011
         + 111   + 10111
         ─────   ─────

   d 101010   **h** 100100
        + 1011   + 1011
         ─────   ─────

8 Work out the following subtractions in binary:

a   11
     −10

e   100011
     − 101

b   101
     − 11

f   11111
     − 111

c   1100
     − 11

g   11011
     − 1011

d   1001
     − 111

h   1111
     − 100

9 **a** Convert the following denary (base 10) numbers into binary:
    i   43
    ii   144
b Convert the following binary numbers into denary (base 10):
    i   10010
    ii   1011101
c Work out the answers to the following binary calculations:
    i   10111
      + 1010
    ii   101101
      − 10100

10 Which one of the following hexadecimal numbers is sixteen times the hexadecimal number B9?
a B916
b B90
c 1904
d 2960

11 Overflow occurs when which one of these happens?
a A computer blows a fuse
b A calculation exceeds the capacity of the computer
c A program contains an endless loop
d A flowchart has to be continued on another page.

12 Convert the following binary numbers to octal numbers (base 8):
a 101
b 101001
c 101111
d 10100
e 101110
f 1111111
g 101111001
h 100101011

13 Convert the following numbers which are in base 8 to binary numbers:
a 7
b 31
c 63
d 100
e 130
f 111
g 200
h 333

14 Convert the following binary numbers to hexadecimal numbers (base 16):
a 1111
b 10111001
c 11000011
d 110111
e 1011101
f 10110100
g 101110111010
h 110000111110

15 Using six bits represent the following numbers using two's complement coding:
a −32
b +31
c −20
d +20
e −11
f −5
g −2
h −1

16 The following numbers are written using six bit two's complement coding. Write down these numbers in base 10 (denary):
a 101100
b 100001
c 0101101
d 011111
e 101101
f 110001
g 100000
h 110110

17 **a** Change the octal number 24 to a binary number.
b Change the decimal number −7 to an eight-bit binary number using two's complement representation.
c How many bits are needed to represent all the characters possible in a two digit hexadecimal number?

18 A computer using an eight bit word can represent integers in the range 0 to +255. Explain how this word may be used to represent integers in the range −128 to +127 inclusive.

19 A computer stores a representation of integers in a four bit word, using two's complement notation.

a What is the largest possible integer represented in a four bit word?

b What number is represented by 1000?

c Show how you would represent the integer −3 in the four bit word.

20 A certain computer uses twelve bit words. The diagram below shows the contents of one word.

0	0	0	0	1	0	1	1	0	1	0	1

Interpret this word:

a As a denary number

b As an octal number

c As a hexadecimal number

21 Using six bits and two's complement coding represent the following numbers:

a −31

b −28

c 14

d −8

e 5

f 3

22 Using an eight bit two's complement number, perform the following subtractions:

a 14 − 7

b 28 − 12

c 34 − 33

d 54 − 6

e 72 − 61

f 100 − 50

g 12 − 12

h 102 − 64

23 What are the largest and smallest (decimal) numbers that can be stored in two's complement using

a six bits and

b eight bits?

24 Using sign and magnitude coding and writing the sign bit on the right, change the following base 10 numbers into their binary sign and magnitude coded equivalents:

a −4

b −10

c 14

d −8

e −26

f 19

25 A computer has a six bit word store. It stores numbers using two's complement. When showing the numerical contents of a storage location, on the VDU screen, they are represented in octal.

a If a store contains 001001 what denary number would this represent?

b How would it store the denary number −27?

c State the largest positive number and the most negative number that this computer can store.

d Why would a six bit word machine be likely to use octal and what would be the binary content of the store whose octal

representation is 35?

e What is the hexadecimal result of adding together the hexadecimal numbers 2 and A?

14
Bits, bytes and words

Coding data

Computers deal with two types of information; data and instructions. For instance, 'Fred Bloggs' would be data whereas 'PRINT' is an instruction. The computer can distinguish between data and instructions.

In the last chapter we mentioned that data is coded in the form of groups of binary digits, each digit having the value of 0 or 1. Rather than deal with each bit individually, it is more convenient to deal with the bits in groups. The size of these groups really depends on the type of computer used.

Using two binary digits, we would only be able to produce four codes i.e. 01, 00, 10 and 11. To find the number of possible combinations of codes from a certain number of binary digits, we can use this formula:

number of combinations = 2^N

where N = number of binary digits used for making up the code.

Suppose we want to find the number of combinations of codes using three bits. We could do this the long way by writing down all the possible combinations. So,

000
001
010
011
100
101
110
111

Or, much easier, we could use our formula:

Number of combinations = 2^3 = 2 x 2 x 2 = 8

Each combination of binary digits can be used to store a **character**. A character is a symbol or letter on the computer keyboard. For example, A, B, C, 0 to 9, ?,", and +, − * are all characters.

Using three binary digits, we can make eight combinations or **character codes**. This would not be

enough, as the alphabet alone needs twenty-six codes.

2^5 or 32 would also not be enough because as well as the alphabetic characters, we need all the numbers, punctuation marks, arithmetic symbols etc.

2^6 or 64 is the least we can use and this is the number of binary digits or bits used by some smaller computers. An example of a 64 character set code using six bits is shown in Figure 14.1. This character code is used by the ICL 1900 series of computers.

Character	Code	Character	Code
0	000000	@	100000
1	000001	A	100001
2	000010	B	100010
3	000011	C	100011
4	000100	D	100100
5	000101	E	100101
6	000110	F	100110
7	000111	G	100111
8	001000	H	101000
9	001001	I	101001
:	001010	J	101010
;	001011	K	101011
<	001100	L	101100
=	001101	M	101101
>	001110	N	101110
?	001111	O	101111
space	010000	P	110000
!	010001	Q	110001
"	010010	R	110010
#	010011	S	110011
£	010100	T	110100
%	010101	U	110101
&	010110	V	110110
'	010111	W	110111
(	011000	X	111000
)	011001	Y	111001
*	011010	Z	111010
+	011011	[	111011
,	011100	$	111100
−	011101	]	111101
.	011110	↑	111110
/	011111	←(new line)	111111

Figure 14.1 *A 64 character set code*

Bits, bytes and words

A **bit** is a single binary digit 0 or 1. A **byte** is a group of bits which are used to represent a character. Using the ICL 1900 character code, the letter A would have the following group of bits forming the byte, 100001. The number of bits forming a byte can vary, but it is usually eight since this is the number that most computers use. Bytes are treated by the computer as a single unit rather than separate individual bits.

A **word** in computing is a fixed number of bits which is treated as one unit by the central processing unit. Words usually consist of a greater number of bits than a byte. The number of bits in a word is sometimes referred to as the **word length**. Word lengths can be fixed or variable. If it is fixed the word length is usually 16, 32 or 64 bits.

Parity checks

Parity checks (checks for errors) are performed on the words or bytes. This is done by adding an extra binary digit to the end (leftmost) bit. This is called a parity bit. If even parity is used, then the leftmost bit will be added to make an even number of 1s in the byte or word. So, if the following eight bit byte had even parity, then the leftmost digit would be a zero to keep the number of 1s even (i.e. 4):

00101011
↑
parity bit

If the above word was incorrectly transferred to another part of the computer and ended up as 01101011, then it no longer contains an even number of 1s (even parity) so an error will be detected.

You can also have odd parity which means the number placed on the left always makes an odd number of 1s in the byte or word. This eight bit word has odd parity.

11010110
↑
parity bit

Parity checks are usually done as data is input into the computer since this is the time when most of the errors are likely to occur.

The computer and bits, bytes and words

What happens to the binary coded information after it has been input into the computer is quite a complicated process. What we will try to do in this section is to give a brief outline of what happens to the binary coded words as they are dealt with by the various parts of the CPU.

You will remember that there are three parts to the central processing unit; the arithmetic and logic unit (ALU), the control unit (CU) and the central memory. We will look at what happens in each of these parts.

Registers

A **register** is a storage unit inside the CPU. Registers are different from storage locations in the main store because they are temporary. There are many types of register in the CPU and each is used to perform a specific task.

The main store of the computer consists of a lot of compartments where information in the form of words is kept. As the information is needed for processing it passes into the processing part of the CPU where it is kept in a temporary storage location register until it is used. Usually the register can store one or two words of binary coded information.

In the main store memory, the words are neatly contained in storage locations. They are also given an address so that they can be located easily when required. The address is a number which tells the computer where to find a particular word. Each storage location has its own address. The number of storage locations is a measure of the power of the computer. If all these locations are used up then some extra backing store is needed, such as floppy disks, hard disks, magnetic tape etc.

Accumulators

An **accumulator** is a special type of register found in the arithmetic and logic unit (ALU). The accumulator is used when the ALU is performing some arithmetic.

Buffers

As coded data is passed around the parts of the computer **buffers** need to be used. Because different parts of the computer work at different speeds, it is sometimes necessary to hold data in a temporary store to compensate for these differences. The temporary store is called a buffer.

Half and full adders

There are series of logical operations which can do

certain arithmetic functions. A **half adder** is a set of logic gates which adds together two binary digits and gives the answer and the carry digit.

A **full adder** is like a half adder except that it adds three binary digits. Full adders need to be used in binary addition when there is a carry digit from another addition for example, the column before. E.g.

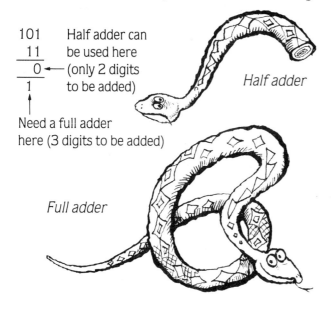

```
101    Half adder can
 11    be used here
  0 ◄── (only 2 digits
  1    to be added)
```
↑
Need a full adder here (3 digits to be added)

Half adder

Full adder

Test yourself

Using the words in the list below, copy out and complete sentences A to I underlining the words you have inserted. The words may be used once, more than once or not at all.

parity   groups   fixed   instructions
binary   buffer   byte   character
data   register

A There are two types of computer information. These are _____ and _____.
B Bits are _____ digits with the value 0 or 1.
C Computers deal in _____ of bits. The size of these varies according to the machine.
D _____ codes are made up using groups of bits.
E A _____ is a group of bits used to make up one character.
F A word is a _____ number of bits which are treated as one unit by the central processing unit.
G _____ checks are used to make sure that words are transferred from one part of the computer to another.
H A _____ is a store inside the CPU.
I A temporary store is called a _____.

Things to do

1 Give definitions for the following terms:
  a Bit
  b Byte
  c Word
  d Word length
  e Address

2 A non-numeric character (e.g. the letter S) held within immediate access store would be represented by which one of these?
  a A file
  b A peripheral
  c A program
  d A number of lists
  e A number of records

3 **a** State the relationship between a 'bit' and a 'byte'.
   b Show the representation of −27 in a sixteen bit word using two's complement notation.

4 Explain briefly why a four bit word would not be suitable for the binary representation of each alphabetic character.

5 The following list is a set of eight bit words written in even parity, one of which contains an error. Copy out the list and put a cross in the box next to the word you think is incorrect.

1	1	0	1	0	1	0	0
1	0	0	0	0	0	0	1
1	0	1	0	1	0	0	0
1	1	1	1	1	1	1	1

6 **a** How many different characters can be represented in a four bit character code?
   b Design your own three bit codes to represent A, B, C, and D, using the third bit for an even parity check.

7 A simple arithmetic unit consists of a buffer, an accumulator, and full adder circuitry.
  a What is a buffer?
  b Give **one** use of an accumulator in an arithmetic unit.
  c Distinguish between the purpose of a full adder and a half adder.

15 Computer logic

Electronic pulses

Data and instructions are both stored by the computer as the binary digits 0 and 1. Sometimes it is useful to think of these binary digits in terms of electric currents. 0 represents no current (or pulse) and 1 represents a current (or pulse) being present (Figure 15.1). These pulses of electricity can be put together to produce **pulse trains** (Figure 15.2)

Figure 15.1

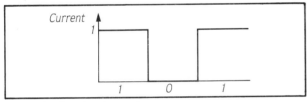

Figure 15.2 *A pulse train*

These electronic pulses are used to carry data and instructions to and from the various components of the CPU. They are also used to pass data and information to and from the peripherals, e.g. keyboard and line printer, which are attached to the CPU. Figure 15.3 shows how this works.

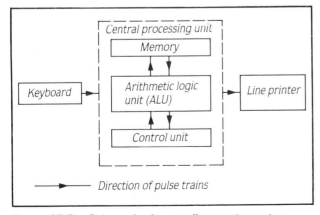

Figure 15.3 *Pulse trains in a small computer system*

In fact computers don't usually use this system because it is difficult to get an electronic component to distinguish between voltage and no voltage. Instead it is easier to produce a component that lets through a high voltage or a low voltage. Low voltage is represented by the binary digit 0, and high voltage is represented by the binary digit 1. Figure 15.4 shows a typical pulse train using high and low voltages.

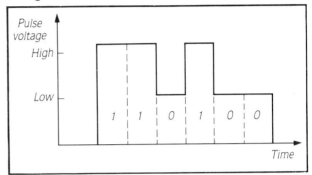

Figure 15.4 *A pulse train using high and low voltages*

Data and information are carried to and from the various parts of the computer system using pulse trains which represent the binary digits 0 and 1.

Logic gates

Electronic pulses can be made to follow sets of rules if they are passed through certain components. These components act like electronic switches and are called **gates**. They either let electricity pass through them or they prevent it from going through, so, they are like an ordinary gate which can be either open or shut.

We can think of logic gates as having two positions: open and shut. We can use the binary digits 0 or 1 to represent whether a gate is open or shut. If the gate is open then this means a 0 and when it is shut it means a 1. Using the binary digits 0 and 1 we can work out what the output will be for different inputs.

The three most common gates are the AND, OR and NOT gates. Other gates such as the NOR and NAND gates are made up by combining two of the basic gates together. More complicated logic operations can be carried out by putting a large number of these logic gates together.

Chips

In modern computers, one or more logic gates are put together to form a **chip**. These chips contain all the electronic circuitry needed for the various operations.

Before the chip, valves were used to act as gates. This made computers bulky, unreliable and expensive. Now, with the use of the silicon chip, computers are small, extremely reliable and inexpensive.

A chip can contain all the components of a circuit which can act as a logic gate. This type of chip is called an **integrated circuit**. When an integrated circuit makes up all the central processing unit (CPU) except the memory, it is called a **microprocessor**.

Logic elements

Logic gates can control the flow of pulses in a certain way. A gate which performs a simple operation is called a **logic element**.

To see how these gates work we can make up a table called a **truth table** or **operation table**. To do this we write down all the different inputs. Then we work out the outputs and fill these into the table.

Logic diagrams

We can show logical operations in logic diagrams. In logic diagrams we draw inputs on the left and label them with letters. Arrowed lines show the direction of the flow of logic. The gate is drawn as a circle with the name of the gate inside the circle. There is only ever one output from a logic gate or a combination of them.

The AND gate

AND gates can have two or more inputs, but they only have one possible output. If all the inputs are 1 then the output will also be 1, but in any other combination the output will be 0.

Figure 15.5 shows an AND gate with two inputs.

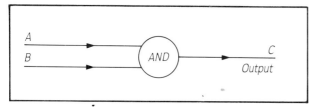

Figure 15.5   *A two input AND GATE*

To draw the operation table for this gate we must first write down in the table all the possible combinations that the inputs A and B can have. For a

two input gate, there will be four. For a three input gate, there will be eight. Then we can work out the output. For this AND gate we get this table:

Inputs		Output
A	**B**	**C**
1	1	1
0	1	0
1	0	0
0	0	0

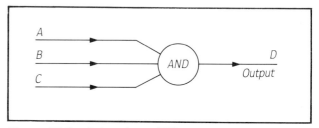

Figure 15.6   *A three input AND gate*

Figure 15.6 shows a three input AND gate. Its operation table would be this:

Inputs			Output
A	**B**	**C**	**D**
1	1	1	1
0	0	0	0
0	1	0	0
0	0	1	0
0	1	1	0
1	0	1	0
1	0	0	0
1	1	0	0

As for the two input AND gate, all the inputs need to be 1 in order to get a 1 out.

Switching circuits for an AND gate

Gates are equivalent to combinations of switches. We can make a simple circuit using switches, a battery and a bulb that will perform in the same logical way as an AND gate (Figure 15.7). The bulb will only light when switches A and B are closed. A and B have to be 1 for the bulb (or output C) to be equal to 1.

We can also make a three input AND gate switching circuit (Figure 15.8). Like before, the current can only flow around the circuit to light the bulb when all the

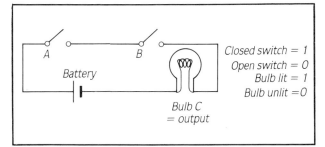

Figure 15.7 *A two input AND gate switching circuit*

Closed switch = 1
Open switch = 0
Bulb lit = 1
Bulb unlit = 0

Bulb C
= output

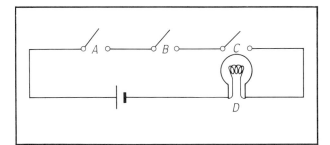

Figure 15.8 *A three input AND gate switching circuit*

three switches are closed. Any other combination of switches (e.g. A open, B open and C closed) means the bulb will not light up.

The OR gate

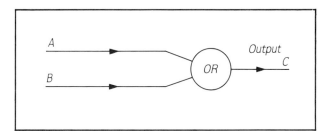

Figure 15.9 *A two input OR gate*

Figure 15.9 shows a two input OR gate. This is its operation table:

Inputs		Output
A	B	C
1	1	1
1	0	1
0	1	1
0	0	0

The output from an OR gate will be 1 as long as one or more inputs are 1. So if any of the inputs is a 1 then the output will also be a 1. Figure 15.10 shows a three input OR gate.

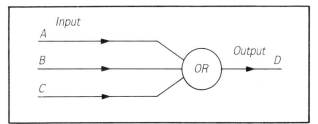

Figure 15.10 *A three input OR gate*

Here is its operation table:

Inputs			Output
A	B	C	D
1	1	1	1
1	1	0	1
1	0	1	1
0	1	1	1
0	0	1	1
0	1	0	1
1	0	0	1
0	0	0	0

OR gate switching circuits

In an OR gate the switches in the circuit are in parallel. In the two input circuit (Figure 15.11), the bulb will light if either of the switches A or B is closed. It will also light if both of the switches are closed. In the three input OR gate switching circuit (Figure 15.12), the bulb will only light when one or more of the switches are closed.

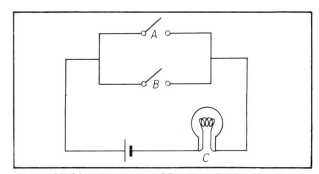

Figure 15.11 *A two input OR gate switching circuit*

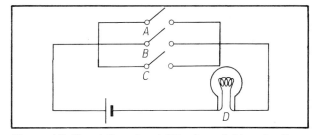

Figure 15.12 *A three input OR gate switching circuit*

The NOT gate

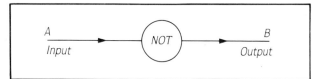

Figure 15.13 *A NOT gate*

Unlike the other gates the NOT gate has only one input. But like the other gates, it has only one output.

Sometimes the NOT gate is called an **inverter** because it has the effect of making the output the opposite of the input. So if the input is 0 then the output is the opposite which is 1, and vice versa.

Because there can only be one input into a NOT gate, it is the simplest of the three gates. Figure 15.13 shows a NOT gate. Its operation table is below.

Input A	Output B
1	0
0	1

NOT gate switching circuits

To draw a switching circuit for a NOT gate we use a two-way switch. In one position (A=1) the switch is open which means the bulb does not light (B=0). In the other position (A=0) the current flows round the circuit and lights the bulb (B=1). Figures 15.14 and 15.15 show this.

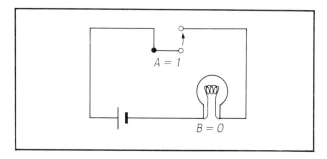

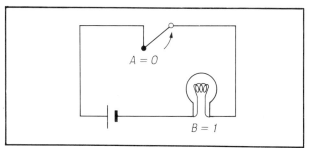

Other logic gates

As well as the three logic gates already mentioned there are two other gates which you will come across. These are the NAND and NOR gates. They are made by combining some of the common logic gates.

The NAND gate

The NAND gate is an AND gate followed by a NOT gate (Figure 15.16). To write its operation table we must follow the input firstly through the AND gate and then through the NOT gate.

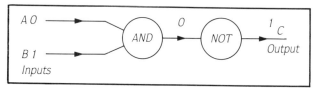

Figure 15.16 *A NAND gate*

When working out combinations of logic gates it is best to write down in pencil the inputs and how they change on going to the right for each combination of input. Then they can be rubbed out and another combination put in. For example, suppose we want to find out what happens when the inputs A = 0 and B = 1 go through the NAND gate. First we can work out what happens when they go through the AND gate. 0 and 1 through an AND gate gives a 0. So this 0 is the input going into the NOT gate. A 0 going into a NOT gate gives an output of 1. You can follow these steps for the other inputs and then complete the operation table:

Input A	B	AND	NOT	Output NAND (C)
1	0	0	1	1
0	1	0	1	1
1	1	1	0	0
0	0	0	1	1

Figure 15.14 *The switch represents the input position 1. There is no connection so the bulb will not light. So the output is 0*

Figure 15.15 *Here the output position = 0. There is now a path for the current to follow so the bulb lights. The output is now 1*

With practice, you will not need to fill in the extra columns. You will be able to just put the input and output in the table.

Inputs		Output
A	B	C
1	0	1
0	1	1
1	1	0
0	0	1

We don't have to draw two gates. All that we need draw is a circle with NAND written inside (Figure 15.17).

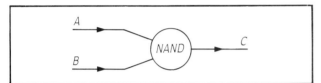

Figure 15.17

The NOR gate

The NOR gate is formed by combining an OR gate with a NOT gate (Figure 15.18). In order to work out

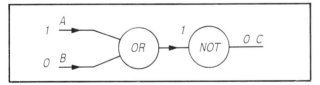

Figure 15.18 *A NOR gate*

the output we go through two steps. First we work out the inputs and outputs for the OR gate. These are now the inputs for the NOT gate. The second step is working out the output of putting these inputs through the NOT gate. This is the operation table:

Inputs		Output
A	B	C
1	1	0
1	0	0
0	1	0
0	0	1

Instead of drawing two gates we can just draw a NOR gate (Figure 15.19).

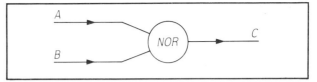

Figure 15.19

Like the AND and OR gates, the NAND and NOR gates may have more than one input and like all gates there is only ever one output.

> **Important note**
> We saw before that 0 and 1 in actual computers does not mean off and on. But it is useful to think of them as switches for explaining logic diagrams. Actually, 0 means a pulse of low voltage and 1 means a pulse of high voltage.

Some other uses of logic diagrams

Any problem which has sets of conditions which have yes or no answers can be solved using logic diagrams. First we have to decide what the inputs and outputs are. As before, we draw the various inputs and the output underneath letters.

Example 1 A hire purchase company will only lend money to a person who is a homeowner and in full-time employment. Draw a logic diagram and a truth table to satisfy these conditions
To work this out first decide on what symbols you are going to use and write them down along with what they mean.
For this example we could use the following symbols:

F = full-time employment
H = homeowner
L = loan

F and H will be the inputs and L will be the output.
If F = 1 this means that the person has full-time employment, but if F = 0 this means they do not have full-time employment. L = 1 means a loan is given and L = 0 means no loan is given.
Now we can see that for the loan to be given a person must own their home AND be in full-time employment. Any other combination will result in the hire purchase company not granting the person the money.

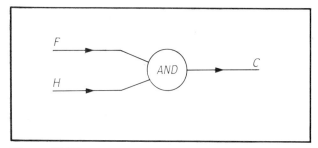

Figure 15.20

Now we can draw the logic diagram for this (Figure 15.20). The truth table is below:

| Inputs | | Output |
A	B	C
1	0	0
0	1	0
0	0	0
1	1	1

Example 2   The Government will give grants to new companies provided they are in an area of high unemployment or are able to take on young school leavers. In addition to this they must be an engineering company. Draw a logic diagram and truth table

We can show the first part of this question using an OR gate. However, first we must decide on a code:

U = area of high unemployment
Y = able to take on school leavers
E = engineering company
G = obtains Government grant

We will also need to use an AND gate for the second part of the question. This will give us the logic diagram in Figure 15.21. We can now draw the truth table.

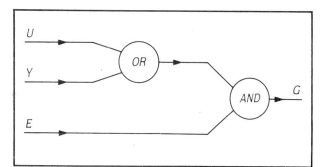

Figure 15.21

| Inputs | | | Output |
U	Y	E	G
1	1	1	1
1	0	0	0
1	1	0	0
1	0	1	1
0	0	1	0
0	0	0	0

You can see from the truth table that there are three possible inputs that will result in the Government giving a new company a grant.

Test yourself

Using the words in the list below, copy out and complete sentences A to J. Underline the words you have inserted. The words may be used more than once.

element	digits	pulse	AND	gates
chip	operation	binary	1	NOT
NAND	peripherals	NOR	logic	low

A *Data and instructions are stored in the computer in the form of _____ _____ 0 and 1.*

B *A _____ current represents 0 and a high current represents _____.*

C *A series of pulses of electric current is called a _____ train.*

D *The pulse trains carry information between the _____ and the central processing unit.*

E *The pulse trains follow certain rules when they pass through electronic switches called _____.*

F *A _____ _____ is a gate which performs a simple logic operation.*

G *_____ OR and _____ are the three basic gates.*

H *Logic gates are combined together to form a _____ made of silicon.*

I *Two other gates, the _____ and _____ gates can be made by combining two of the basic gates together.*

J *To see how these gates work we can draw an _____ table.*

Things to do

1 The following truth table is a truth table of an AND gate. Fill in the missing parts:-

Inputs		Output
0	1	0

2 Which column A, B, C or D of the truth table describes the output of the logic gate shown in the diagram?

X	Y	A	B	C	D
0	0	0	0	0	1
0	1	0	1	1	0
1	0	0	1	1	0
1	1	1	0	1	0

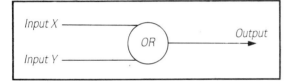

3 'Train' is the term used to describe which one of these?
  a Related program statements
  b Computer connections
  c High speed teleprinters
  d A sequence of pulses
  e Links between computer peripherals

4 Fill in the truth tables for the following logic circuits.

a

Inputs		Output
A	B	C
1	0	
0	0	
0	1	
1	1	

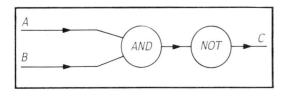

b

Inputs		Output
A	B	C
1	0	
0	0	
0	1	
1	1	

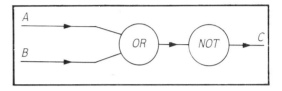

c

Inputs			Output
A	B	C	D
1	1	1	
0	0	0	
1	0	0	
1	0	1	
1	1	0	
0	0	1	
0	1	0	
0	1	1	

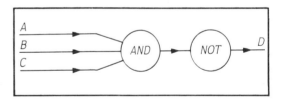

d

Inputs			Output
A	B	C	D
1	1	1	
0	0	0	
1	0	0	
1	0	1	
1	1	0	
0	0	1	
0	1	1	

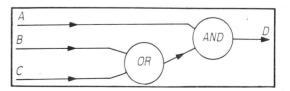

5 The following truth table shows the input and output for the illustrated logic circuit. Write in the circles the names of the gates that are represented.

Input		Output
A	**B**	**C**
0	0	1
0	1	1
1	0	1
1	1	0

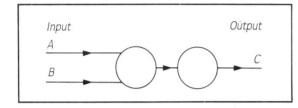

6 Write down the truth tables for the combinations of logic gates in the diagrams.

a

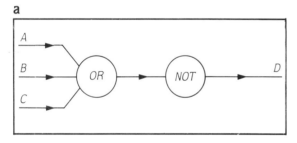

b

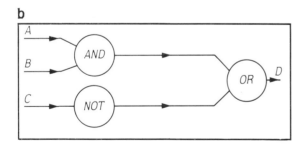

c

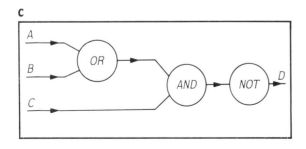

d

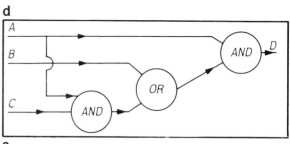

e

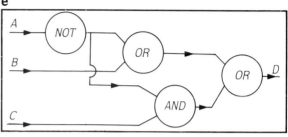

7 a Draw a truth table which represents a NOT logical element.

b Copy and complete the truth table for the network shown below.

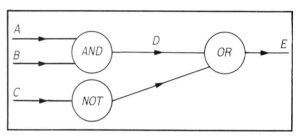

A	B	C	D	E
0	0	0		
0	0	1		
0	1	0		
0	1	1		
1	0	0		
1	1	0		
1	1	1		

c Draw a suitable logic diagram for the truth table below.

A	B	C
0	0	1
0	1	1
1	0	0
1	1	1

d How could three NOT gates and one OR gate be arranged to produce the same output as one AND gate?

8 Using the following circuits, complete the truth table for the output at X, Y and Z given the inputs A, B, C.

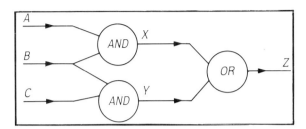

A	B	C	X	Y	Z
0	0	0			
0	0	1			
0	1	0			
0	1	1			
1	0	0			
1	0	1			
1	1	0			
1	1	1			

9 The output from the logic diagram with the inputs as shown is which **one** of the following?
A   Logic 0
B   Logic 0 and logic 1
C   Logic 1
D   Nothing at all
E   Logic 1 or logic 0

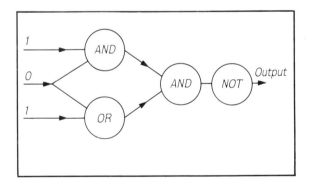

10   a Construct the truth table for the following logic diagram.

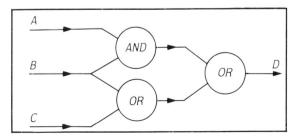

A	B	C	D

b Which of the inputs has no effect on the final output?

11 Fill in the truth tables for the following circuits.

a

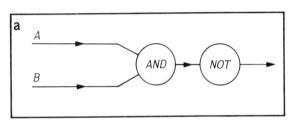

A	B	C

b

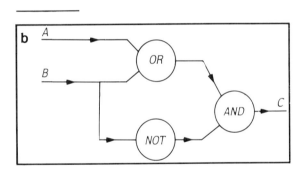

A	B	C

12 Write down the definitions of the following words:

a Logic gate
b Integrated circuit
c Microprocessor
d Logic element
e Gate
f Operation table

13 **a** Describe briefly the function of AND, OR and NOT gates.

b Copy and complete the following truth tables for each of the outputs in the logic circuit given.

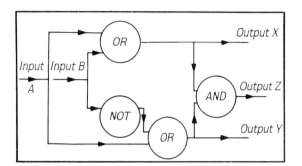

A	B	Output X
0	0	
0	1	
1	0	
1	1	

A	B	Output Y
0	0	
0	1	
1	0	
1	1	

A	B	Output Z
0	0	
0	1	
1	0	
1	1	

14 **a** Copy the truth table and complete the first part of it to show the action of the following circuit.

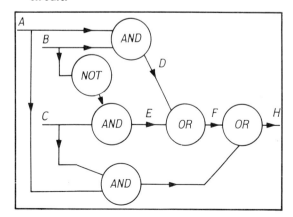

						Good circuit		Faulty circuit	
A	B	C	D	E	F	G	H	G	H
0	0	0							
0	0	1							
0	1	0							
0	1	1							
1	0	0							
1	0	1							
1	1	0							
1	1	1							

b Now suppose that the AND gate which has inputs from A and C develops a fault so that G is always 0. Complete the second part of the truth table for this faulty circuit.

c What do you notice about the outputs from the two circuits? What effect does the faulty gate have?

d Draw a logic circuit that behaves in the same way as the given circuit but uses only four gates.

e Make a truth table for the following circuit.

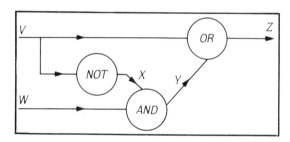

f What would happen if the NOT gate developed a fault and always gave an output of 1?

g Draw a logic circuit which behaves in the same way as the given circuit but uses only one gate.

15 Using the following circuit, complete the truth table for the outputs at R, S, T, X and Y.

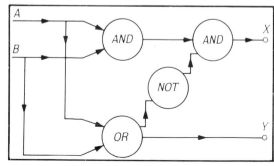

A	B	R	S	T	X	Y
0	0					
0	1					
1	0					
1	1					

16 The table shown below is an operation table for the logic circuit shown. Using the information contained in the table, decide what type of logic gates they are. (Hint: work backwards from the output.)

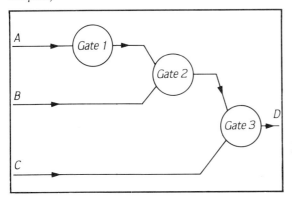

Inputs			Output
A	B	C	D
0	0	0	0
0	0	1	1
0	1	0	0
0	1	1	1
1	0	0	0
1	0	1	0
1	1	0	0
1	1	1	1

17 In order to gain access to a computer system, the person who wants to use the computer has to do the following.
They must key in any one of three key words using these codes:
A = 1st keyword
B = 2nd keyword
C = 3rd keyword
K = key used
G = gained access to the computer
Draw a truth table for all the combinations of the above, then design a logic circuit to fit your truth table.

18 Complete the truth table for this logic circuit:-

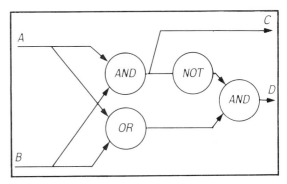

A	B	C	D

19 Construct a truth table for the outputs at C and D for the following circuit.

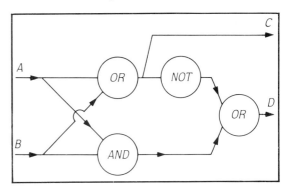

20 In a lottery, the winning ticket must either contain an odd number consisting of three figures or be blue. Answer the questions below using the following codes:
B = blue ticket
E = even number
T = three figure number
W = winner
a Construct a truth table, to show all possible results and indicate with a ★ each winning combination.
b From your truth table or otherwise, construct an efficient logic gate diagram for the winning combination.

21 a Construct a truth table for each of the following logic gates:
   i   AND
   ii   OR
   iii   NOT
   iv   NAND
   v   NOR

b Show that the two circuits below are equivalent.

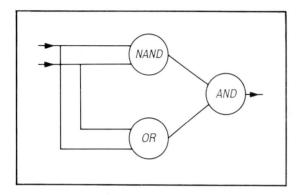

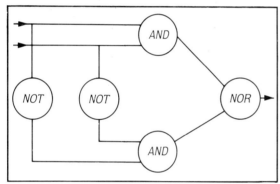

22 A Finance Company will grant a loan to applicants who have a bank account or are married house owners.

a Using the codes
B = bank account
H = house owner
S = single
L = loan
draw a truth table to determine those who are qualified for a loan.

b From the truth table, or otherwise, construct a logic diagram to satisfy the above condition.

23 A bank uses a double security system, based on key-operated switches. The manager, the chief cashier and his deputy each have a key. The door to the vaults can be opened by using any two of the three keys, but the door to the strongroom can only be opened if the vault door is open and all three keys are used to operate the strongroom lock. Design and sketch a logic circuit to satisfy the above conditions, using standard logic elements. Ensure that your diagram is fully annotated.

24 Your school is setting up a drama club. The secretary, a computing expert, is designing a machine to produce membership cards automatically. The machine will have five buttons labelled as follows:
A = member of staff
C = IVth and Vth year pupils
D = pupil studying drama
E = pupil studying English
F = VIth form pupil
Prospective members push the buttons which describe themselves and the machine will produce a membership ticket if they are in one of the following categories:
a Member of staff
b IVth or Vth year pupil studying drama
   VIth form pupil studying English or drama
Draw a diagram of the logic circuit required inside this machine.

16
Boolean expressions

Figure 16.1 *George Boole*

Long before computers and calculating machines were ever thought of, a mathematician was developing a system for mathematical logic. He was called **George Boole** and between 1847 and 1854, he developed **Boolean algebra** for representing logical systems (Figure 16.1).

Boolean algebra can be applied to any problem that has a true/false answer. As you can see, this is very similar to binary representation, where we use bistable systems which can only have two states e.g. ON and OFF, low current and high current, etc. This link with two state systems has made Boolean algebra very important in understanding computer logic.

We saw in the last chapter that there are three main types of logic gate, with two additional gates. These gates can be put together to form a **logic expression**. Sometimes, these logic expressions are called **Boolean expressions**, after George Boole the

inventor of Boolean algebra. Let's now look at some simple Boolean expressions.

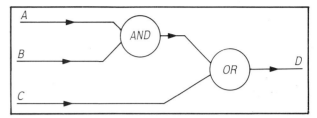

Figure 16.2

Suppose we had the logic circuit shown in Figure 16.2. Before we can work out the output at D we have to work out what happens to the two inputs A and B when they pass through the AND gate. This is done first. As in computer programming and ordinary mathematics, anything that is done before anything else is always put in brackets. You always do what is in the brackets first. So, because the AND operation is performed on the two inputs A and B first, we have to put this expression in brackets. So the logic expression for the logic circuit in Figure 16.2 is

D = (A AND B) OR C

This equation is the logic expression or Boolean expression.

Example 1 Write a Boolean expression for the logic circuit in Figure 16.3

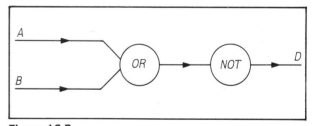

Figure 16.3

The Boolean expression is

D = NOT (A OR B)

Example 2 Draw a logic circuit for the following Boolean expression

C = (NOT A) AND B

Figure 16.4 shows the answer for Example 2.

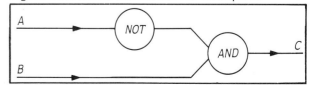

Figure 16.4

Example 3 Write the corresponding Boolean expression for the logic circuit in Figure 16.5

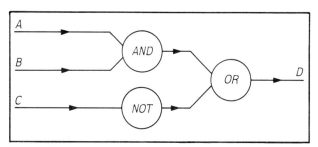

Figure 16.5

The answer is

D = (A AND B) OR (NOT C)

Example 4 A logic cicuit is shown in Figure 16.6. Write down the logical expression for this circuit

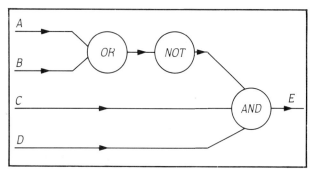

Figure 16.6

The answer is

E = (NOT (A OR B)) AND C AND D

Example 5 A cruise missile can only be launched if the Prime Minister and any two of three cabinet ministers give their permission. Using the codes below

a Draw a truth table (operations table) showing all the possible combinations for the inputs and output.
b Write down a Boolean expression for L in terms of P, A, B and C.
c Draw a logic circuit that is capable of carrying out this expression.

Codes

P = Prime Minister's permission
A = senior cabinet minister A's permission
B = senior cabinet minister B's permission
C = senior cabinet minister C's permission
L = cruise missile launched

To write the truth table we can write a 1 or 0 under each column depending on whether or not permission has been granted. 0 can show that permission has not been granted and 1 can show that permission has been granted. Likewise, a 1 under the column marked L can mean that the missile can be launched.

We can start off by writing the column headings and then filling in all the possible inputs. After this has been done, we can decide what the output, L, will be by considering the conditions. We must have 1 in the P column and two more 1s in either A, B or C. This is the truth table for this problem.

P	A	B	C	L
1	1	1	1	1
1	0	0	0	0
1	1	0	0	0
1	1	1	0	1
1	0	1	1	1
0	1	0	0	0
0	0	1	1	0
0	0	0	1	0
0	0	0	0	0
0	0	1	0	0
1	0	0	1	0
0	1	1	0	0
1	1	0	1	1
0	1	1	1	0
0	1	0	1	0
1	0	1	0	0

For the second part of the question, we know that only two of the three senior cabinet ministers' permission will do. We can write this as:

(A AND B) OR (B AND C) OR (A AND C)

We must also have the Prime Minister's permission, but the expression above must be bracketed because it must be found out first. So, the final Boolean expression is:

((A AND B) OR (B AND C) OR (A AND C)) AND P = L

Remember that we always work from the outer brackets inwards.

Figure 16.7 shows one of the many logic circuits which could do this operation.

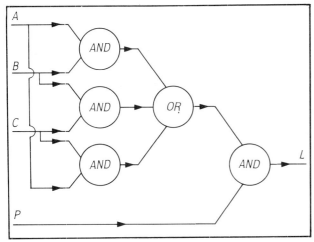

Figure 16.7

Example 6 Construct an operations table and draw a logic diagram for the following Boolean expression

(X AND Y) AND (NOT Z) = A

In this example it is easier to draw the logic diagram first and then to use it to work out the truth or operations table afterwards. Figure 16.8 shows the logic diagram.

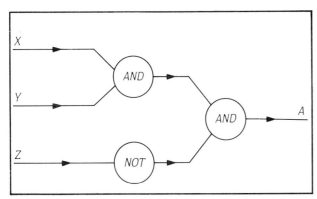

Figure 16.8

X	Y	Z	A
1	1	1	0
1	1	0	1
1	0	1	0
0	1	1	0
1	0	0	0
0	1	0	0
0	0	1	0
0	0	1	0

Test yourself

Using words from the list below, complete sentences A to E. Underline the words you have inserted. The words may be used more than once.

false   gate   Boole   NOT
NAND   Boolean

A *Boolean algebra is a form of mathematical logic invented by George _____.*
B *It can be used in any system which has a true or _____ answer.*
C *There are three main types of logic _____, the AND, OR and _____ gates.*
D *By combining various logic gates together we can write a _____ expression.*
E *In addition to the three main gates there are two other gates, the _____ and NOR gates.*

Things to do

1 *Write down the truth tables showing the operation of an AND gate and an OR gate.*

2 *Draw logic circuits to represent each of the following expressions:*
   a *(A AND NOT B) OR C*
   b *A AND (B OR NOT C)*

3 *The logical statement X = NOT (P OR Q) could be obtained by using two inputs P and Q into which one of these gates?*
   a *An AND gate followed by a NOT gate*
   b *A NOT gate followed by a OR gate*
   c *A NOT gate followed by an AND gate*
   d *An OR gate followed by a NOT gate*
   e *An OR gate followed by an AND gate*

4 **a** *Write down the Boolean expression for the circuit shown in the diagram.*

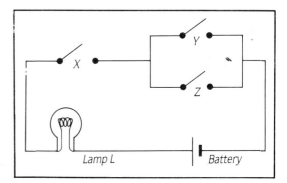

   b *Draw the logic diagram corresponding to this circuit and from it, construct a truth table showing the output L for the various inputs of X, Y, and Z.*

5 Write down the Boolean expressions for the following logic circuits.

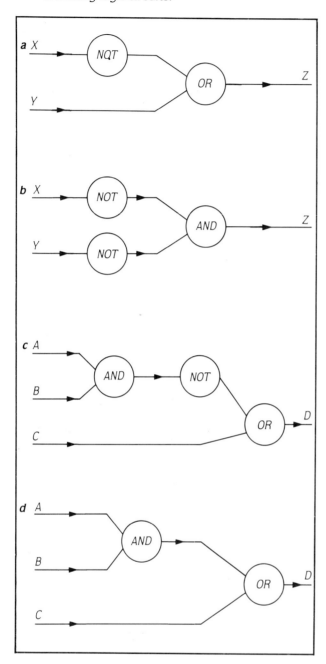

6 Draw logic circuits for the following Boolean expressions:
  a A OR B OR C
  b A AND B AND C
  c (X OR Y) AND Z
  d (X AND Y) OR Z
  e (A OR B) AND (C OR D)

7 All the sheep belonging to Farmer Giles have escaped from his farm to a nearby hillside, where they have joined other sheep. He wishes to recover all his sheep and knows the following:
NOT one of his sheep is black and he believes these to be unlucky, AND all his sheep are branded 'G', OR have a collar.
Using the following:
B = black sheep
G = branded 'G'
C = has a collar
F = belongs to Farmer Giles
Draw a truth table from these conditions to show those sheep owned by Farmer Giles. From your table, or otherwise, produce a Boolean expression to represent those sheep owned by Farmer Giles.

8 The list below shows several methods of travelling.
Boat
Plane
Car
Bicycle
Train
Bus
The characteristics of these modes of travel are shown below:
A ⇒ has 4 wheels exactly
B ⇒ runs on rails
C ⇒ flies
D ⇒ floats
F ⇒ has 2 wheels exactly
D ⇒ has many seats (more than 4)
E ⇒ travels by road
  a By looking at the logic circuit drawn below, and working backwards from the output to the input, find the mode of travel represented by the output G when G = 1.

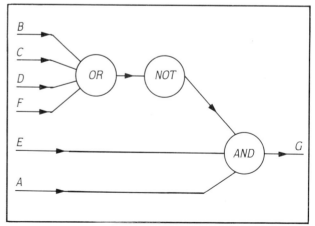

  b Write down the Boolean expression corresponding to the above diagram.

9 Mike the mad motor-cyclist has the following rules of his own for when he is approaching traffic lights.

Any time a red light is showing he will STOP.

If there is an amber light showing and he is in a hurry he will GO.

If he is not in a hurry and either red or an amber is showing he will STOP.

a Complete a truth table using as input:

A = an amber light is showing

R = a red light is showing

H = Mike is in a hurry

and output S = Mike will stop,

b From your truth table, or otherwise, draw a logic diagram to illustrate the above statements.

c Write the corresponding Boolean statements.

10 To be awarded a school's prize a pupil must either finish top in any subject or have not been absent on any day for a whole term and been late on less than three occasions.

Using as input:

T = a pupil who has finished top

A = a pupil who has been absent

L = a pupil who has been late on three occasions or more

and output

P = a pupil who will be awarded a prize

a Draw a truth table

b Draw a logic diagram

c Using the truth table or otherwise, write a corresponding Boolean expression.

11 The following conditions are used to determine whether applicants for appointment should be called for interview.

i   A female applicant will only be called for interview if she is single and has less than 2 years experience.

ii A male applicant will be called for interview either if he is single with 2 or more years experience, or if he is married with less than 2 years experience

In your answers to the following questions, use the variables:

F = female

M = married

E = 2 or more years experience

a Draw a truth table to represent the above conditions.

b State the Boolean expression for the truth table.

c By using AND, OR and NOT gates only, construct two logic networks, one for the male applicants and one for the female applicants to represent the above conditions. State the Boolean expression for each.

12 When a certain type of light aircraft with retractable undercarriage (i.e. the undercarriage can be raised or lowered) is coming in to land, the following safety checks are made on the state of the undercarriage.

If only the left-hand or right-hand wheel is down a bell rings.

If neither wheel is down a buzzer sounds. (N.B. If a wheel is still retracted, it is not shown.)

Using the following symbols:

L = left-hand wheel retracted

R = right-hand wheel retracted

B = bell rings

Z = buzzer sounds

a Form a truth table for the above conditions.

b Write down the Boolean expression using AND, OR and NOT gates.

c Describe how this circuit could be used to carry out a function within a computer.

13 'A woman over 60 or a man over 65 is entitled to a pension.' Use the following coding:

For input:

A represents the proposition 'you are over 60'

B represents the proposition 'you are over 65'

C represents the proposition 'you are a male'

For output

D represents the proposition 'you are entitled to a pension'

a Draw up the truth table for inputs A, B and C, and for output D.

b In the truth table two lines are logically impossible. Which are they?

c Write down a Boolean expression for D in terms of A, B and C.

d Hence, construct a logic circuit to accept A, B and C as input and to output D. Use only AND, OR and NOT gates and indicate on the diagram the Boolean expression after each gate.

17
Computer peripherals

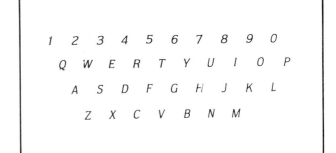

Figure 17.2 *The alphanumeric keys on a keyboard*

Peripheral devices

To get data in and out of the computer, we need **peripheral devices**. Peripheral devices are devices that are attached to, and controlled by the central processing unit. They are not contained inside the CPU. The word 'peripheral' means 'on the outside of'. So a peripheral device is a device on the outside of the CPU.

The peripheral devices provide the two-way communication between the computer and the person using it, the **user**. Peripheral devices can be divided into two: those for input and those used for output. Some peripherals can be used for input and output.

Peripheral devices include paper tape readers. punch card readers, VDUs and keyboards, MICRs, OCRs, printers, bar code readers etc. Figure 17.1 shows which of these are for input and which are for output.

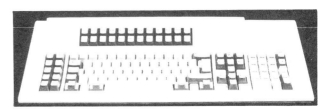

Figure 17.3 *A computer keyboard*

keyboard. They do have some additional keys to cope with arithematic functions and some other functions. The keys containing the letters of the alphabet from A to Z and the numbers 0 to 9 are sometimes referred to as the **alphanumeric** keys (Figure 17.2). Figure 17.3 shows a modern computer keyboard.

The **visual display unit** (**VDU**) allows information to be output on a screen similar to that of a television, when it is used with a keyboard (Figure 17.4).

Input	Output
Paper tape reader	Printer
Punch card reader	Graph plotter
Magnetic tape unit	Magnetic tape unit
Magnetic disk drive	Magnetic disk drive
Magnetic ink character reader	Microfilm/Microfiche
	VDU
Optical character reader	Paper tape punch
Bar code reader	Voice synthesizer
Voice input unit	
Light pen	
Laser scanner	
Document reader	

Figure 17.1 *Input and output devices*

VDU and keyboard

This is the combination of peripheral devices which you are probably most familiar with. Data can be input directly into the computer via a **keyboard**. Most computer keyboards are very similar to a typewriter

Figure 17.4 *A VDU and keyboard*

Card readers

A **card reader** is a hardware device which reads data off punched cards. Using punched cards as input media is an old fashioned method. It is very time consuming and wasteful. Figure 17.5 shows a punched card. Figure 17.6 shows a card reader.

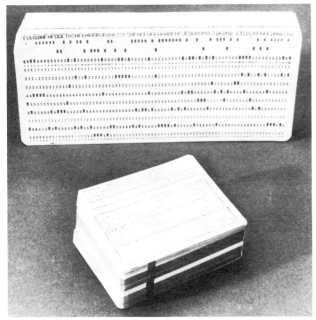

Figure 17.5 *Punched cards. The largest ones are more common*

Punched tape readers (paper tape readers)

Paper tape is also not used very often as input media. It is slow and too expensive. A **punched tape reader** is the peripheral device that reads information contained in the tape (Figure 17.7). We now have much better ways of putting information into the computer such as key to disk, MICR, OCR etc.

Document readers

A **document reader** is a device that can read information off specially prepared documents. There are two types of document reader. One is a **mark reader** which can understand marks made at certain places on a document. The other is a **character reader** which can read actual letters.

Mark readers

Marks in documents can be read in two ways. One method is **mark sensing**. This brushes electrical contacts across the paper. If the contacts touch a pencil mark then a current can flow between them because the pencil lead conducts electricity. This method is used for marking multiple-choice question papers.

A newer method of mark reading involves directing a thin beam of light onto the document and sensing the light reflected by the document. If there is a dark part (pencil mark) then very little light is reflected. This is called **optical mark recognition** (**OMR**).

Mark reading is ideal for documents such as meter reading sheets which the Gas or Electricity man marks in when he comes to read the meter (Figure 17.8). No other data preparation stage is needed so fewer errors are introduced. Documents are read at very high speeds, much faster then typing speed (Figure 17.9).

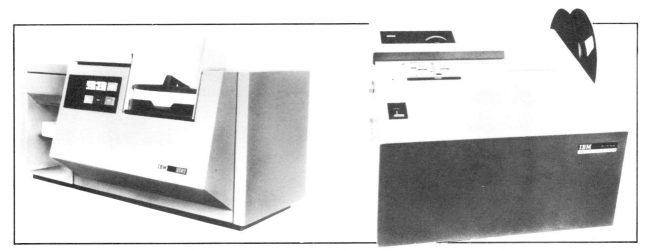

Figure 17.6 *A punched card reader*

Figure 17.7 *A paper tape reader*

142071983

Mr M. Mouse
10 Disney Drive
Anytown

PREVIOUS READING	12000
EXPECTED HIGH	20000
EXPECTED LOW	14000
PRESENT READING	14378

CUSTOMER ACCOUNT NUMBER	PREVIOUS READING	PRESENT READING
0 0 0 0 0 0 0 0 0	0 0 0 0 0 0	0 0 0 0 0 0
1 1 1 1 1 1 1 1 1	1 1 1 1 1 1	1 1 1 1 1 1
2 2 2 2 2 2 2 2 2	2 2 2 2 2 2	2 2 2 2 2 2
3 3 3 3 3 3 3 3 3	3 3 3 3 3 3	3 3 3 3 3 3
4 4 4 4 4 4 4 4 4	4 4 4 4 4 4	4 4 4 4 4 4
5 5 5 5 5 5 5 5 5	5 5 5 5 5 5	5 5 5 5 5 5
6 6 6 6 6 6 6 6 6	6 6 6 6 6 6	6 6 6 6 6 6
7 7 7 7 7 7 7 7 7	7 7 7 7 7 7	7 7 7 7 7 7
8 8 8 8 8 8 8 8 8	8 8 8 8 8 8	8 8 8 8 8 8
9 9 9 9 9 9 9 9 9	9 9 9 9 9 9	9 9 9 9 9 9

Figure 17.8 *A meter reading sheet with mark sense boxes. Information is coded by shading in the boxes*

Optical character readers

Optical character readers can recognize actual letters and numbers. The process of reading is called **optical character recognition (OCR)**.

Sometimes the documents read in this way are typed, but they can also be handwritten. If the documents used are handwritten then, just like humans, the reader can only read it if it is very neat. OCR is used for producing bills and is a very quick method of getting information into the computer (Figure 17.10).

Figure 17.9 *An optical mark reader*

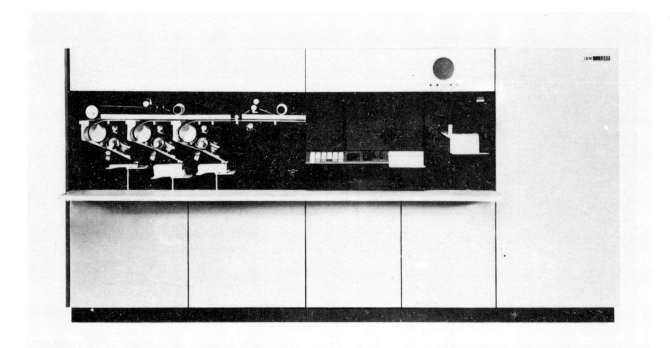

Figure 17.10 *An optical character reader*

Magnetic ink character readers (MICR)

This reader can read the characters printed in magnetic ink on cheques. It is extremely fast and it can handle large amounts of work accurately.

Bar code readers

This peripheral device can understand the pre-coded data in a bar code. There are two types of bar code reader. In one type a light pen called a **wand reader** is passed across a series of lines. In the other type objects are passed across a light pen fixed into a unit.

The bar code reader is an excellent device for data capture because it is very quick and can do several jobs at once. Bar code readers are used in shops and libraries. Figure 17.11 shows the bar code on a library ticket. Figure 17.12 shows a bar code reader being used in a library.

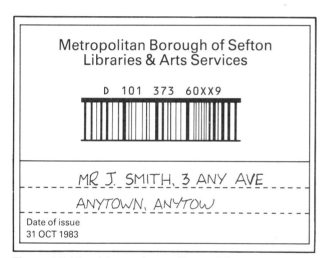

Figure 17.11 *A bar code on a library ticket*

Figure 17.12 *Using a bar code reader in a library to record books borrowed and returned*

Printers

Printers are an important part of most computer systems. They produce visual records of the information on paper which is permanent and can be posted. Often, information must be printed for legal reasons.

It is hard to think of a business use for a computer where a line printer would not be needed. Bank statements, invoices, sales figures, stock lists, payroll slips, accounts etc. are all examples of information that needs to be output on a printer.

There are two types of printer: **line printers** and **character printers**. Line printers can type a complete line at a time whereas character printers can only print a single character at a time. An ordinary typewriter is a character printer.

Line printers

Line printers are the most common type of printer used in computer systems. They work at much faster speeds than character printers because they print a whole line at a time. Some line printers can print the lines backwards on the return journey and save even more time.

The way in which the line printers work depends on the speed and the type of printing quality required.

There are two types of line printer: **drum printers** and **chain printers**.

Drum printers

A drum printer consists of a drum which has rows of characters along its length (Figure 17.13). The printer paper is placed over the carbon with the drum

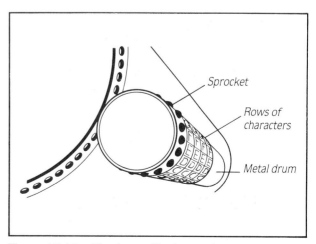

Figure 17.13 *The drum off a drum printer*

underneath. Hammers strike the paper against the carbon and the drum and the characters are printed out in alphabetical order. For example, the word COMPUTER would be printed out like this:

```
C
C       E
C M     E
COM     E
COMP    ER
COMP TER
COMPUTER
```

Figure 17.14 shows the parts of a drum printer.

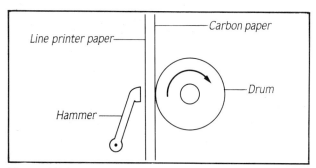

Figure 17.14   *How a drum printer works*

Chain printers

Chain printers are similar to drum printers because both use the impact method (hammers push the paper against the carbon and the drum).

The chain rotates and the hammers strike out the character and a whole line is printed very quickly (Figure 17.15).

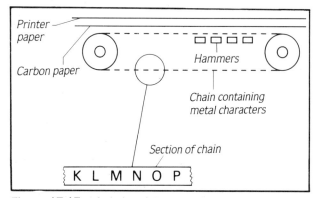

Figure 17.15   *A chain printer*

Dot matrix printers

There is another type of printer called a **dot matrix printer** which is usually used with smaller computers such as microcomputers.

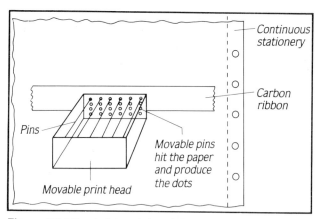

Figure 17.16   *A dot matrix printer*

The dot matrix printer is another impact printer and the characters are made up of a series of dots formed when rods in the print head press against the carbon and the paper (Figure 17.16). Because of the dot nature of the characters, dot matrix produced print is not as neat as print produced by other methods. Figure 17.17 shows a dot matrix line printer.

Figure 17.17   *A line printer*

Character printers

Character printers produce one character at a time and, as a result, are generally slower than line printers. However, what they loose in speed they generally make up for in print quality. The print produced by these printers looks as if it has been produced by a good quality typewriter rather than by a computer.

There are many types of character printer, each relying on a different method of print production. Which one is chosen really depends on the speed and quality of print you require.

Daisy wheel printers

The **daisy wheel printer** consists of a wheel with lots of arms attached to it, a bit like the way petals

Figure 17.18 *Daisy wheels and printer ribbon cartridges*

are attached to a daisy (Figure 17.18). At the ends of these arms are two characters, one above the other (Figure 17.19). The daisy wheel rotates and a hammer presses the carbon and paper against the arm.

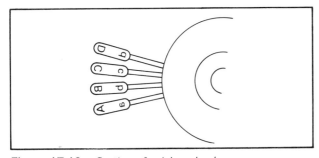

Figure 17.19 *Section of a daisy wheel*

Daisy wheel printers tend to be slow but they can be used where the standard of printing must be high. This type of printer is ideal for use with a word processor where business letters are produced. The slowness would not be important in most office situations, but it would be a problem where the volume of printing is high. Another problem with the daisy wheel printer is noise. Like most impact printers, they are very noisy and this can cause problems in small offices.

Other printers

Laser printers

Laser beam printers are extremely expensive – £10 000 upwards! This means that they are only used by large organizations with large amounts of work. One of the advantages of these printers is that

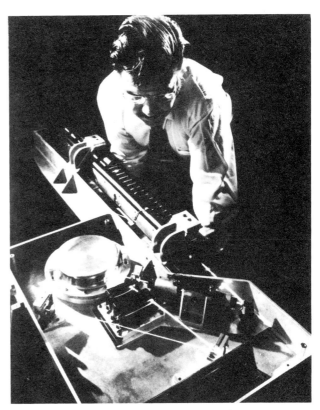

Figure 17.20 *Inside a laser printer. The laser hits a rotating metal drum to form characters. This laser printer can produce about 10 000 11" sheets of printed paper an hour*

they are noiseless. The reason for this is that they are non-impact printers which means they don't have hammers hitting the paper and creating noise. Another advantage is that they can do different sizes of type.

Laser beam printers are ideal for producing written material that needs to be produced in large quantities all at once. They are used for Giro cheques, electricity, gas and water bills and rates. Figure 17.20 shows the inside of a laser printer.

Ink jet printers

In an **ink jet printer**, tiny drops of ink are sprayed onto the paper to form characters as the paper moves. A new technique has also been developed that can produce any pattern you want so that you are not just limited to characters. One advantage of this type of printer is that pre-printed stationery with the company name on it etc. does not need to be used as all the printing can be done using the printer. Another advantage is that it is a non-impact printer, so it is quiet.

Graph plotters

A **graph plotter** allows the computer to draw pictures on paper. These pictures may be graphs, pie diagrams, maps, three dimensional drawings etc.

A computer with a graph plotter is a very useful system for an architect, draughtsman or engineer, because drawings on the VDU can be altered on the screen without having to redraw the drawing. When the drawing is correct it can be printed out.

The graph plotter consists of a pen which moves across the paper. There are two types of graph plotters: **flat bed plotters** (Figure 17.21) and **drum plotters** (Figure 17.22). In the flat bed plotter, the pen is hanging down from a bar and can move in all directions. In the drum plotter, the paper moves and a pen moves along a bar.

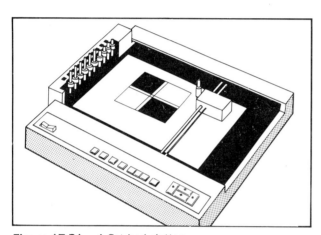

Figure 17.21   *A flat bed plotter*

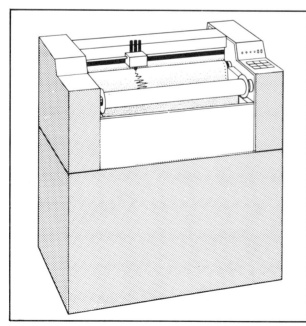

Figure 17.22   *A drum plotter*

Graphical display unit and light pen

A **graphical display unit** is similar to a visual display unit. It can display both text and graphics. But it is better than a VDU because you can draw fine lines on it and if you plot curves they don't look as if they are made up of a series of squares.

Graphical display units are now used more and more for showing information pictorially. Pie diagrams, histograms, cumulative frequency distribution and graphs can all be shown very accurately and sometimes in colour.

Objects in three dimensions can be drawn and then rotated so that they may be viewed from different angles. If necessary, the diagram can be altered using a **light pen**. A light pen is a pen which senses light emitted (let out) by a VDU or graphical display unit.

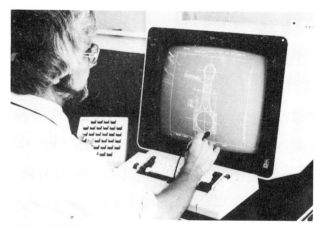

Figure 17.23   *Using a graphical display unit and light pen to design the connecting rod for a diesel engine*

Using a light pen, it is possible to draw lines and characters on the screen. It is also possible to alter diagrams that are not correct.

A graphical display unit used with a light pen is a valuable device for engineers, scientists and architects. A field called **CAD** (**computer aided design**) enables engineers and architects to design new products using these two peripheral devices (Figure 17.23).

Point of sale terminals (POS)

A **point of sale terminal** (**POS**) is really a computerized till. It is a very quick and effective way of recording purchases. The terminal looks a bit like a till but there is usually a wand reader attached to it.

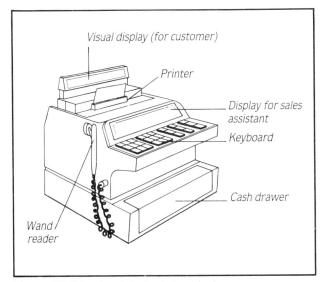

Figure 17.24 *A point of sale terminal*

This is passed over the bar code on the goods (Figure 17.24). Sometimes the reader is under a glass panel on the check-out desk instead.

The point of sale terminal can read coded information contained in the bar code. It adds up the items and produces an itemized receipt like the one in Figure 17.25.

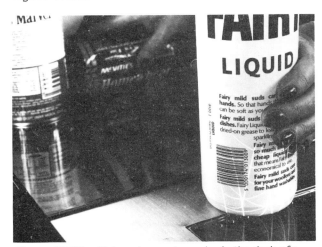

Figure 17.26 *Using a bar code reader in the desk of a point of sale terminal*

The advantage of POS terminals is that they can save a lot of time and money. You don't have to stick price labels on each article because by reading the bar code the computer knows what price to charge. The person at the till no longer has to type in the price of each article so they can work faster (Figure 17.26). Also the computer can deduct each item from the stock as it is sold so this makes stock-taking simpler. Some POS systems can re-order stock automatically if it reaches a certain minimum level.

```
    CHICKEN CURR       .68½
    POTATOES           .29½
    IRISH STEW         .39
    POTATOES           .20
    WHOLE MUSHRM       .38
    AMER GINGER        .23
    PASTE              .24½
    NOODLES            .39½
    CRNISH PASTY       .36
    WHOLE MUSHRM       .38
    BALANCE DUE       4.77

    CASH              5.00

    CHANGE DUE         .23

 23/10/84 15:52 1208 0001   2      1006
      **  THANK YOU - COME AGAIN  **
```

Figure 17.25 *An itemized receipt*

Test yourself

Using the words in the list below, copy out and complete sentences A to S underlining the words you have inserted. The words may be used more than once.

character	dot matrix	document reader
graph plotter	laser	CPU	keyboard
line	hard	bar code	daisy wheel
light pen	characters	wand reader
ONR	mark reader	word	CAD
bar code reader	POS	peripheral
input	punched tape

A A _____ device is a device which is under the control of the _____ but outside it.

B These devices can be divided into two; output and _____ devices.

C The most common combination of input and output devices is the VDU and _____.

D Card readers and _____ _____ readers are not used much nowadays because they are very wasteful.

E A _____ _____ can understand letters placed in boxes on a specially prepared document.

F Marks placed on a document can be read by a

_____ _____.

G This form of reading is called _____.

H An OCR can understand _____ on a document.

I A _____ _____ _____ is often seen in large supermarkets. The shop assistant uses a _____ _____ to pass a beam of light across a _____ _____ on the goods.

J A _____ printer can be used to obtain a _____ copy.

K A _____ printer prints one line at a time, but a _____ printer only prints a single character at a time.

L The _____ _____ printer produces characters made up of a series of dots.

M For high quality print, it is best to use a _____ printer.

N A _____ _____ printer is slow but produces very high print quantity. It is often used in conjunction with a _____ processor.

O If large quantities of printed material are needed very quickly, such as electricity bills etc. then a _____ printer can be used.

P The computer can be used to display pictures and graphs on paper. The output device needed to do this is called a _____ _____.

Q A graphical display unit used with a _____ _____ can be used to alter drawings on the screen.

R _____ enables engineers and architects to design new products.

S A computerized till is often called a _____ terminal.

Things to do

1 A computer consists of a central processing unit and peripheral equipment.
  a Explain the meaning of the word peripheral.
  b Give one reason why peripherals are necessary.
  c Which peripherals could be used to help with the following?
    i Sending daily figures from an agency to the computer based at Head Office
    ii Drawing a hard copy diagram of the sales of goods over a period of a month

2 Which of the following may be used only as an output device?
  a a punched card reader
  b a line printer
  c a magnetic drum
  d a mark sense card reader

3 Name these bits of hardware:
  a The parts of the computer consisting of the immediate access store, the arithmetic unit and central processing unit.
  b A device suitable for reading the special marks on bank cheques.
  c A terminal device, incorporating a cathode ray tube, on which both line drawings and text can be displayed.
  d A device used by data preparation staff to check for correct punching of data on cards or tape by repeating the keyboard operations.
  e A backing storage device only appropriate for serial access usage.

4 What computing device might be used for:
  a Designing a car?
  b Outputting lists of books by title, author and publisher for libraries?
  c Scanning a bar code on a grocery item?

5 Give **one** advantage and **one** disadvantage of a VDU compared with a line printer.

6 Laser printer   teletype
  drum line printer   micro film output
  a Place the output devices above in order of their introduction to common computer use. List them with the earliest first.
  b For each of the above devices, list their advantages and disadvantages compared with the others.

7 The following statement contains two misuses of terminology. Identify and correct each misuse.
  'The data, input using a line printer, was stored in the central processing unit before being processed by a disk drive.'

8 What do the following abbreviations stand for?
  a VDU
  b OMR
  c OCR
  d CAD

9 **a** What, in a computer installation, is meant by a peripheral?
  b Some peripherals are classed as 'fast' peripherals and others as 'slow' peripherals. Classify the following as 'fast' or 'slow.'
    i A card reader
    ii A magnetic tape unit

10 Copy the table below and put a tick in the appropriate columns to clarify the following peripheral devices. You can use more than one tick per row.

	Input	Output	Internal store	Backing store
Keyboard				
Graph plotter				
Bubble memory				
VDU				
Line printer				
Document reader				
Floppy disk				
Paper tape reader				

11 **a** Why are peripherals an essential part of most computer systems?
    b Give **one** example of an output peripheral.
    c VDUs and hard copy output devices have different functions. Give one use of each to illustrate clearly their different functions.

12 The following are all output devices:
    Graphical display unit
    Teletypewriter
    Laser printer
    On-line card punch
    In each of the situations below, state which of the above output devices would be most suitable and give one reason for your choice.
    a A mail order company producing a very large number of customer statements overnight
    b A cartographer (map-maker)
    c A member of a city transport department who is organizing the bus routes

13 The diagram shows the flow of data to and from various peripheral devices attached to the central processing unit (CPU). Write down the names of suitable devices which could be used for A, B, C and D.

Device	
A	
B	
C	
D	

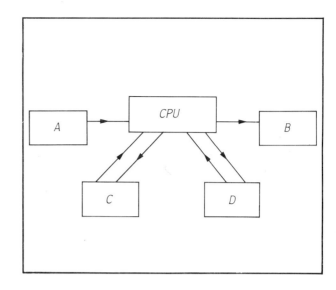

14 A great many printers are now available, ranging from small, slow devices, to versatile, fast printers. Describe various types of printer which are now in use, giving an indication of their operating speeds and paying particular attention to:
    a The different facilities which they provide
    b Typical applications for which they are appropriate

15 A doctor wishes to install a computer system to help him in the running of his practice. he has quite a large number of patients and he would like to store their records in the computer.
    a Assuming he has decided on the CPU, what peripherals would you suggest he buys?
    b For each of the above peripherals you have listed, explain what use each of them could be put to.
    c What other jobs, apart from storing patients records, could be done using the computer.

16 Describe what type of printer you would use to do the following jobs. For each one you have chosen, explain your choice.
    a Suitable for typing out pupils programs on a microcomputer in a school.
    b Producing high quality typed letters on a word processor
    c Printing a very high volume of material, i.e. all the bills for the water rates at once

17 **a** What is a point of sale terminal?
    b What are the advantages of using it?
    c Point of sale terminals can be divided into two types. What is the difference between the two types?

18 Suggest a use for each of the following peripheral devices:

   a Optical character reader

   b Magnetic ink character reader

   c VDU and keyboard

   d Document reader

   e Daisy wheel printer

   f Laser printer

   g Bar code reader

   h Graph plotter

   i Graphical display unit and light pen

19 Two girls leave school and start jobs in two different self-service stores. One store uses a cash register and the other has a point of sale terminal with a bar code reader at the checkout counter:

   a What is a bar code?

   b If the girls are going to work at the checkout counters, give two tasks that the girl using the cash register will do that will be unnecessary for the girl at the point of sale terminal.

   c Choose **three** ways in which the use of the point of sale terminal will make the store more efficient. Give a reason for each choice.

   d Give two probable reasons why the store with the cash register has not yet updated their equipment to include a terminal.

18
Backing store

There are two types of storage used by a computer: **backing storage** and **main storage**. Main storage is the name given to the circuits inside the central processing unit that store information and data which is needed immediately by the computer. Usually the storage space in the main store is very small compared to the storage space needed, so some additional storage space is necessary. It would be possible to build a computer with a large main store but this would be very expensive and as only part of the information would be needed at any one time it would also be wasteful. It would also be volatile, so the information would disappear when the computer was turned off. So this additional storage is outside the CPU. It is referred to as the **backing store**.

There are many types of medium (materials) that can be used for backing store. The one you choose really depends on the price you want to pay and the amount of storage capacity you need. Two common backing store media are magnetic tape and magnetic disks (Figures 18.1 and 18.2)

Figure 18.1 *Tape is one common backing store medium*

Figure 18.2 *Disk is another*

Magnetic tape

The magnetic tape which is used in backing storage for large mainframe computers is very similar to the tape used by reel-to-reel tape recorders, except that it is wider. The tape consists of plastic coated with iron oxide. This can be magnetized in one of two directions, so it represents a binary code.

The main advantage of magnetic tape storage is that it is a cheap way of storing a lot of information and it does not take up much space.

The disadvantage of tape is that it only allows **serial** or **sequential access**. What this means is that to get to one part of the tape it may be necessary to run through all the tape if the information is on the end. This can be a very time consuming process, since the search for data could take several minutes.

A magnetic **tape unit** is a device which is used to record information onto the tape or to read information from the tape (Figure 18.3). It consists of read/write heads similar to the ones in an ordinary tape recorder (Figure 18.4). The tape travels through vacuum columns. These produce very little friction with the tape when it rapidly accelerates or decelerates. Tapes can be taken off the tape units when they are not required and are usually kept in a tape library.

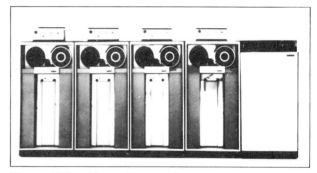

Figure 18.3 *Magnetic tape units*

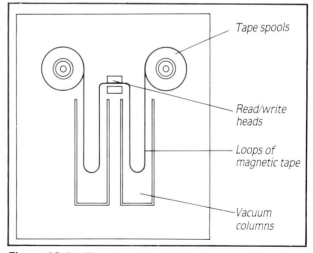

Tape spools

Read/write heads

Loops of magnetic tape

Vacuum columns

Figure 18.4 *The parts of a magnetic tape unit*

Magnetic disk

Magnetic disks consist of a thin metal disk coated

with magnetic material on both sides. The information and data is put on and taken off the disk in much the same way as for tape. Magnetic disks can be hard or flexible. The flexible disks, mainly used on microcomputers are often called **floppy disks** or **diskettes**. We will look at floppy disks separately.

Magnetic disk storage costs more than magnetic tape storage but is a much better way of storing information and data that is needed regularly. If the information is needed immediately it will need to be held on-line. This means it must be connected to, and directly under the control of the CPU. Magnetic tape tends to be too slow for on-line storage. However, magnetic disk provides a **random access medium**. This means that the data or information held on the disk can be found almost immediately because you don't need to go sequentially through the data before the item you want is found. Using magnetic disk, you go straight to the data. This method of access is referred to as **random** or **direct access**. To understand this better, suppose you had an LP record and a cassette tape of the same piece of music. If you wanted to find the fifth piece of music on the LP it would be easy. You would just put the stylus down in

the right place. This is an example of random access. If you wanted to find the fifth track on your cassette though, it would not be so easy. You would have to go through all the other tracks to get to the fifth track. This is an example of serial or sequential access. Figure 18.5 shows the difference between these two types of access.

In order for the computer to go straight to the information, a catalogue needs to be produced which tells the computer where on the disk or disks the data can be found. The data needs to be recorded onto the disk in a predetermined way.

The data is arranged on the disk in circular tracks. These are very small areas which are magnetized in one direction or the other to represent 0s and 1s. The first track, which is the outermost one, contains the directory. This tells the computer what data is held on the disk. The tracks are normally arranged in blocks or sectors and they have gaps between them. Data can only be taken off the disk when it is working at full speed. It takes a bit of time for the disks to reach this speed. So the gaps are places where the disks accelerate up to full speed before they reach the tracks containing data. Figure 18.6 shows the parts of a magnetic disk.

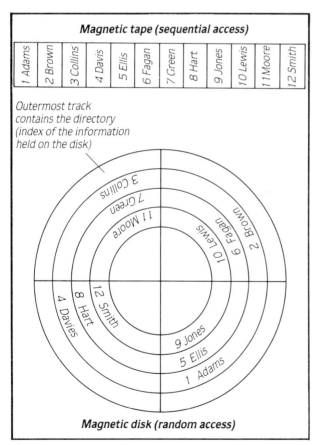

Figure 18.5 *How information is stored on magnetic tape (sequential access) and magnetic disk (random access)*

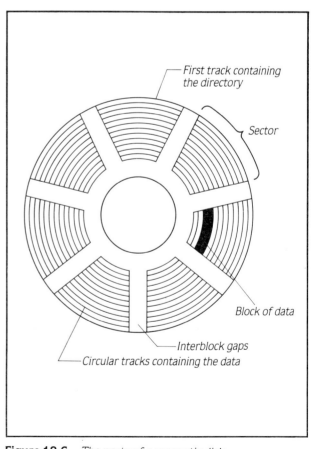

Figure 18.6 *The parts of a magnetic disk*

Figure 18.7 *Putting an exchangeable disk unit into a disk drive*

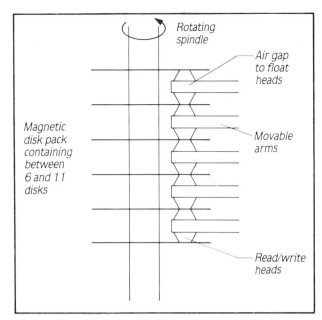

Figure 18.8 *A magnetic disk pack in a magnetic disk drive*

Disk drive unit

Figure 18.7 shows an operator putting a disk into a **magnetic disk drive unit**. A disk drive unit is the name given to the piece of hardware that is able to read information off the disk and record information onto the disk. The disk drive rotates the magnetic disk or disk packs at an extremely high speed. The movable arms containing the read/write heads look for information on the disks or place information onto them. The disk operating system also keeps an account of space utilization (how the space has been used) so that if a program doesn't use all the space on a disk, then other programs can be put in the empty spaces.

Figure 18.9 *Exchangeable disk packs. The first pack is empty and the second contains 11 disks.*

Disk packs

Disks packs are used when large quantities of data need to be stored. These disk packs usually contain about eleven disks in a single plastic case. The whole pack can be placed on the spindle of the disk drive unit (Figure 18.8). Sometimes. these packs of disks are inside the drive and cannot be removed. These are called **fixed disks**. When the packs can be removed, they are called **exchangeable disk packs** (Figure 18.9).

In order to find an item of information contained on a disk pack, the movable arms first read the first track which contains the directory. This directory is similar to an index in a book. Once it has been read, the movable arms will know on which disk, which side, which track and on which sector the information can be found. The movable arms can then go directly to the place on the disk where the information is held, ignoring all the other information. This direct accessing saves a lot of time compared to serial accessing (accessing in order).

The **disk operating system** is responsible for the storage of information on the disks and allows the computer to gain access to the information in as short a time as possible. The disk operating system is an actual computer program which co-ordinates all the functions of the disk drive.

Floppy disks (diskettes)

Floppy disks are becoming one of the most popular

means of storing information. They are used mainly by microcomputers although some mainframe machines use them.

A floppy disk is a disk made out of flexible plastic coated with iron oxide, just like the coating on a cassette tape. Like the hard disk, this coating can be magnetized in two directions so it can be used to store information.

The disk is contained inside a cardboard envelope, there is a liner which removes any debris on the disk surface and also lubricates the disk as it rotates. There are two sizes of disk: 5¼″ and 8″ diameter. Most microcomputers use the smaller disk.

To read and write the data off and onto the disk, a floppy disk drive unit is used. The read/write head moves along the short cut in the cardboard envelope towards the centre. It can find, read and write data at extremely high speed.

Like hard disks, floppy disks are a random access medium. Because the floppy disks have to be small, the data needs to be packed together very closely. Because of this, floppy disks can be very sensitive to dust and changes in temperature, so for some large computer systems, floppy disks would not be reliable enough for storage.

The amount of storage capacity depends on the recording density (how near the tracks and sectors are to each other). A typical disk drive with a disk of 5″ diameter, can hold between 150 and 500 k bytes of information. Some disks can hold information on both sides. The write protect notch at the side of the disk can be covered with tape to prevent erasure.

Figure 18.10 shows the parts of a floppy disk. Figure 18.11 shows a floppy disk being put into a disk drive.

Floppy disk drive unit

The **floppy disk drive** is the unit which rotates the floppy disk and enables the read/write head to put information on or take information off the disk. Most disk units contain two disk drives because one of the units can be used to record information off the other.

Quite often, the disk drive units will be used to store information in the form of files. These file things like stock lists, names and addresses, payroll information etc.

The disk operating system, (DOS) keeps a directory of the files on the disk. It also controls the information storage and retrieval.

Cassettes

Cassettes can be used as a cheap alternative for disks with microcomputers (Figure 18.12). The cassettes are the same as those used in an ordinary cassette recorder. The trouble with using cassettes is that the loading of a program takes quite a long time. Also, the reliability of loading is not always what would be desired. Because of the slowness and the unreliability their use is usually restricted to home computers.

Figure 18.13 shows the similarities and differences between the main types of backing store.

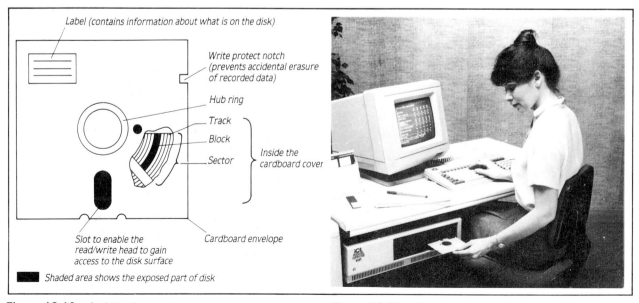

Figure 18.10 *Inside a floppy disk*

Figure 18.11 *Putting a floppy disk into a disk drive*

Magnetic tape	Magnetic disk	Floppy disk	Cassette tape
Cheap	Expensive	Fairly cheap	Very cheap
Serial (sequential) access	Random (direct) access	Random (direct) access	Serial (sequential) access
Very large storage capacity (10 – 60 megabytes)	Very large storage capacity (2 – 60 megabytes)	Medium storage capacity (0.25 – 1.5 megabytes)	Very small storage capacity
Slower access time	Fast access time	Fast access time	Very slow access time
Fast transfer rate	Very fast transfer rate	Fairly slow transfer rate	Very slow transfer rate
Exchangeable	Exchangeable or fixed	Exchangeabe	Exchangeable

Figure 18.13 *Comparison between the main types of backing store*

Figure 18.12 *Data cassettes for microcomputers. There are like ordinary cassettes but they are made to a higher standard and are usually shorter in length*

Other backing store media

Magnetic cartridges

Where very large quantities of information are kept, a lot of time is wasted in obtaining a disk or tape to put into the drive. Because of cost considerations, it is not always possible to keep the tape and disks on the drives permanently. A file librarian would have to look up the file.

Using **magnetic cartridges** provides an ideal way of keeping data stored so that the computer can find it rapidly and read it without needing human intervention (Figure 18.14).

The data is stored in spools of tape which are housed in cartridges about the size of a small tin. They are stored in a honeycomb arrangement and can be picked out when required by an electro mechanical picker (Figure 18.15). Vast quantities of data can be kept in a very small amount of space using this mass storage system.

Figure 18.14 *Magnetic cartridges. The pen gives you an idea of their size*

Figure 18.15 *The main storage system is arranged like a honeycomb*

Bubble memory

Bubble memory is a new type of storage device which can store huge quantities of information in an extremely small space (Figure 18.16). The data is stored in binary coding in the form of magnetic bubbles in a chip. If a bubble is present, then it represents the number 1, and if it isn't present, then it represents 0. The magnetic bubbles can be moved

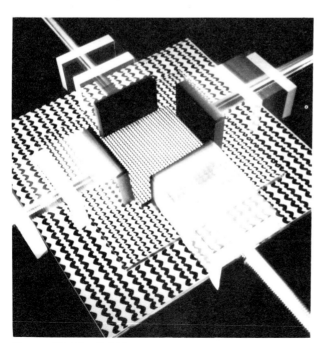

Figure 18.16 *Bubble memory*

along the chip and the data contained can be read sequentially. Using this method huge quantities of information can be stored permanently in a small space. The bubble memory is non-volatile, so when the computer is switched off, the stored information is not lost.

Microfilm and microfiche

Off-line information can be stored in the form of either a photographic slide (called **microfiche** Figure 18.17) or photographic film in the form of a reel (called **microfilm**). Pages of print taken off the screen of a VDU can be greatly reduced in size.

Computer output in microfilm (COM) is ideal for situations where information is kept that doesn't go out of date quickly such as books in a library etc.

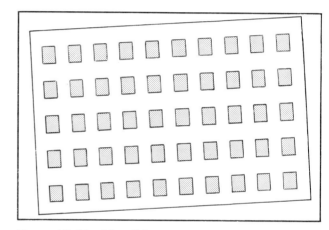

Figure 18.17 *Microfiche*

Test yourself

Using the words in the list below, copy and complete sentences A to H. Underline the words you put in. The words in the list can be used more than once.

bubble memory   floppy disk   sequence
magnetic   magnetic tape   exchangeable
directory   random access   microcomputers
disk pack   disk operating system   serial

A   *There are two types of access to data, _____ access, which means the information is accessed sequentially and _____ _____ where the information is accessed immediately.*

B   *A _____ disk is a random access medium whereas _____ _____ is a serial access medium.*

D When the information is accessed in _____, a serial access medium is required.

E A flexible magnetic disk is called a _____ _____. They are generally used by _____ and the smaller mainframes.

F A series of magnetic disks contained inside a plastic case is called a _____ _____. Sometimes these packs can be removed. They are then called _____ disk packs.

G To locate an item of information a _____ _____ _____ is used. The first track always contains the _____ which contains information about what files are held on the disk.

H _____ _____ is a new type of storage medium which stores information inside a chip.

Things to do

1 Explain what each of the following words or phrases means:
   a Backing store
   b Off-line storage
   c On-line storage
   d Disk drive
   e Exchangeable disk pack

2 **a** i What is a sequential access file?
   ii Give an example of a medium suitable to hold a sequential access file.
   iii Give an example of an application where a sequential access file would be appropriate.
   b i What is a random access file?
   ii Give an example of a medium suitable for a random access file.
   iii Give an example of an application where a random access file would be appropriate.

3 Here is a list of media which may be used as backing store. They can be divided into SERIAL and RANDOM ACCESS media.
   Magnetic tape
   Cassette tape
   Bubble memory
   Floppy disk
   Exchangeable disk pack
   Magnetic cartridges
   a i What is meant by 'serial access'?
   ii What is meant by 'random access'?
   b Divide the above list of media into two; one

of serial access media and one of random access media.

   c For each medium, state a suitable application which would use it. State the reasons for your choices.

4 **a** What is meant by serial access to a file?
   b Why is it not possible to use direct access to a file held on magnetic tape?

5 A computer is to be used to store all pupils' timetables so that individual timetables can be inspected at any time. Say which backing store medium you would recommend and explain your choice.

6 The list below contains **one** medium which could be used for internal storage and **three** media which could be used for external storage. Select the words from the list to complete the sentences.
   Visual display unit
   Magnetic tape
   Light pen
   Accumulator
   Logic circuits
   Buffer
   Bubble memory
   Can be used for internal storage _____
   Can be used for external storage _____
   Can be used for external storage _____
   Can be used for external storage _____

7 State, with reasons, which backing store medium you would choose for holding files for the following applications:
   a Finding how much money a bank customer has in her account
   b Preparing a company's payroll in alphabetical order
   c Holding out-patient files in a hospital, that may only be used a few times in a person's lifetime
   d Holding in-patient files in a hospital, that could be needed at any time immediately
   e Holding information about holidays in a travel agent's

8 The following parts of this operation all refer to a magnetic disk store.
   a What is the shape of each recording surface?
   b With what is each recording surface coated?
   c What is a track?

d What are carried on the arms which move between the recording surfaces?

e Why do the arms move?

f After the arm has been moved to the correct position, there may be a delay before information can be read. Why is this?

g Describe how information is arranged on a track.

h Explain what is meant by a 'cylinder' of storage.

i Name a magnetic backing store which is faster than a disk store.

j Name a magnetic backing store which is slower than a disk store.

9 A computer uses two types of store: immediate access store and backing store. Why do computers need backing store as well as immediate access store?

10 a The diagram shows part of a school's pupil file held on magnetic tape. Write in the empty circles the correct letters to show each of the following.

    A   A block
    B   A record
    C   A field

b What does the circle labelled D show?

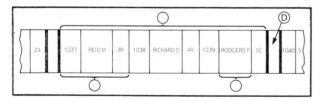

11 The diagram shows a cross-section of a magnetic disk store.

a What are the parts labelled A and B called?

b What three items of information are needed by the computer to enable it to find data stored on a disk?

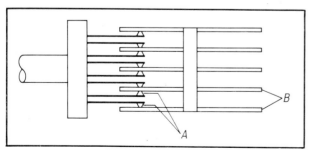

c Why are magnetic disks often preferred to magnetic tape as a means of storage?

d Although many people prefer disks, why do

most computer installations use magnetic tape as well?

e Describe **two** methods of making sure that data stored on magnetic tape is not accidentally lost.

12 A large school has details of all its pupils on a computer system. On which medium would it be best to store the data for rapid random access?

    a Punched cards
    b Paper tape
    c Magnetic tape
    d Floppy disk
    e Mark sense cards

13 It is not practical to use magnetic tape as the backing storage medium for an airline seat reservation system operating in real time because:

    a The average access time would be too slow
    b It would be too expensive
    c It would take up to much room
    d It would require too many operators
    e It would be unable to store all the data

14 The following words or phrases refer to storing data on magnetic disk. Explain what each of the following words or phrases mean:

    a Track
    b Block
    c Sector
    d Inter-block gap
    e Directory

15 a Compare magnetic tape storage with magnetic disk storage. In your answer discuss methods of data access, speed of data retrieval, the amount of data stored and a typical application implemented on each storage medium with reference to the suitability of the chosen storage medium for each application.

b Name the different types of magnetic tape and disk storage media commonly used as backing store. Indicate which are used as backing storage for mainframe and which are used for microcomputers.

16 Which of the following would be useful for serial access storage only?

    a Magnetic disks
    b ROM
    c Line store
    d Magnetic tape
    e RAM

19
Organization of data

If you had a large amount of data (e.g. files on people) then you would probably keep it in some sort of order. You would probably put it in files in alphabetical order according to surname. This would be very useful if you wanted to find a particular person's file. Organization of data is very important, both in manual and computerized systems. In computerized systems, correct organization of data becomes extremely important because, unlike manual systems, the information is accessed in many ways. Using manual systems, the file on a person would usually be accessed alphabetically. Using a computerized system, however, it would be possible to find the information in many ways. For example, suppose we knew the postal area of where a person lived but we didn't know his surname. It would be possible for the computer to print out a list of people living in that postal area. Or if we only knew the name of the road, then the computer could give us a list of people who live in the road.

As you can see from this example, a computerized system is much more versatile than a manual one. Because the information can be accessed in many ways using a computerized system, the data needs to be highly organized.

There are many advantages of using computerized storage rather than manual storage. Probably the main advantage is the speed of access to the information. In a manual filing system, there is always the danger that a file might not be put back into its correct place. Finding a misplaced file can be an awesome task.

Computerized filing systems also take up much less space than manual ones as Figures 19.1 and 19.2 show. This results in some cost savings since smaller premises can be used. It is much easier to alter information with a computerized system and any out of date information can be erased and the tapes or disks can be used again.

Figure 19.1 *In a manual filing cabinet everyone relies on the file being put back in the right place. This is not necessary with a computerized filing system*

Figure 19.2 *The paperless electronic office. There are no filing cabinets. All the information is held on floppy disks*

A computerized system offers a much better way of holding information and we will soon see computerized systems replacing filing cabinets in most of our offices. Soon, we will have paperless offices with all the records being done on computers.

How data is divided up

Data can be subdivided into the following groups:

Bits   [Smallest amount of information]
Characters
Fields
Records
Files   [Largest amount of information]

Bits

A **bit** is a binary digit 0 or 1. Groups of bits are used to represent data instructions. A single bit is the smallest item of data. Usually, sets of bits are used to make up a character.

Characters

Groups of bits, usually about six, are used to represent **characters**. Characters are letters, numbers and symbols, which can be input, stored and output by a computer.

Fields

A **field** is an area on a file which contains a single piece of information. Examples of fields include name field, address field, order number field, etc. The type of fields that you get on a file depends on the file itself.

Records

A **record** is a set of related information about a thing or an individual. A student record would contain information about one particular student. The record could probably be divided into fields. A payroll record could contain information about a particular employee's pay, tax deduction, national insurance contributions, pension etc. A sales record would contain all the sales made to a particular company.

Files

A **file** is a collection of records that gives a complete set of information about a certain subject. A sales file would contain all the sales made by a company. A purchase file would contain all the information about purchases made. A payroll file would contain a set of records which together formed information about the company's complete payroll. (Figure 19.3 shows some data organized into files, records and fields on a sales record.)

Key fields

A **key field** is a field which is used to identify a particular piece of information. Usually, the key field chosen is unique to the particular piece of information. But this may not always be possible. For example, if a surname is used as a key field, it may not have to be used with another key field. Suppose we were using surnames as key fields and we wanted some information on a Mr Smith. The computer could list all the information it had on all the Mr Smiths on its files. There could be a lot of Mr Smiths, so the computer would need additional information to

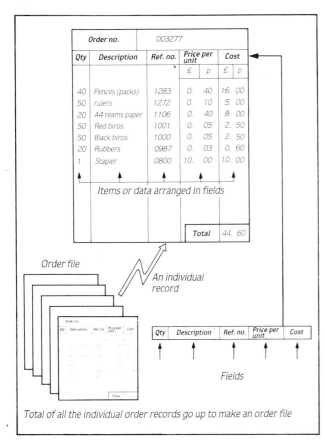

Figure 19.3 *A typical sales record showing the arrangement of files, records, fields and items*

Surname	Smith	Key field
Forenames	John Paul	
Street	1 Any Street	
District	Crosby	Fields
Town	Liverpool	
Post code	L23 6TA	Key field

Figure 19.4 *An address file showing key fields*

Account number	Name of firm	Address of firm	Credit limit	Amount outstanding
0120	—	—	—	—
0126	—	—	—	—
0128	—	—	—	—
0129	—	—	—	—
0132	—	—	—	—
0140	—	—	—	—
0151	—	—	—	—
0161	—	—	—	—
0163	—	—	—	—
0165	—	—	—	—
0168	—	—	—	—
0170	—	—	—	—
0181	—	—	—	—

Key field

Directions of search

Figure 19.5 *Using a key field to find a record*

narrow the choice down. Another key field could be used, such as address or postal code (Figure 19.4).

Sometimes, it is possible to use a unique key field if there is no possibility of confusion. For example, order numbers, account numbers, cheque numbers, are all unique pieces of information. The problem with these is that people don't always use code numbers, they much prefer to use names and words. You only have to look around you to see how many people use postal codes correctly.

The whole purpose of using a key field is to find a particular record in a file in as short a time as possible. So the key field should preferably be one

which is unique to the record needed or one which will narrow the choices down as quickly as possible. Most computer systems nowadays can locate records using more than one key field.

Suppose the accounts department of a firm wants to know how much a customer owes or how much credit she can have. They could use the system shown in Figure 19.5 to arrange the records. A record could consist of the amount outstanding, account number, name of firm, address of firm and the credit limit. Each of these would be a field. Each customer could then be given a unique account number. There would be no two firms with the same number. This account number could be used as a key field. In other words, it can be used to locate a particular record. So, if we wanted to find the credit limit of a company, we could type the account number into the computer. The computer would then search along the key field (i.e. the account numbers) until it found the right one. The information contained in the record could then be displayed on the screen.

Sorting and merging

Sometimes it is necessary to arrange items of data into a certain, predetermined order. To do this we perform a process called **sorting**. Computers are very quick at sorting and they can sort into many different orders. Usually, the key fields are sorted

Name	Form	Mark
Grant L	4A	7
Blain A	4C	8
Rigby E	4B	9
Burke B	4A	9
Dillon L	4A	5
Ratcliffe A	4C	9
Williams K	4B	8
Garry J	4B	6

Sorting according to surname

Name	Form	Mark
Blain A	4C	8
Burke B	4A	9
Dillon L	4A	5
Garry J	4B	6
Grant L	4A	7
Ratcliffe A	4C	9
Rigby E	4B	9
Williams K	4B	8

Sorting according to form

Name	Form	Mark
Grant L	4A	7
Burke B	4A	9
Dillon L	4A	5
Rigby E	4B	9
Williams K	4B	8
Garry J	4B	6
Blain A	4C	8
Ratcliffe A	4C	9

Sorting according to examination mark

Name	Form	Mark
Rigby E	4B	9
Burke B	4A	9
Ratcliffe A	4C	9
Blain A	4C	8
Williams K	4B	8
Grant L	4A	7
Garry J	4B	6
Dillon L	4A	5

Figure 19.6 *Sorting a class into alphabetical order, form and examination mark*

Sometimes we want to combine the contents of two files together to form a single file. The process of combining two files together is called **merging**. Before the two files can be merged, the data in each file must be in order. So, before merging we must **sort** each file into order. After the two files have been merged, the new file will also be in order. The reason for needing both files in order is that, if magnetic tape is used as storage media, and the files are not in order, then one of the tapes would need to be constantly rewound to find the information.

With computers, it is very easy to sort a file into lots of different orders according to the key fields. In Figure 19.6 a typical class in a school is being sorted according to surname, form and examination mark.

Merging is the process of making a new file from two other files. The information on each of the old files is brought together to make a new file. In order to merge two files, both files will need to be in order. If the files contain names then the names in each file will need to be in alphabetical order. The new file produced in the process of merging, will also be in alphabetical order. Files are usually merged according to one of their key fields. In Figure 19.7 the key field used would be the surname.

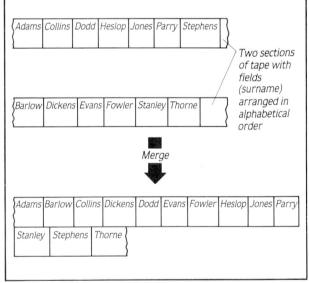

Figure 19.7 *A section of two files being merged according to the key field, 'surname'*

Master files and transaction files

The **master file** is the main file containing all the records about a particular subject. For example, a sales master file will contain all the information about the accounts. Because there will be many transactions (pieces of business), the master file needs to be regularly updated. All the transactions which take place in a day or sometimes a week are placed on a file which is called the **transaction file**. The transaction file is combined with the master file to produce a new **updated file** (Figure 19.8). The new updated file now becomes the master file.

The grandfather – father – son principle

There is always a slight chance that the data contained on a master file may be destroyed. It might be destroyed by an operator error, a power failure, fire or even theft. For a large company. this could prove disastrous. But using the **grandfather – father – son principle** it is possible to recreate the master file if it is destroyed.

The principle works like this. Basically, three generations of files are kept. The oldest master file is called the **grandfather** file and it is kept with its transaction file. These two files are used to produce a new master file called the **father** file which, with its transaction file, is used to create the most up-to-date file, called the **son** file. The process is repeated and the son becomes the father and the father becomes the grandfather and so on. Only three generations are needed and the other files can be re-used. Figure 19.9 shows how this procedure works.

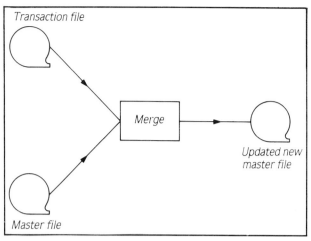

Figure 19.8　*Merging files*

Systems flowcharts

A **systems flowchart** shows what happens to data when it is input, processed and output by a computer system. Systems flowcharts are a bit like the flowcharts in Chapter 7 except that there are a few more symbols and they refer to data processing. Figure 19.10 shows some of the symbols used.

Systems flowcharts show us what type of input

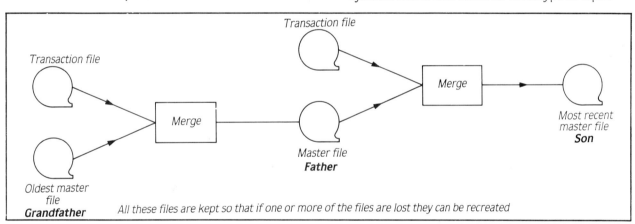

Figure 19.9　*The grandfather-father-son principle often used for file security*

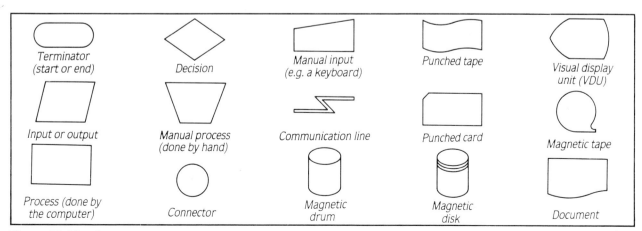

Figure 19.10　*Symbols used in systems flowcharts*

and output mediums are used and also what sort of backing store is being used. The process boxes tell us what is happening to the data during processing.

Before any computer system is decided on, the systems analyst (the person who plans the work to be done by the computer) draws a systems flowchart.

Figure 19.11 shows how we represent sorting a magnetic tape using a systems flowchart. Figure 19.12 shows the systems flowchart for merging two magnetic disks.

Updating

Figure 19.13 shows **updating** using magnetic tape. You can see, using the systems flowchart, that the information in the source documents (orders, accounts, new additions etc.) is keyed into the computer via the keyboard. This information is added to, or changed (updated) on the master file to produce a new updated master file.

If a company has a head office with lots of branches, then the branches may send in their master files to update the head office's master file. Figure 19.14 shows the systems flowchart for this.

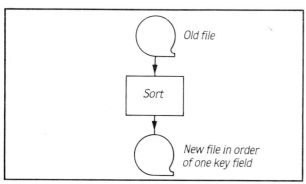

Figure 19.11 *Sorting a magnetic tape*

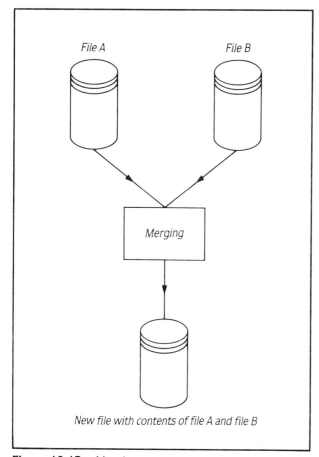

Figure 19.12 *Merging two magnetic disks*

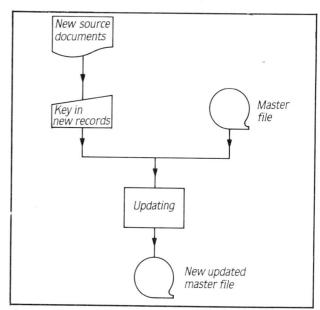

Figure 19.13 *Updating using magnetic tape*

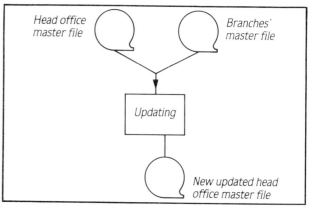

Figure 19.14 *Changes at a branch must be passed on to the Head Office so that the Head Office master file can be updated. After updating this file becomes the new updated Head Office master file*

Using a transaction file to update more than one master file

Sometimes, one transaction file will be used to update several master files. Suppose a sale is made. The details of the sale will be recorded on the sales transaction file. Naturally, these details will be needed to update the sales master file. An invoice (bill) will need to be issued, so the accounts master file will also need to be updated to debit the customer's account by the amount on the invoice. Also, since the goods have been bought they will reduce the amount of stock. The stock master file will also need to be updated.

Rather than use three separate transaction files to update each of the master files, we can use just one transaction file, the sales transaction file, to update all three.

You can see the systems flowchart for this in Figure 19.15.

Some systems flowcharts

A typical payroll system using punched clock cards as input media and magnetic disks as storage media

In this computer system, the punched cards produced when the employees clock in and out every day are used as the input media to calculate their wages. The payroll program and tax tables are held on one disk and the employees' master file containing details on each employee, is kept on the other. The computer uses the contents of these two files along with the information contained on the employee's clock cards to work out the gross pay, tax, national insurance, net pay etc.

A hard copy of the information is obtained in the form of a payslip on a line printer. Once this has been done, a new updated master file is produced. Figure 19.16 shows the systems flowchart.

A computerized theatre/concert booking system

In a typical system, the booking agent types into the computer the venue number, concert date and concert time. The records of all the concerts are held on disk and, because they are on-line, these are accessed by the computer very quickly. The computer then outputs the availability of seats on a visual display unit. If seats are available then a booking can

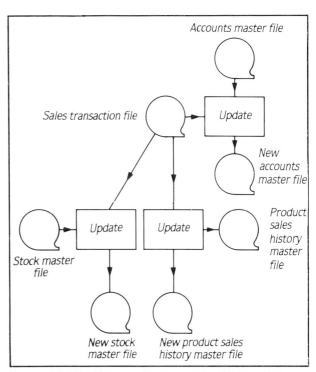

Figure 19.15 *Using a sales transaction file to update three master files*

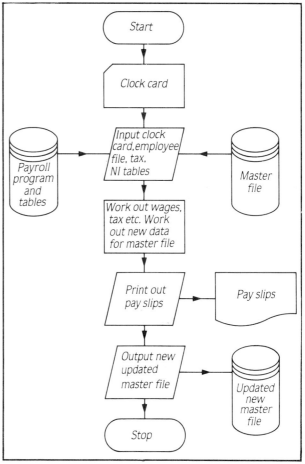

Figure 19.16 *A typical payroll system using punched clock cards as input media*

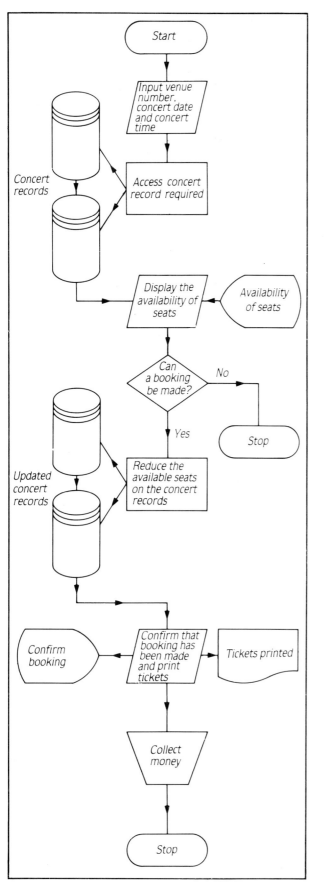

Figure 19.17 *A computerized theatre/concert booking system*

be made. The details are typed into the computer and because it is a real-time system, the computer automatically updates its files by reducing the number of available seats. Then the computer confirms that a booking has been made and the tickets are issued on a line printer. It is then up to the booking clerk to perform the manual process of collecting the money.

The systems flowchart for this system is shown in Figure 19.17.

Test yourself

Using the words in the list below, copy out and complete sentences A to Q. Underline the words you put in. The words in the list can be used more than once.

accessed	master	quickly	record
sorted	files	characters	misplace
organization	key field	unique	
merging	space	bit	file
sorting	transaction	alphabetically	
son	grandfather		

A In a normal office, information is kept in _____ which are usually arranged _____.

B _____ of data is much more important in computerized systems because the information can be _____ in many ways.

C The main advantage of holding information on a computer is that it can be accessed much more _____. Also it is impossible for the computer to _____ a file.

D Another advantage is that the system takes up much less _____.

E The smallest amount of data is a _____.

F These are grouped together to form _____.

G A field is an area on a _____ which contains a single piece of information.

H A _____ is a set of related information about a thing or an individual.

I The largest amount of information about a certain subject is called a _____. It consists of a collection of records.

J A _____ _____ is a field used to identify a particular piece of information.

K It is best if the key field is _____ so that no confusion occurs.

L Arranging items of data into a certain order is called _____.

M When two files are combined together, the process is called _____.

N Before files are merged, each needs to be
_____.

O A file containing all the records about a particular subject is called a _____ file.

P A file which contains the changes or transactions is called a _____ file.

Q So that a master file can be re-created if it is destroyed the _____ – father – _____ principle is used.

Things to do

1 a The following is a list of amounts of information. Put the list in its correct order with the lagest amount of information at the bottom:
Files
Records
Bits
Fields
Characters
b Write a sentence about each of the above to show you know what they mean.

2 Using a suitable example, explain the relationship between a file, a record and a field.

3 Barclaycard keep records of all their customers on magnetic tape in the form of <u>customer files</u>. On each <u>master file</u>, details such as name, address, amount owed, minimum payment and date due are kept. The customer pays a certain amount of money each month and every month the computer centre receives a tape called the <u>transaction file</u>, which contains details of all the payments which have been received from all the customers.
   The transaction tape is <u>processed</u> with the master tape to produce a new <u>up-to-date</u> file which now has all the new amounts on it.
a Explain what is meant by the following words which are underlined in the above passage:
Customer file
Master file
Transaction file
Processed
Up-to-date
b Often computer systems make use of the grandfather – father – son file system. What does this mean?
c Why is the above system used?

4 Mrs Jones is a patient at a large hospital. She has to visit the hospital each month. After each visit, details are written out on paper and added to her already bulky file, which is returned to the appropriate place in the hospital records department. This department takes up a whole floor of rooms with shelves from floor to ceiling in each room, each shelf crammed tight with files like Mrs Jones's.
Explain how the introduction of a computer might help hospital staff and benefit the patient.

5 A firm has a computerized payroll system for dealing with workers' pay. The workers' records are held in a master file on magnetic tape: records are held in alphabetical order. Imagine that a number of new people have started work for the firm: their records will therefore have to be added to the master file.
a Explain why these records are usually sorted into the same sequence as those already on the master file.
b Why is it not possible for the amended master file to occupy the same tape as the original master file?
c Give **one** further advantage of putting the amended file onto a new tape.
d The diagram below shows the updating of a serial file. Copy the diagram and label each file.

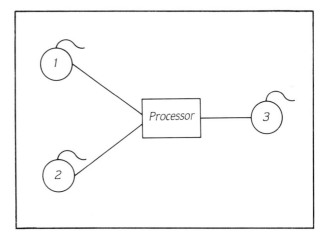

6 Draw systems flowcharts and explain the following processes:
a Sorting
b Merging
c Updating
Explain with the aid of a systems flowchart, the grandfather – father – son principle which is used for file security.

7 Within the forseeable future, your local doctor may use a computer to maintain patients records.

  a What **three** items of data, apart from name, age, sex and address, will be included on a patient's record?

  b State **three** peripherals that the doctor could need. For each of your choices give your reason for choosing it.

  c The patient's records will be <u>updated</u> regularly, from a <u>transaction file</u> completed by the doctor. Explain the meaning of the underlined words.

  d Give the advantage of using such a computerized system.

  e State **two** other ways in which the doctor may use the computer.

8 This is a computer print-out of a section of an employee's file in a large factory:

Name	Sex	Age	Department
Watkins J.	F	25	Typing
Watkins J.	F	32	Typing
Watkins J.A.	M	43	Machine shop
Watkins J.L.	M	27	Machine shop

  a Describe this file in terms of fields and records.

  b In the interrogation of this file, how could confusion between the four surnames be avoided?

9 At present most schools have manual systems to keep records on each pupil during their time at school. With cheaper technology these systems may soon be changed to computerized systems.

  a Describe the information which might be held in such a system and indicate, by giving meaningful names to the files, the files which could be held.

  b In creating the files, some information may be translated into codes. What are the advantages and disadvantages of this?

  c What safeguards should be taken to ensure the security of pupil records?

  d Discuss briefly what advantages, for both pupils and school administration, the new computerized system might have over the previous system.

10 Mr Smith has an account with a large clothing firm. The company uses a computer for its accounting system, and the 'record' of Mr Smith's account is kept on the Sales Ledger Master File.

  a What single item of data distinguishes his record from all others?

  b Give **two** other items that would be held in this record.

  c Give **two** items of data that are regularly updated on the file.

  d What are the **three** most recent versions of a regularly updated file called?

11 Draw a systems flowchart for an airline booking system which uses as input the flight number, date, class of seats and number of seats.

20 Computer languages

The programs for computers can be written in many different languages just as humans can communicate with each other in different languages. The language used by most microcomputers is BASIC. Some other computer languages are COBOL, FORTRAN and ALGOL.

Why we need computer languages

Computer languages have been developed over the last ten years. This has made programming computers a lot easier. Computer languages are needed because they allow the person using the computer to tell the computer what to do. The very early computers such as ASCC and ENIAC had the program stored in the electrical components. They were only able to do one job. To program the computer to do a different job it would have been necessary to completely rewire it.

The earlier computers were used mainly by scientists for performing millions of complicated calculations. As a result of this the computer languages used to supply instructions to the computer were for scientific uses. They were not much use for business uses such as file handling.

When computers got a lot cheaper business languages began to be developed. These languages had facilities such as extensive file handling and scheduling of processing which were not needed in the scientific languages. Also in the business world, less experienced staff would be using the computers, so the languages needed to be simpler.

High level languages

A **high level language** is a language geared towards solving problems. This means that rather than taking notice of how the computer was designed to solve the problem, we take more notice of the type of problem to be solved. So high level languages are **problem orientated**. The low level languages take account of design features of the computer and are **machine orientated**.

High level languages are much easier to write than low level languages because the program instructions are similar to instructions written in English. 'High' in the name 'high level language' doesn't mean that it is more complicated. It means that the language is more problem orientated. One statement in a high level language can be used for several instructions in a low level language. So it takes less time to write a program using a high level language.

Because high level languages work independently of the machine, it is fairly easy to modify (adapt) the program so that it will run on a completely different computer.

There are many high level languages. Which one is chosen really depends on the sort of job that you want to do. High level languages are usually either business languages or scientific languages.

Most business programs are written in a language called COBOL (**common business orientated language**) because of its extensive file handling ability. Other business languages include RPG II and BASIC (**beginner's all-purpose symbolic instruction code**). Scientific languages include ALGOL (**algorithmic orientated language**), FORTRAN (**formula translation**) and BASIC.

BASIC which is a high level language that you are probably familiar with, is an ideal language for people who are learning programming. It can be used for writing business and scientific programs but it takes longer and has some limitations which the other languages do not have.

Low level languages

Low level languages are usually machine dependent. This means that one computer's low level language is different from another's. This means that it is not easy for a programmer (someone who writes programs) to move from one machine to another as she will have to learn a completely new language. Low level languages are machine orientated and one low level program instruction has to be written for every machine instruction. This tends to make the programs very long and tedious to write. So low level languages are seldom used nowadays and easy to understand high level languages such as BASIC are used instead.

Machine code

Machine code is a machine language with instructions in a binary code that can be understood directly by the computer hardware. No other programs are needed.

The main problem with programming in machine language is that codes are very difficult to memorize and having to look them up every time can be very tedious. Also understanding what the series of 0s and 1s mean is almost impossible (Figure 20.1).

Figure 20.1 *Machine language has very little in common with everyday English. A high level language such as BASIC has easy to understand instructions*

Test yourself

Using the words in the list below, copy out and complete sentences A to H underlining the words you have inserted. The words may be used more than once.

directly   BASIC   high level
languages   machine   COBOL   dependent
FORTRAN   high

A *Computer _____ enable humans to communicate with the computer.*

B *The language that is most commonly used in schools is called _____.*

C *A _____ _____ language is a problem orientated language.*

D *Low level languages are said to be _____ orientated and machine _____.*

E *_____ is a common business language used because of its good file handling.*

F *ALGOL and _____ are scientific languages.*

G *BASIC is a _____ level language.*

H *Machine code consists of a binary code. It is understood by the machine _____.*

Things to do

1 *Which of the following is not a computer language?*
   a *BASIC*
   b *RPG II*
   c *FORTRAN*
   d *CPU*
   e *COBOL*

2 *Which **one** of the following is a high level language?*
   a *Compiler*
   b *Assembler*
   c *CESIL*
   d *ALGOL*

3 *The programming language specially designed for commercial work is which **one** of the following?*
   a *ALGOL*
   b *BASIC*
   c *COBOL*
   d *FORTRAN*
   e *PASCAL*

4 FORTRAN is an example of which **one** of these?
- **a** A low level language
- **b** An assembler code
- **c** A machine code
- **d** A high level language
- **e** A compiler

5 Name two examples of high level languages other than BASIC.

6
- **a** Distinguish between high level and low level computer languages.
- **b** At a particular computer centre, certain programs are written in low level language. Suggest why this might be so.

7 As a programmer I have the choice of writing my programs in a low level language or in a high level language. Each of them has its advantages and its disadvantages. In the table following, enter **one** advantage of each.

	Low level language	High level language
Advantage		

8 There are various levels of programming used to communicate with a computer:
Machine code   Low level   High level
Explain the difference between the above three levels referring to storage space required, ease of programming and debugging, ease of use and any other relevant information.

9 Most programs are now written in high level languages. Give **two** reasons why low level languages are still used.

10 FORTRAN and COBOL are two widely used programming languages.
- **a** Explain where their main applications lie and why it is not easily possible to interchange their use.
- **b** Explain their relationship with machine code and briefly indicate why it is impracticable to use machine code as an everyday language.

11 The following list is a list of computer languages:
COBOL   BASIC   FORTRAN
From the above languages, select which one would be suitable for each of the following applications:
- **a** Teaching pupils in a school computer programming
- **b** Calculating mathematical tables
- **c** A computerized catalogue of all books in a library
- **d** Stock control in a factory

For each one, say why the language you have chosen is suitable.

12 Older computers needed to be programmed in 'machine code'. The computers of today now use easy-to-understand computer languages such as BASIC, FORTRAN and COBOL. These languages are called 'high level languages'. They are easier to use than 'low level languages' because they have statements which are very similar to English statements.
- **a** What is meant by 'machine code'?
- **b** Why is it difficult to write a program in machine code?
- **c** What do the following abbreviations stand for?
  - i BASIC
  - ii FORTRAN
  - iii COBOL
- **d** What is meant by 'high level' and 'low level' computer languages?

21
Systems software

Systems software is the name for specialist programs that enable the hardware of a computer system to function correctly. It is essential that any computer should have adequate systems software. Some computers have better systems software than others. Along with the hardware and the applications programs the systems software allows the computer to perform useful work. (Applications programs are programs for a particular task such as payroll, stocktaking etc.)

The systems software is not just one program. It consists of a number of programs each responsible for a particular task. The programs include **translation software**, **compilers**, **assemblers**, **interpreters** and **executive program** or **operating system program**.

Translation software

Translation software is the name given to the group of programs that enable instructions to be converted into machine code. The computer hardware can only understand machine code and since it is very difficult to write programs in machine code, it is usual to allow the computer to convert the program using translation software. Programs which translate instructions into machine code are called **translators**. There are three types of translators. They are **assemblers**, **compilers** and **interpreters**.

Compilers

Compilers are programs that can translate a program from a high level language to machine language. The high level language program is often called the **source program**. The compiler converts this source program into a machine program called an **object program**.

The compiler changes each high level instruction into several machine code instructions. The whole program is translated completely with a compiler before the machine language program is carried out.

Assemblers

Assemblers are translator programs supplied by the computer manufacturer. They translate **assembly language** instructions into machine code. **Assembly language** is a low level programming language which is easy to translate into machine code. One instruction in assembly language usually corresponds to one machine code instruction.

Figure 21.1 shows the relationship between assemblers and compilers.

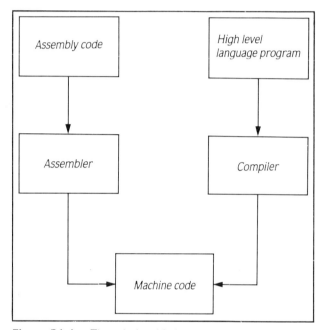

Figure 21.1 *The relationship between assemblers and compilers*

Interpreters

Interpreters are translator programs that translate and execute each instruction in turn from a high level language into machine language. For example, suppose we wanted to input a number. The interpreter would convert the high level BASIC instruction into machine code which the computer can understand.

Executive program or supervisor program

The executive or supervisor program is also called the operating system. An operating system consists of a series of control programs. These programs co-ordinate all the parts of the computer.

The operating system is permanently stored by the computer and controls such things as use of coding store, input and output devices. It also controls the internal operations.

Test yourself

Using the words in the list below, copy out and complete sentences A to I underlining the words you have inserted. The words may be used more than once.

executes   assembly   operating   object
low   systems   translators   machine
interpreters   source   translator

A   The _____ software enables the hardware of the computer system to function correctly.
B   Programs which convert instructions to machine code, are called _____.
C   There are three types of translators. They are assemblers, compilers and _____.
D   High level language programs are often called _____ programs, and machine language programs are called _____ programs.
E   A _____ converts each high level language instruction into several machine code instructions.
F   _____ language is a _____ level programming language which is easy to translate into machine code.
G   The executive program is also called the _____ system.
H   Each instruction in assembly language corresponds to several _____ code instructions.
I   An interpreter translates and _____ each instruction in turn from a high level language to machine code.

Things to do

1   Explain what is meant by the following words:
    a   Hardware
    b   Software
    c   Object program
    d   Source program

2   A program which translates and executes a source program one instruction at a time is known as which of these?
    a   A compiler
    b   An interpreter
    c   A utility program
    d   An operating system
    e   An executive program

3   The output from a compiler is called which **one** of the following?
    a   Object code
    b   Source code
    c   Assembly code
    d   Mnemonic code

4   Which **one** of the following is an example of software?
    a   A floppy disk
    b   A compiler
    c   A magnetic disk
    d   A peripheral

5   An instruction that can be recognized and used without translation is written in which **one** of these?
    a   Assembly code
    b   CESIL
    c   Machine code
    d   PASCAL
    e   COBOL

6   What do the following sentences describe?
    a   The process of translating a low level language into machine code.
    b   The process of translating a high level language into machine code.
    c   Inserting test data and using it to test all the paths through the program.

7   a   Why is machine code not practical as an everyday computer language?
    b   What do you understand by the term 'high level language'?
    c   Give **two** advantages of high level language over low level language.
    d   What is an assembler?
    e   What is a compiler?
    f   Certain high level languages have been developed to suit particular applications. Name **three** different applications and the language used in each case.

8 Write down the meanings of the following words or terms:
   a Systems software
   b Translation software
   c Compilers
   d Assemblers
   e Interpreters
   f Executive program

9 Below are two lists. List A gives type of software and list B jobs that could be carried out by some of the software. Opposite each job, write down the letter corresponding to the type of software you would use for that job.
   List A
   a Compiler
   b Executive program
   c Assembler
   d Operating system
   e Application package
   f Utility program
   List B
   i   Translating low level language program into machine code.
   ii   Copying a program from one magnetic tape to anoher.
   iii Processing a company's complete stock control system.
   iv   Issuing a warning message when the line printer runs out of paper.

10 a Explain the difference between a high level language and a low level language.
    b Give **two** advantages of a high level language over a low level language.
    c Name the software used to change source programs to object programs in each case.

11 a i   Briefly explain the need for programming languages.
          ii   Explain the meaning of the terms 'machine orientation' and 'problem orientation'.
          iii What is an interpreter?
    b What are logical errors and syntax errors? Explain what steps you could take to avoid them.
    c Briefly describe the difference in the way the computer uses interpreter basic and compiler basic.

12 Comment on the differences between, machine code, assembly language and high level language.

22 Applications software

The software, along with the hardware, allows the computer to do a useful job. Computers are now performing many different jobs or **applications** and for each particular application, software needs to be written to tell the computer what to do.

Most of the computers in businesses are performing similar tasks such as accounts, stocktaking, payroll (working out wages), wordprocessing (writing letters) etc. Each of these is an application. There are many other applications such as computer aided design (CAD) which enables computers to design buildings and pieces of machinery and sales forecasting where sales for each month can be predicted by using trends from previous years (Figure 22.1).

Applications software is the term given to a series of programs used with the hardware for a particular application. Applications software usually comes complete with instruction manuals, flowcharts etc.

There are three main ways in which companies can get applications software. Firstly, they can get it from the computer manufacturer who supplies the hardware. Secondly, they can employ programmers to write it for them, or thirdly, people in small businesses can write the software for themselves.

Applications packages from the manufacturer who supplies the hardware

When small to medium sized businesses buy a computer, they usually buy the software at the same time. The person that they buy it all from is usually the computer manufacturer. They can buy the hardware and software as a complete package.

Applications packages are programs which do a particular type of job. The likelihood is that a person who is an accountant will want to do the same job as another person who is also a accountant. Rather than each person developing the software himself or

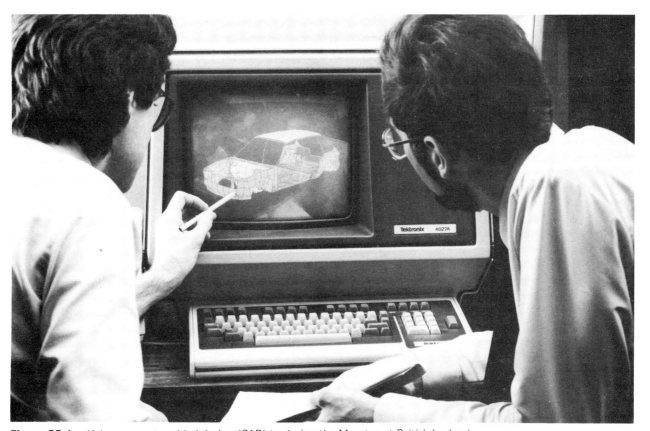

Figure 22.1 *Using computer aided design (CAD) to design the Maestro at British Leyland*

131

contracting someone to do the job for him it is much cheaper to share the costs between them. The major computer companies will supply particular packages of software which can be used by people performing a particular type of job. So an accountant would buy an accountancy package and a retail store would buy a retail package. The main advantage with this is that the costs are much less (because they are shared between so many people) and the programs are usually much better.

The only real disadvantage with applications packages is that you don't always get what you want. The packages are usually a compromise. But in spite of this applications packages are used by the majority of computer users and give small businesses an ideal introduction to computing.

Employing programmers to write applications packages

If a company or organization is large, then it may well be that they employ computer programmers who can program the computer themselves. This is called **developing software by the user**. It has the advantage that it will be tailor-made to do exactly what the person wants it to do. The program is made to fit the job and not the other way round.

One of the disadvantages of the user writing the program is cost. Programmers demand high salaries and program writing can be a long process. So, this method is only really used by larger companies and organizations.

If the organization does not employ programmers itself then it can go to a **software house** for the programs. Software houses are companies that employ programmers. They specialize in writing computer programs. They act as consultants and anyone who requires a particular program written can go along to them to get it written. Software houses can be very expensive, but if there is no suitable applications package then you may have no choice but to go to them.

People in small businesses writing software themselves

A person in a small business might decide that he would like to write his own program. Many good applications programs have been written in this way.

However, writing good business programs is a very specialized and time consuming task. Usually, the person regards the writing as a bit of a hobby so the saving of money is not his prime concern.

Documentation

Documentation is the name given to the instruction booklets and paperwork that comes with a computer program. It explains the purpose of the programs and tells you what to do if any errors occur.

Good programs always have clear documentation which is easy to understand. Included in the documentation is a flowchart, an explanation of the various parts of the program, the actual computer language listing and some test data which can be used to check whether the computer program is working correctly.

Program libraries

Sometimes, we might want to sort a list of names into alphabetical order or write out a list of names and exam marks in rank order. These tasks are performed fairly regularly. Some computers have what are called 'program libraries', where such programs are held permanently in store by the computer. These programs are sometimes called **utility programs**.

Utility programs are likely to be used as part of a number of different applications packages, because the jobs they do need to be done in many different applications.

Test yourself

Using the words in the list below copy out and complete sentences A to F underlining the words you have inserted. The words may be used more than once.

documentation   application   software houses hardware   applications   utility computer bureaus

A _____ *software allows the computer* _____ *to do a useful job.*

B *Payroll, stocktaking, invoicing and accounts, are all examples of* _____ .

C *The cheapest way to buy software is to buy an* _____ *package.*

D All the instruction booklets and paperwork which comes with the computer program is called the _____.

E _____ _____ are companies which specialize in writing computer programs.

F Programs which are often used and are held permanently in the computer are called _____ programs.

Things to do

1 List **four** main steps involved in documenting a computer program, and describe why a program should be documented.

2 Which of these is an example of an 'applications package'?
  a The operating system
  b A payroll program
  c BASIC
  d The compiler
  e A data base

3 **a** What is meant by the term 'program package'?
  b Give **two** advantages and **one** disadvantage of using a package rather than writing your own programs.

4 A computer system requires 'software' to enable users to make the best use of the equipment. Large systems will require an 'operating system' together with other types of software depending on whether 'high' or 'low level languages' are used. These systems may also have 'utility programs' and 'applications packages' available.

  a What do you understand by the term 'software'?
  b What is the function of the 'operating system'?
  c Give **two** operations which 'utility programs' may be required to perform, and hence explain the function of a utility program. State **two** further examples of utility programs.
  d By reference to a particular applications package, discuss the advantages and disadvantages of using an applications package.

5 Explain how an applications package would be developed from an original idea to a commercial reality.

6 **a** What is a utility program?
  b Give an example of a task that a utility program might perform.

7 **a** Explain the purpose of an 'operating system' used as a large main frame computer.
  b Pre-written applications programs may be bought for use on a computer system. What would you look for before buying such a program?
  c How would you test such an applications program?

8 Describe **two** applications packages designed for use in numerical or scientific computing. Indicate ways in which the packages have been designed to be of general use. Mention any advantages which might be gained by writing new programs for a particular application rather than using an existing package.

23
The people who work with computers

People who work inside the computer room

The computer industry will soon be the largest industry in the country. Because of the widespread introduction of computers, many new types of jobs have been created which did not exist before. Also many people whose jobs did not involve computers in the past are now using them to do their jobs more efficiently.

In this section we will look at the more traditional jobs in the computer industry and then look at how computers are increasingly used by more people. But before we look at the jobs, we must remember that computer systems can be very different. Some are very large and others are small. Obviously the size of the system influences the number of staff working with it. For example, in a small system few staff are needed so the jobs they do in connection with the computer will be more varied.

First let's look at the people who would be involved in computers in a large company which has a computer department where people are employed in clearly defined jobs. The people who work in a large computer department include people with these job titles: systems analysts, programmers, computer operators, data preparation operators and file librarians. Over these people will be the operations manager and the data processing manger.

The systems analyst

Before a computer is used in a company, most of the work will have been done manually. That is, people will have dealt with a lot of the routine paperwork involved in running a business. To perform this work quickly and efficiently, a system will have been used. In other words, someone will have sat down to decide how all the bits of paper that come about in the day-to-day running of an office should be dealt with. They would have looked at how information is passed and processed from one department to another.

When a company decides to replace their manual system with a computerized system, a person called a **systems analyst** is employed. A systems analyst's job is to look at how the various jobs are done manually, and to see if any of these jobs could be done by a computer.

When it has been decided that a computer should be installed, the system analyst has to design the computer system so, sometimes, system analysts are called **systems designers**. They have to decide on what equipment to use and the number of peripherals such as line printers, VDUs and terminals to use.

After the computer has been installed and is working correctly, the systems analyst constantly looks for ways of improving the system. This may include finding new tasks for the computer to do and altering programs to make the system more efficient. He will also be looking at the next computer system. It is common to find one computer being dismantled while another is being used and yet another, newer, computer is being connected up!

The systems analyst's job is an extremely skilled one. He needs to have extensive knowledge of computers and what their capabilities are. He also needs a thorough knowledge of the working of the organization he is working for. A lot of the time is spent talking to the people who use the computer, called **users**, to find out what it is that they want the computer to do.

The programmer

Programmers are the people who instruct the computer. They tell it what to do and also how to do it. They usually start writing a program by drawing a flow diagram which helps them to decide on the flow of logic. Once the flowchart has been drawn, they will then start to write the program. Usually, they write the program on paper first, mainly because the computer is being used for other jobs. Once the program has been written, it will be tested. Very few computer programs work first time and any errors, or bugs as they are often called, will need to be corrected. Quite often, the computer program will need to be corrected many times before it works properly. The process of getting rid of the bugs is called **debugging** (Figure 23.1).

So that other people or programmers can alter the program, the programmer goes through a stage called **documentation**. This means she will write down an outline of the way the program works so

Figure 23.1 *Debugging!*

that other people can use the program.

A lot of routine programming jobs are performed from time to time. For example, after a Budget, a lot of changes to programs need to be made concerning National Insurance contributions, VAT, tax etc.

Quite often, several programmers write the program together. Each one writes part of the

program – called a **module** – and they get together to assemble the whole program. Some programs can take over a year to write. Obviously when a lot of people are involved in the writing of a program, many errors are likely to occur.

There are two types of programmer; the systems programmer and the applications programmer. The applications programmer writes programs to do various tasks or applications. The systems programmer writes the programs to control the computer system.

The computer operator

Computer operators operate the computer (Figure 23.2). In large companies the computer will be kept running twenty-four hours a day, so computer operators quite often work in shifts. However, with the increased speed of the computers and the ease of operation, many firms now find that they can get all their work done during the day. This avoids having a shift system and having to pay shift workers extra money for the inconvenient hours that they work.

The job of a computer operator involves typing in information to the computer via the keyboard. The computer operator also has to feed the programs into the computer. These may be in the form of magnetic disk, magnetic tape, paper tape or punched cards. The computer operator also makes sure that the computer has everything necessary to perform the task e.g. that there is paper in the line printer. She loads input and output devices.

Figure 23.2 *Computer operators at work in the computer room. Notice the magnetic tape units on the left and the magnetic disk units on the right. The operators' consoles are in the centre of the room*

The computer operator sits at an **operator's console** which usually contains a keyboard, a VDU and sometimes a line printer. A computer log is kept in which the operator writes down information about the programs she has used. This information includes the name of the program and the starting and finishing times. The log is usually in the form of a book kept next to the computer. In some systems, the log is kept by the computer itself.

Data preparation operator

Data preparation operators convert written information into a form that can be read by the machine, such as punched cards or paper tape. Usually the operators work from specially designed input documents which have been designed by the systems analyst.

It is essential that information is correct before it goes into the computer. To make sure that no wrong keys have been pressed, data preparation operators work in pairs. One of them prepares the medium, for example, the punched cards or paper tape, by keying in the information from the source documents. The other operator keys in exactly the same information. If the two operators key in exactly the same information, then the task has been done correctly. If the two lots of information don't match exactly, then the operators are told by the machine to go back and check what they have done. This process is called **data verification**. It can eliminate most of the errors.

Although some computer systems still use paper tape and punched cards as input media, the modern method is to enter the data into the computer using a keyboard or a VDU. This system is often called a **key-to-disk system** (Figure 23.3). Key-to-disk data entry involves a person typing in the information on to the screen of a VDU using a keyboard. The operator checks to make sure it has been typed correctly and, if it has, it goes on to magnetic disks.

Using key-to-disk methods of inputting data has meant that data preparation is now often done by clerical staff outside the computer department.

The librarian

The **librarian** is the person who is in charge of all the software for the computer. He makes sure that it is placed in the right place after it has been used and mends it if it needs any repairs.

The librarian is also responsible for maintaining catalogues and indexes of all the files kept so that they can be located quickly (Figure 23.4). He also keeps duplicate files in case of damage or for security.

The computer (or data processing) manager

The **data processing manager** is the person responsible for the overall running of the data processing department. In a commercial organization, he would be a senior manager who is directly responsible to the directors of the company for all the computing activity of the company. As well as being responsible for the technical side of things he also needs to be able to organize staff and appoint new staff.

The data processing manager will usually have had

Figure 23.3 *Key-to-disk operators keying in information via keyboards*

Figure 23.4 *The file librarian keeps tapes and disks in a certain order so that they can be found quickly*

experience in the three branches below him i.e. systems analysis, programming and operations.

The senior systems analyst

The **senior systems analyst** is usually a member of the junior management team. She is responsible for all the systems analysts under her.

The senior programmer

The senior programmer is responsible for the organization of the programming department. He has control over the two types of programs; systems and applications.

The operations manager

The operations manager usually has a lot more staff than the other members of junior management. A lot of her time will be spent in the day-to-day management of staff. Generally, the operations manager will be working with less qualified staff and a lot of her time will be spent in training.

Figure 23.5 shows how the data processing department in a large organization works.

People who work with computers outside the computer room

As well as the personnel of a typical computer department, there are also a lot of other people who work with computers. These people usually work outside the company. They are employed in production (which involves research, design and construction), sales and marketing, and engineering.

Computer production

Research
The few people employed in this area have changed the face of computing. This group of people are constantly trying to make computers faster, smaller, more efficient and cheaper. Over the last few years, they have achieved their aims. Quite often, the people involved in research have set up their own companies to produce computers and their associated peripherals.

Research is very important. At the moment people in research are looking at computer automation in factories using robots and methods of storing much larger amounts of information in a small space. New data capture methods are constantly being investigated because this is an area where a lot of

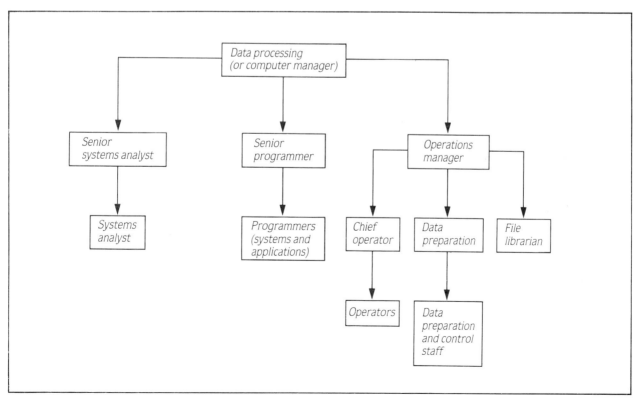

Figure 23.5   *How the jobs in a large data processing department are organized*

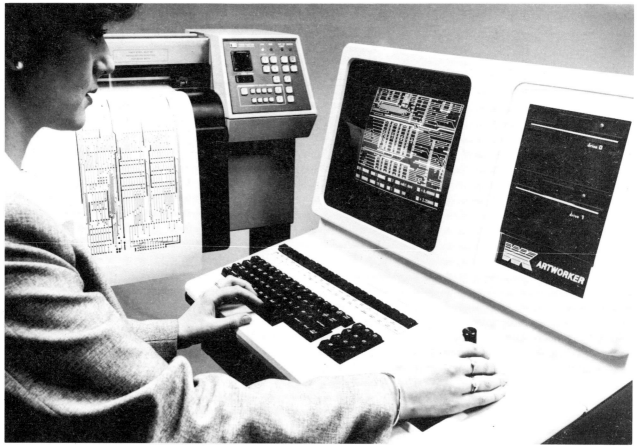

Figure 23.6 *Using a computer to design the electronic circuitry for another computer*

money could be saved. Voice recognition systems are also being looked at. One day it will be possible for a person to dictate information directly into a computer.

Computer design

Once the ideas have come from the research team, the next step is to sit down and design the actual computer (Figure 23.6). The computers are designed by **computer designers** (sometimes called computer architects). They have an intimate knowledge of the computer market and can make decisions that will result in the best possible computer at a particular price. In an extremely competitive market, it is extremely important to get this stage right and avoid costly mistakes.

Once the hardware has been designed, it is then left to the systems programmers to write the systems software to operate the hardware.

Computer construction

Like motor cars, computers consist of many individual components. These components are often manufactured separately and then brought together for the final assembly. Some computer manufacturers construct and assemble all their own components. Others construct some parts but buy in some components such as silicon chips, which are very difficult to make and need very expensive machinery and very clean conditions.

Some computer manufacturers use robots to connect up the many wires involved in the complex circuitry (Figure 23.7). In the future, it will not be uncommon to see computer controlled robots making computers.

It is vital that the construction of computers is done as accurately as possible in order to avoid costly mistakes when the machine is on the customer's premises (Figure 23.8).

Computer sales and marketing

Computer salespeople have the job of selling the computer hardware and software to the customer. A computer sale can be a lengthy process. The salesperson usually starts off by trying to convince the potential customer that they have a need for a computerized system (Figure 23.9). If they already

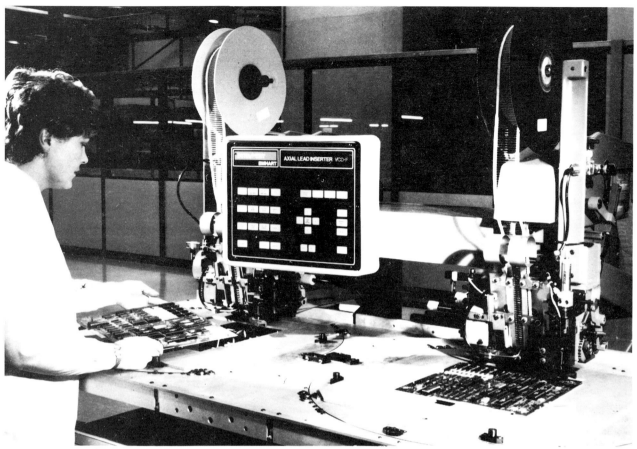

Figure 23.7 *Putting resistors into printed circuit boards containing integrated circuits*

Figure 23.8 *Testing a computer before delivering it to a customer*

Figure 23.9 *Salespeople need to persuade people that they really need a computer*

have a system, it may well be that it is out of date, so the salesperson will be looking to introduce a better system.

Quite often, the customer will want to see a computer doing a job similar to his own. If the salesperson has a customer doing a similar job, then she will take the potential customer to see it.

If the customer requires special programs, rather than a standard package, then the salesperson will arrange for these to be written. Finance can also be arranged by the salesperson. She will then be responsible for all the work leading up to the installation of the system and sometimes for the work afterwards. Before the computer is installed, staff will need to be taught how to use it. The salesperson will either instruct the staff herself, or she may arrange for them to go on a training course.

All in all, computer selling is a very complicated job because it needs the skills of systems analyst, programmer, operator and salesperson.

Computer engineers

To operate or program a computer it is not necessary to know anything about the complex electronic components contained in it. However, the computer engineer needs this technical knowledge in order to service or repair them. The computer engineer also helps in the installation of the system.

Computers today are extremely reliable, but when one does go wrong, it is essential that the computer is repaired as quickly as possible. Because the computer is sometimes used twenty-four hours a day, the computer engineers usually work shifts. Nowadays, the computers are designed so that they have various test points which the engineer attaches his meters to (Figure 23.10). They will tell him on which circuit board the fault lies so that the complete circuit board can be replaced. It is much quicker and cheaper to replace the whole circuit board rather than try to locate the faulty component on a board containing thousands of them.

The most up-to-date computers can even maintain themselves! In some IBM computers, there is a separate service processor which continually monitors the computer operations and the environment (voltages and temperatures). This can sometimes detect and then correct a failure. The service processor can also analyse the symptoms of an error and will instruct the engineer as to the cause of the problem. It is even possible for a specialist engineer, who is hundreds of miles from the

Figure 23.10 *This computer engineer is testing the slot in the circuit boards inside the CPU*

computer, to link into the computer via the telephone lines, to try to find the cause of the problem, and if possible, fix it!

Test yourself

Using the words in the list below copy out and complete sentences A to K underlining the words you have inserted.

engineers   programmer   computer
data preparation   users   system analyst
operator   line printers   flowchart
documents   repairs   librarian   verified
program   bugs   debugging

A When a company thinks of installing a computer system a _____ _____ looks at the manual systems to see if they could be performed more efficiently by a _____.

B He will consult the _____ to see what their requirements are.

C The person who tells the computer what to do and how to do it, is the _____.

D Usually the programmer will first draw the _____ and then write the _____.

E The program is then tested and any _____ are corrected. This process is called _____.

F The programmer then fully _____ the program.

G The _____ operates the computer making sure that the right programs are being used and there is paper in the _____ _____.

H If necessary, data is prepared by the _____ _____ operators.

I Data is also _____ by these people.

J The _____ keeps all the software catalogued and indexed. She also _____ damaged programs.

K The computer _____ maintain and repair the computer and its peripheral equipment.

Things to do

1 The person with the responsibility for the day to day efficiency of the computer and the operating staff is which of these?
   a Computer operator
   b Chief programmer
   c Systems analyst
   d Operations manager
   e Field engineer

2 Which of these people has the job of changing magnetic tapes and disks?
   a A computer engineer
   b A data preparation operator
   c A computer operator
   d A systems analyst
   e An operations manager

3 Which of these jobs does a computer programmer do?
   a Investigates problems that may be eased by using a computer
   b Writes instructions in a language a computer will accept
   c Organizes the efficient use of computer personnel
   d Prepares data onto punched cards or tape
   e Runs computer programs and inputs data when required

4 a Give **one** job which is part of the work of a data processing manager.
   b Give **one** job which is done by the chief programmer but not by the programming team.

5 a What is a file librarian's job?
   b Name **two** items in a program user manual that would be of special interest to the file librarian.
   c Who would do the file librarian's job in a small computer installation?

6 The data processing department in a large company is to be split into two sections, those who prepare the programs and those who run them.
   a Name **three** different job titles from the running section.
   b Briefly describe the job of a systems analyst.

7 A firm has advertised for a computer operator, a data processing manager and a maintenance engineer.
   a For each of these jobs:
      i Describe what the job involves.
      ii State the qualifications and experience you would expect an applicant to have.
      iii Describe the relay, hours of work and promotion prospects which the job would give.
   b Give the job titles of **two** other members of the firm's computer staff.

8 Who would use a computer console in the course of their work?

9 a Draw a diagram/organization tree to show how the following jobs in a computing department are related:
      Programming manager
      Data processing manager
      Senior systems analyst
      Senior applications programmer
      File librarian
      Systems analysts
      Applications programmers
      Operations manager
      Data preparation supervisor
      Senior systems programmer
      Chief operator
      Operators
      System programmers
      Data preparation Operators
   b List **three** activities which are performed by operators during the course of their work.
   c List **three** activities which are performed by programmers during the course of their work.

10 Describe how a commercial data processing department might be organized. Include in your answer a brief description of:
   a A typical computer installation, e.g. one you have visited
   b **Four** different jobs in the DP department
   c How the different jobs are related
   Credit will be given for clear diagrams where appropriate.

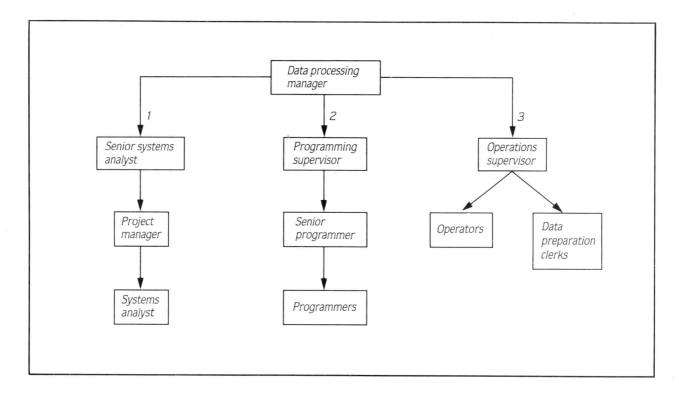

11 The organization of a computer department in a large commercial company is shown in the above diagram.
Choose **one** of the three labelled branches and give a detailed description of the person in the most senior position.
Show how this person is reponsible to the data processing manager and also describe his relationship with each of his subordinates.

12 In a large computer organization, the following personnel are employed:
 a File librarian
 b Computer operator
 c Systems analyst·
Write **three** paragraphs describing the tasks undertaken by each of the above personnel.

13 Read the passage carefully and then answer the questions below.
'In 1965, a firm installed a computer and issued the following instructions:
Each branch will complete an order form for every customer. These forms will be posted to the <u>data preparation</u> department at Head Office. At Head Office, the information from each form will be punched onto paper tape. The tapes will be <u>verified</u> and then read in to the computer.'
Last week, a representative of the firm said that the instructions were now out of date, since in 1975, new <u>hardware</u> had been installed in the Head Office to speed data input. Also, further improvements were planned for 1979 which would enable the branches to communicate directly with the computer at Head Office.

 a What is meant by each of the following terms which are underlined in the passage above?
   i   Data preparation
   ii Verified
   iii Hardware
 b Give **one** example of hardware that could have been installed in Head Office in 1975 to speed up data input.
 c Name equipment that would have to be installed at the branches to enable them to communicate directly with the computer at Head Office.
 d Why would this new system be an improvement over the 1965 system?

14 Describe the personal qualities and educational qualifications you would need to do the following jobs in computers. Explain in each case why the qualifications and personal qualities are required in relation to the type of work that is required.
 a Computer programmer
 b Computer operator
 c Systems analyst

15 Use the information contained in this chapter to decide who would do the following tasks.

  a Establish how a job could be done better using a computer
  b Maintain and keep records of all the available software
  c Persuade someone that a computer could do their job more efficiently and cheaply.
  d Load input and output peripherals and backing store devices
  e Verify tapes and punch cards before they are input into the computer
  f Look into new ways of storing information and making computers faster, smaller and cheaper
  g Use the key-to-disk method to input information straight into the computer.

16 All new computers use the 'key-to-disk system' for the input of information into the computer. The advantage with this method is that it cuts out a lot of the work that was previously necessary, such as the punching of cards and paper tape. Also, because there is less handling of the information, less errors are introduced. More people are able to use the computer using this system and there is a tendency for job descriptions to become blurred.

Read the above passage and answer the following questions:

  a Explain what is meant by a 'key-to-disk system'.
  b Why does this system reduce the amount of work that was previously done in preparing the data?
  c Punched cards and paper tape used to be very wasteful. Why was this?
  d What is the storage medium used in the key-to-disk system?
  e Why is it necessary to avoid people handling the information as much as possible before it goes into the computer?
  f Why are jobs in the computer department becoming more blurred?

24
Adopting a computer system

In this chapter we will look at the steps involved in adopting a computer system, from the initial ideas to the final system running and performing its jobs correctly. To make it simple, we will assume that the company is medium sized and has not used a computerized system before. The steps are:

Systems analysis and problem identification
Feasibility study
Project approval
Designing the computer system
Training personnel
Writing instruction manuals and documenting the system
Implementation
Monitoring the 'live' system

Systems analysis and problem identification

A company that has not used a computer before will usually employ a systems analyst or computer consultant to look at the existing manual systems to see how they could be performed more efficiently using a computer. The systems analyst has to look at the existing system and decide what problems the computer needs to solve (Figure 24.1). Only by analysing the system thoroughly will he discover what it is that the computer needs to do.

The sort of tasks the systems analyst will look at are the preparation of accounts and payroll, stocktaking, invoicing, order entry etc. Each task will be looked at closely to see what input is needed, what processing is done and what final output is needed.

Systems analysis can take quite a bit of time because it is essential that the systems analyst understands exactly what the computer has to do. This usually involves a lot of meetings with the people who will be using the computer to find out what they would like to get out of the computer. If they haven't used computers before, their expectations of the

Figure 24.1   *Finding the problem!*

system might be unreasonable. It is up to the systems analyst to decide in conjunction with senior management on the best method to solve a particular problem.

Most firms, even the very small ones, can now afford some sort of computer system. The cost of the initial computer system is rapidly recovered because efficiency and productivity increase.

Usually, a company or organization introduces computerized systems slowly so that the staff and management can get used to them. Mistakes can be very costly and it is not worth rushing into anything. Partial computerization usually starts off with simple tasks such as payroll. Nowadays, wordprocessing is a good introduction to computerized systems for small businesses.

When the systems analyst has carefully performed the systems analysis he submits a **feasibility study** to the senior managers or the directors of the organization.

The feasibility study

In the feasibility study, the systems analyst looks at which manual system it would be feasible to computerize. This will depend on many things, such as the volume of work, the repetitiveness of the work and the qualifications of the available staff.

Usually, if the benefits which will be got from the computerized system outweigh the cost of buying the hardware and software, then the feasibility study is likely to be approved. Although cost used to be an important factor, it has now become much less important because over the last ten years computers have got cheaper.

Project approval

Once the feasibility study has been completed, the stage comes where it is possible to decide whether to go ahead with the project or to abandon it. The decision is made by senior managers or directors.

Cost considerations are not the only ones. Lack of suitably qualified staff could cause problems and sometimes the staff and their trade unions try to oppose certain computer systems.

Designing a computer system

When the systems analyst has got together all the information about what is required from the potential system, he sits down and sets about designing the system in detail. He puts forward sets of proposals about different systems.

In these sets of proposals, he will put forward ideas about the system. Included in these ideas will be the number of VDUs, backing storage type and size, CPU size, number and type of line printers etc.

He will also decide what type of processing would be best, whether it should be batch or real-time processing. The type of input medium needs to be decided. It is now common to use key-to-disk and it would be virtually impossible to buy a system which still used paper tape or punched cards.

It may well be that other really up-to-date methods of data capture could be used such as magnetic ink character recognition (MICR) or optical character recognition (OCR).

What the systems analyst has to bear in mind is that the system may need to be expanded in the future, so he must take this into account at the design stage. Usually, the computer system is designed in this order:

Outputs (results)
Inputs (data)
Files (files)
Procedures (programs)

Outputs

These are the actual results of using the system. In the case of a manufacturing company the results may include production of payslips for its employees, sets of accounts for the accountants, invoice and despatch notes and stock lists. It is essential that a clear idea about the results is obtained before the system is designed as this is the purpose of installing the system in the first place.

Inputs

This is the data supplied to the computer. What data is needed for input really depends on the output (results). Obviously, any information used in the output will need to be input.

There are many ways of inputting information into the computer and which method of data capture is selected depends on the type of application and to some extent, cost.

Files

All the data in the computer will need to be arranged in some sort of logical order in the same way as you would expect to keep papers in an office. Sets of related items of data are collected together to form files. The results will be used to decide what files will be needed and the systems analyst will decide on how to collect the various files together.

In the old system, files will probably have been kept in lots of filing cabinets under different headings. In a large organization these filing cabinets may be in different rooms. File conversion involves transferring information contained on paper to magnetic tape or disk in the computer (Figure 24.2). A program will be written for creating files in the computer. Conversion will involve keying in information into the computer via the keyboard. Usually, the old files will still be kept for a while just in case anything goes wrong.

Procedures

Once the systems analyst has decided on the other design features he will have an idea of the procedures that need to be followed. He will then have some idea of the flow of information around the system. This will allow him to draw systems flowcharts and computer flowcharts for writing the programs.

Once the systems analyst has definitely decided on what the computer system has to do, he can look at the suppliers who could supply the equipment. Sometimes, the analyst will tender for the equipment. This means he outlines what is required of the system and the computer manufacturers submit detailed descriptions and prices of the hardware and software needed for the job. Then it is up to the managers or directors to decide which manufacturers to use.

It is essential that great care is taken in the selection of equipment. It may well be that one company makes the best CPU but another company makes better line printers. So, a computer system can be made up of equipment from several companies. One of the disadvantages with this is maintenance – many people could be involved in the systems repair.

Training personnel

Once a computerized system has been decided upon, the personnel, who may have had no previous experience of computers, will have to be trained.

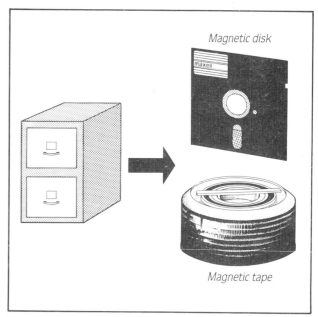

Figure 24.2 *File conversion involves converting information on paper to magnetic storage media such as tape or disk*

Usually, the computer manufacturer or supplier will have a training centre, where the various levels of staff can be sent. Alternatively, a training officer from the computer manufacturer is sent to the company's premises to train the staff.

Different levels of staff will attend different courses since they will be using the computer for different things. Programmers and systems analysts need to have the greatest knowledge of the computer so they will go on courses that go into the system in greater detail. Although these people will obviously already know a great deal about computers, they may not fully understand the new model because various computers can be very different.

Staff who are going to be operators will be sent on a course to learn how to operate the computer. They will also need to know what to do if anything goes wrong.

It is very important that the staff are fully trained because they are much less likely to be sceptical about the introduction of the computer and many costly mistakes can be avoided.

Writing instruction manuals and documenting the system

It is essential to document any computer system fully. The documentation is produced so that the personnel using the computer at any level from operators to systems analysts will be able to understand the system should anything go wrong. The computer documentation will be different for the different levels of personnel. A systems analyst will be concerned with the system as a whole, whereas an operator will only be concerned with her own particular terminal.

Apart from fully documenting the system so that any errors can be corrected, it is also essential to document for future use. Changes will probably be made to the system at a later date and then the documentation might be needed when the system is improved or upgraded.

Instruction manuals will also have to be prepared. These act as a refresher for experienced users and can help them find out how to correct anything that goes wrong. These manuals can also act as training manuals to teach inexperienced personnel or experienced personnel who may have worked on different machines how a particular system operates. Unfortunately, instruction manuals can be very complicated and there is no real substitute for proper training.

If you have your own computer you will realize just how hard some of these manuals can be to understand (Figure 24.3). It is important that the training manuals are easy to read and understand.

Figure 24.3 *Many instruction manuals are too complicated!*

Implementation

Implementation involves putting the theory behind the computer system, into practice. If all the steps before implementation have been performed correctly, then the implementation should go smoothly. Usually a company that hasn't used a computer system before will start by partial implementation. This means that the computer will just be used to perform a few tasks to begin with. After the successful implementation of part of the system, other jobs can be put into the computer.

Before implementation, a team is formed by the personnel directly connected with the computer system. The systems analyst is usually the team leader. Many meetings of the team are arranged so that the team members can give the systems analyst some feedback as to how the implementation is going. Any little unforeseen problems that arise can be quickly sorted out.

There are two main ways to implement a computer system. They are **parallel running** and **pilot running**.

Parallel running

Parallel running is a system where the manual system is run alongside (i.e. parallel to) the computerized system. All the tasks are performed manually as well as by the computer. Obviously this involves a lot of extra work but it does provide back up if anything goes wrong with the computer system.

The results of the computer system can be checked against those obtained manually. After a period of parallel running, when the management are happy that all is well, then the computer system can take over on its own. This is referred to as **going live**.

Parallel running used to be used a lot more than it is today, because people were very sceptical about having records on computers rather than on paper. Also, computers weren't as reliable as they are today and the software was not so good. Probably, the main reason for parallel running was the fear that a catastrophic mistake might occur due to the lack of experience of the personnel involved and the whole company's records might be wiped clean.

Mistakes like this did happpen at first and newspapers were quick to report them. Some of these mistakes involved computers adding tax to people's wages rather than taking it away, and producing bills for extremely large or small amounts. A lot of these problems would have been prevented if more careful validation and verification techniques had been used.

Pilot running

There are two types of pilot running. One system uses the new computerized system with an old set of data. The results are known because the task has already been done manually, so they can be checked against the results from the computer. Generally, this method is preferred to parallel running because it is easier to control.

The other system involves phasing in different jobs gradually. One job is put into the computer, and when it is working correctly, other jobs can be put in. This has the advantage that full implementation is broken down into small, easily manageable steps. Unfortunately, some computer systems are so complex that it is impossible to do just one job to start with because all the jobs are interconnected. Each job depends on others being done at the same time. This is mainly a problem with large real-time systems.

Monitoring the 'live' system

Throughout implementation, the project team meets and discusses each stage. After implementation, the project team still meets but not as often. It reviews the system to see if there have been any problems, and to see how well the system is working. Once everyone is satisfied that all is well, then the system will be adopted. When the system is adopted, only system maintenance will be required. This involves checking that all the bugs in the software have been found and that the files are accessed adequately and that they are regularly updated.

Test yourself

Using the words in the list below, copy out and complete sentences A to R underlining the words you have inserted. The words may be used once, more than once, or not at all.

phasing   pilot running   design   data
systems analyst   outputs   trained
old   review   procedures   project
approval   feasibility study   files
documented   parallel   instruction
implementation   process   processing

A A _____ _____ is the person who looks at the manual system to see which parts to computerize.

B She looks at the manual system in terms of three stages: input, _____ and output.

C When she has completed her analysis, she will submit a _____ _____ to the senior management or directors.

D _____ _____ is the stage where the decision about going ahead with the computerization is made.

E Once approval has been obtained, the systems analyst starts to _____ the computer system.

F The computer system is usually designed in the following order _____, inputs, _____ and procedures.

G _____ are the results obtained from the computer system.

H Inputs are the _____ supplied to the computer for _____.

I Files are _____ arranged in a logical order.

J _____ are the programs and steps that need to be followed.

K The personnel of any new computerized system will need to be _____.

L It is essential that all computer systems are fully _____.

M _____ manuals for the staff will also need to be prepared.

N _____ involves putting the theory of the computer system into practice.

O There are two main ways of implementing a computer system. They are parallel running and _____ _____.

P Parallel running involves running the manual system _____ to the computer system.

Q _____ _____ involves either running the computer system with an _____ set of data or _____ in jobs gradually.

R System _____ involves the project team meeting to discuss any problems.

Things to do

1 Before a computer system is installed, a systems analyst would be called in to ensure that the requirements of the customer would be met. Put these stages into the correct order and briefly summarize the work involved at each stage.
   Project approval
   Training

Feasibility study
Detailed system design
Monitoring the 'live' system
Implementation
Problem identification

2 A small business has just installed a computer system and in order to implement it they decide to do 'parallel running'.
  a What is 'parallel running'?
  b Why is 'parallel running' often done?

3 An old-established engineering company has decided to buy a computer. They plan to buy applications packages from a software bureau to enable them to use the computer for payroll and stock control. Many of the company's employees are worried about the introduction of the computer because:
  i they are unsure of the effect that the computer will have on the payroll and stock systems already in operation, and
  ii they fear redundancies.
  a Define the terms 'software bureau' and 'applications package'.
  b Suggest reasons why the payroll and stock control systems have been selected by the company as the initial uses of the computer.
  c The fears mentioned above are common in companies introducing computers. Do you think that the introduction of a computer in this company will produce the effects the employees fear? Give reasons for your answer. You should include in your answer the benefits that the computer is likely to bring.
  d What should the management do to overcome the employees' fears and ensure that the payroll and stock control continue to run smoothly? Write your answer as if you are the systems analyst advising the company on the introduction of the new system.

4 Carefully read the following passage and then answer the question:
Consultants analyse clients' business systems and, where appropriate, select computer hardware, software and communications equipment to best meet the customer's requirements. They produce detailed systems and program specifications, design test data and are involved in user procedure and training.

What do you understand by the phrases:
  a 'detailed systems and program specifications',
  b 'user procedures and training'?

5 **a** For the successful design and installation of a computerized system, a systems analyst must deal with various groups of people. Name **three** of these groups.
  b A systems analyst could be responsible for the introduction of the new computerized system after the software has been written and tested and the hardware produced. Name and describe **one** method of introducing this new computerized system.

6 A school shop which sells foodstuffs, books, stationery etc. has a manual sales system. It is felt that it would be advantageous to computerize the system to make accountancy, stock control and re-ordering more efficient.
  a Explain each of the following steps involved in the design and implementation of a new system:
  feasibility study; system design; changeover; parallel running; pilot running; monitoring.
  b Draw a flowchart for the daily accounting part of the system showing the steps involved in producing the daily statement below.

Item no.	Sold	In stock	Unit cost	Total cost
2341	30	150	£0.25	£7.50
2349	5	50	£1.25	£6.25
3456	4	60	£3.99	£15.96

Total daily sales.............£55.60

7 When a new computerized system is first suggested, a systems analyst is usually employed to carry out a feasibility study and to prepare a report for management.
Assuming that it is decided to continue with the computerization, state and describe the other steps involved on the part of the systems analyst in the successful computerization of a previous manual system.

25
Security and computer systems

Deliberate breaches of security

The security of computer systems has always been a problem. There are various ways in which the security can be breached. Here are some of them.

Unauthorized access to confidential information

A lot of information about a particular company's accounts can be contained on a computer. Obviously, the directors and management want to keep this information very confidential. One way round this problem is to keep certain key files in a safe and only allow certain key staff access to them. Another system uses passwords and codes. Certain files containing information can only be accessed if a certain password or code is put into the computer.

Unauthorized access is a big problem because if people are to use the computer, they must have access to it. Probably, the best way round the problem is to select computer staff very carefully.

Tapping computer information travelling along telephone lines

It is possible to tap information travelling along telephone lines and even alter it (Figure 25.1). This problem can be avoided by using a **modem**. This transforms data into a modem code before it is transmitted along the telephone lines. The modem at the other end of the line then decodes the information at its destination. If anyone tries to interfere with these devices, they sound an alarm and the data is stopped from going along the lines.

Alteration of accounts by staff

This is very difficult to prevent. Computer fraud is on the increase and, in America, the FBI have estimated that it costs $300 million a year.

To discover any fraud that is taking place, it is necessary to do long and complicated audits. This can be very expensive. It is best to try to prevent fraud by taking as many precautions as possible. This sometimes includes keeping programs away from the computer and constantly changing operators around so that they are not always doing the same job.

Damage to magnetic storage media by digruntled staff

This can be quite a problem. Employees who have been sacked have been known to damage records held on magnetic media by running a magnet across the surface. This ruins the information held on them and can cost a lot of money. Ways around this include duplicating the information (which is usually done anyway) and keeping the copies in a fireproof safe (Figure 25.2).

Accidental damage

Damage by fire or smoke

If a fire were to start in a computer room, a lot of damage could be done not only to the hardware but also to the software. The software would contain files essential to the running of the company so its loss

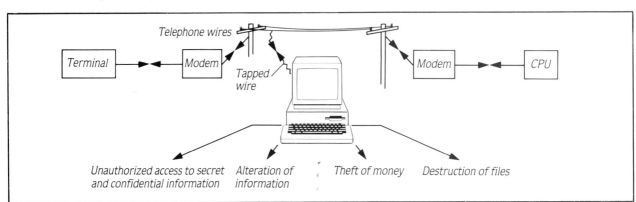

Figure 25.1   *Some consequences of tapping computer information travelling along telephone lines*

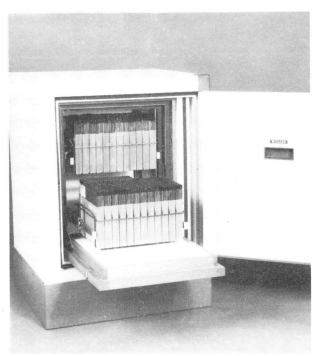

Figure 25.2 *Keeping floppy disks in a fireproof safe prevents theft or alteration of disks by staff and loss by fire*

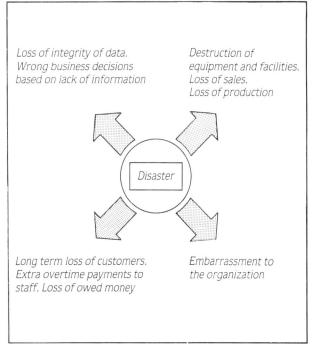

Figure 25.3 *How computer loss can affect a large company*

could prove disastrous (Figure 25.3). Most large companies are completely computer dependant, and it could take years to recover from the loss. Smoke can also damage the hardware and software and even just the heat will do great damage.

Quite often, the process of putting the fire out can cause more damage than the fire itself. Ordinary water can completely ruin computer systems.

In order to prevent damage by fire, it is best to try to first avoid the risk of fire by taking precautions such as making the complete room a no smoking room. If a fire does start, then it should be detected immediately and attempts should be made to extinguish it automatically. This may involve using an automatic sprinkler system which sprays carbon dioxide gas instead of water.

Accidental erasure

There is always a chance that data can be accidentally erased from a magnetic disk or tape in error or by an inexperienced operator. To prevent this, magnetic tapes have write-protect notches on them which means you cannot accidentally write data onto the tape. Floppy disks have a notch on the side in much the same way as a video tape (Figure 25.4). The large disk drives have special hardware devices which prevents erasure.

Figure 25.4 *The write/protect notch on a floppy disk*

The security of file data

It is essential for every organization that uses computers, that their data files and other software should not be lost completely. This loss could come about by fire, floods, earthquakes, war, bomb attacks, disgruntled staff, accidental erasure, a fault in the equipment etc.

To make sure that the loss is not total, copies of all the relevant files should be held in a fireproof safe or even another building nearby. This is probably the

151

best and safest way of safeguarding the data.

Another way we can safeguard files is by using the **ancestral file system**. Here, one file is used with a transaction file to produce a new file. The original file is called the **master file** and this is the **father file**. The father file along with a **transaction file** (which contains recent changes) are used to create a new master file called the **son file**. The father file and the transaction file are kept together and stored in a safe place. If the son is lost or corrupted (altered incorrectly) then the father and transaction files can be used to produce a new son file. The son file can now be the father file to produce another new son file. The original father file is now referred to as the **grandfather file**. In this way we can produce generations of files. It is usual only to keep the last two generations and all the old files can be used again.

Test yourself

Using the words in the list below, copy out and complete sentences A to G underlining the words you have inserted. The words may be used once, more than once or not at all.

tapped   re-created   son   fireproof
automatic   passwords   father
transaction   codes   modem   ancestral

A   _____ or _____ can be used to prevent unauthorized access to confidential information.

B   *Information travelling along telephone lines can be _____ and to prevent this a special _____ is used which jumbles the information up.*

C   *Unhappy personnel could destroy files using a magnet. To prevent this copies should be kept in a _____ safe.*

D   *Fire can completely destroy a computer system. _____ sprinkler systems which use carbon dioxide are used to put a fire out should one develop.*

E   *The _____ file system makes sure that if a master tape or disk is destroyed it can then be _____ .*

F   *The recent changes are kept on a file called a _____ file.*

G   *Three generations of files are kept along with the transaction files. They are called the grandfather, _____ and _____ files.*

Things to do

1   *Security of data is very much a problem for computer users.*
   a   i   *Give **three** reasons why this is so.*
     ii   *Outline **three** applications of computer usage where security is particularly important.*
   b   *The public at large is concerned about the privacy of information that is stored in computers.*
     i   *Give **two** examples of privacy invasion.*
     ii   *Give **two** example of how privacy can be protected within a computer system.*

2   a   *Why must access to the data in a data bank be subject to strict security?*
   b   *Give **three** methods of achieving this security.*

3   *Explain what precautions you could take in order to protect valuable data files from the following:*
   a   *Destruction*
   b   *Theft*
   c   *Unauthorized access*

4   *A mistake by a new computer operator or an electrical fault causing a fire could result in the loss of all the data on a master file.*
   a   *What is a master file?*
   b   i   *What precaution could be taken to prevent total loss by fire?*
     ii   *Give a different precaution to prevent total loss by operator error.*

5   *You are the last person to leave the computer area at night. State **four** precautions you should take to ensure the security of the installation, apart from turning off the lights and locking the door.*

6   a   *A doctor is thinking of keeping all his patients' records on a computer. He is very worried about the confidentiality of the records contained by the computer and is worried about unauthorized access. Write a short paragraph about why his fears are unfounded and how the confidentiality could be assured.*
   b   *The same doctor is also worried that, because he doesn't know much about computers, he might accidentally erase some of the*

important records. Write a short paragraph to explain to him how he could avoid this happening.

7 Explain how the ancestral file system is used as a security measure in case one of the files is destroyed by fire, accidental erasure etc.

8 **a** List **five** types of disaster or events which could lead to the loss of information contained by the computer.
 b For the above listed events, describe how total loss in each case can be avoided.
 c For each loss, describe what effect it could have on the company.

26
Wordprocessing

Wordprocessing is probably the biggest application of microcomputers. A lot of smaller companies feel that they are unable to use computers because they don't know enough about them and they don't have specialist staff. Wordprocessors are very simple to use. They are an excellent introduction for newcomers to computing. This is probably the main reason why they have become so popular. One other reason is that they are extremely cost effective. A typical wordprocessing system costs £4000. This cost can rapidly be recovered by the increased productivity which the wordprocessor produces.

What is wordprocessing?

A wordprocessor is a small computer used for storing, editing and printing text (i.e. written material). Instead of writing a letter on paper and then amending it before typing up the final copy, you can use a wordprocessor to type it out on a line printer. If the letter is a fairly standard one which is used a lot, then once the letter has been written it can be stored on a disk for future use. If the wordprocessor operator needs to use the letter again, she will not have to retype the whole letter. She just needs to alter the name and address of the person who it is sent to.

The printer which types out the final letter from a wordprocessor works a lot faster that a typist could. The wordprocessor can set out the text so that it looks neat. The margins down the sides of the page are in a straight line and the headings can be centred (Figure 26.1). Some wordprocessors can even detect spelling mistakes made by the typist and correct them in the finished letter or text. Any document which needs to be printed such as insurance certificates, legal contracts, books etc. can be printed using a wordprocessor.

OPTICS

Introduction

This pack contains programs in four central optics topics in CSE and O-level physics:

1. Refraction and apparent depth
2. Convex lenses
3. Concave lenses
4. Long and short sight in the eye

Each program provides a dynamic ray diagram which can be used to explore the principles involved. The programs can be used as demonstration programs by a teacher in front of a class. There are also versions to enable pupils to use the programs for practice. In the practice versions of the programs, certain variables are fixed by the computer and pupils can obtain readings, plot their own graphs and so determine the hidden variable.

The programs can obviously be used as a complete sequence in teaching about refraction and its consequences going from first principles through to practical application. Each program is, however, completely self-standing and they can be used either individually or in any sequence the teacher chooses.

The programs are not intended to replace practical experiments but rather to provide an additional complementary teaching resource.

Figure 26.1 *Some text produced by a wordprocessor*

What are the advantages of wordprocessing?

Wordprocessors can store whole letters or just certain paragraphs so the typist just has to fill in the missing parts. This saves a lot of time. The wordprocessor sets out the letter automatically so this saves time too. Any mistakes the typist makes can easily be corrected on the screen before a hard copy is made on the line printer. If a sentence is missed out or needs to be inserted, then this is easily done.

These advantages mean that wordprocessing saves a great deal of time and money. The letters produced by a wordprocessor generally look neater and are better presented than the same work on a typewriter. Less skilled people can use wordprocessors because mistakes can easily be corrected and no planned setting out of the page is needed. Probably, the overall result of all these advantages is that fewer typists are needed to produce much better results.

Disadvantages of wordprocessing

The main disadvantage of wordprocessing is that fewer typists are needed. It is estimated that in a company which does a lot of standard work e.g. invoices, statements and legal contracts, a wordprocessor can do the work of between 2½ and 5 typists.

Wordprocessors also make the typist's job less skilled. Some wordprocessors can check on their operators by recording the number of keystrokes in a given time.

The hardware of a wordprocessor

The hardware of a typical wordprocessing system is made up of:
A central processing unit (CPU)
A visual display unit (VDU)
A keyboard (like a typewriter but with some extra buttons for features such as delete sentence, insert word etc.)
A backing store (usually floppy disks)
A very good quality line printer. This is usually a daisy wheel printer because it produces good quality type that looks the same as an ordinary typewriter. Where a lot of fast work is needed, a dot matrix printer is sometimes used, but then the text looks as though it has been done on a computer.

Figure 26.2 shows a typical wordprocessing system.

Software for wordprocessing (WP)

Like computer programs, wordprocessor programs are bought as packages. Which package you use really depends on how many features you require. Most of the software packages have **insertions**, **deletions** and **corrections**. These are very useful features and allow you to type in text and then make insertions, deletions and corrections before the text is printed out. Some software allows you to do what is called a 'global search and replace'. This allows a particular word or name to be highlighted so it can be altered or replaced. Figure 26.3 shows a typical menu for a wordprocessor.

Sort

This allows the text to be sorted alphabetically.

Figure 26.2   *The hardware of a typical wordprocessing system*

```
-- Main menu --                        8/5/84   10.01

C = Create a new letter or document
E = Edit an existing letter or document
P = Print a letter or document
 I = Index of letters and documents on file
D = Delete a document
F = Finished using the system
M = More main menu selections



Type the letter and then press RETURN
```

Figure 26.3   *A typical menu for a wordprocessing system*

Ability to copy from other documents

This allows you to store standard paragraphs that come up all the time in between letters. By touching a single key these paragraphs can be inserted as required.

Dictionary/spelling check

Some wordprocessors can do what is called dictionary or spelling check (Figure 26.4). They have a dictionary kept in the memory and all the words keyed in are checked with the dictionary. Any words

Figure 26.4 *A wordprocessor with a built-in dictionary*

mispelled are highlighted on the screen so that they can be retyped. If the word is not one included in the computer dictionary then the word is still highlighted so that the typist can check that it is spelt correctly.

Test yourself

Using the words from the list below, copy out and complete sentences A to I. Underline the words you put in. The words in the list can be used more than once.

delete	store	VDU	quickly
keyboard	skilled	line printer	
neater	spelling	unemployment	
microcomputers	print		

A *Wordprocessing is an application that is widely used on _____.*

B *A wordprocessor is a small computer which can _____, edit and _____ text.*

C *Letters and documents are typed directly onto a _____ where they can be edited before finally being printed on a _____ _____.*

D *Wordprocessors produce written material much more _____ than conventional methods.*

E *Some wordprocessors can detect _____ mistakes.*

F *Written material produced by a wordprocessor is generally _____ than material produced by typists.*

G *Usually, less _____ people are needed to operate a wordprocessor.*

H *Without doubt, wordprocessors do cause _____.*

I *A typical wordprocessing system consists of a CPU, a VDU, backing store and a _____ which has some additional keys such as _____ sentence.*

Things to do

1 Which of the following are the main users of wordprocessors?
   a Engineers
   b Booksellers
   c Shopkeepers
   d Secretaries
   e Factory workers

2 Explain what is meant by a wordprocessor. Why have wordprocessors become so popular in recent years? What factors have led to their popularity?

3 a Describe **two** ways in which wordprocessing machines can be used to help improve the working life of an office typist or secretary.
   b Why is it likely that an office manager would welcome the introduction of a wordprocessing machine?
   c Why might some typists be worried by the introduction of a wordprocessing machine?

4 Outline the hardware configurations of a typical wordprocessing system.

5 Wordprocessing is the application of computer technology to typewriting.
   a Where is the text stored as it is typed?
   b Where is the text stored afterwards?
   c Give **three** examples of the types of commands that are available to the operator.
   d What will be shown on the screen in addition to a selection of the available commands?
   e In what form is the final copy of the text produced?
   f The Minutes of a meeting have been typed on a wordprocessor and stored on a disk. The draft copy shows one mistake. In the middle of a long paragraph, the word 'the' has been typed in twice.
      Briefly describe how the operator would correct the Minutes.

6 It has been said that the use of wordprocessors could lead to mass unemployment amongst typists. Do you think this is true? Give reasons. What types of jobs do wordprocessors do best?

7 Explain in detail some of the features that you would look for if you were thinking of buying a wordprocessor system.

27
Communication networks

Prestel (viewdata)

Prestel or **viewdata** is a two-way information service operated by British Telecom. Prestel is an instant information service. It gives the user access to a vast quantity of information held on computers. The system contains a variety of information for business and domestic users.

Figure 27.1 shows the structure of the system. It is connected via a modem to a telephone line. The modem converts the information into a form that can be transmitted along the telephone lines. Using a remote control keypad, the television can be connected via the telephone lines to the Prestel computer database where all the information is held on disk. Using the keypad, the user can select the pages of information that he requires by pressing the relevant keys (Figure 27.2). The remote control keypad is very easy to operate and no special skills are needed. For the business user, the screen and the keypad are all in one unit.

The Prestel system works like this. When the user has contacted the computer using a key on the keypad, he keys in his personal identification number. There is a small cost to contact the computer. This is the cost of a local telephone call. Some of the pages are also charged for. The charge for the page is shown at the top right hand corner of the screen.

The first page which comes up on the screen is page OO. This is the main index. There are nine options on this page. Only one option can be selected at a time. After an option has been selected, ten more options are displayed. When one of these has been selected, more options are displayed. This continues until the user gets the information he requires. This happens in as short a time as possible.

Using this system, it is possible to find specific items. For example, if you want to find out the name of a play on in a theatre in London, you would page general interest, then entertainment, then theatres and finally theatres in London. This paging system allows you to get the information you require in an extremely short period of time (Figure 27.3).

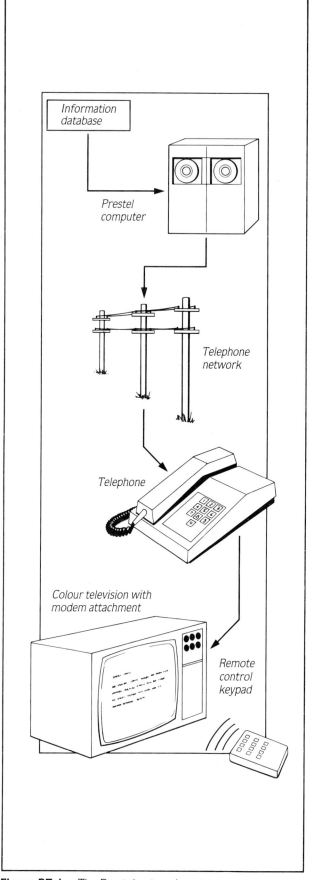

Figure 27.1 *The Prestel network system*

Figure 27.2 *The Prestel system is 'interactive'. This means that the user can communicate with the computer via the keyboard. This user is using the teleshopping service to order goods from home*

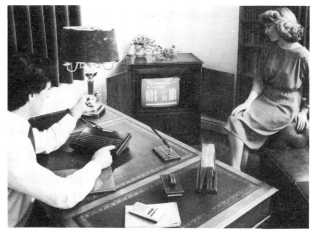

Figure 27.4 *Homelink is a service for some Prestel users. It is run by the Nottingham Building Society and the Bank of Scotland. Customers can access their own bank and building society accounts from home*

Figure 27.3 *Prestel customers can keep up-to-date with the news 24 hours a day. Teletext only works when television programmes are on the air*

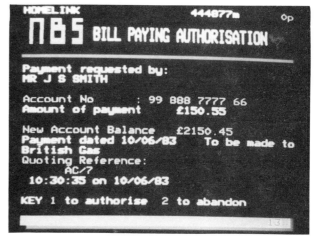

Figure 27.5 *Paying a gas bill using Homelink*

What information is held on Prestel?

The answer to this question is 'almost everything'. The Prestel pages are constantly being updated and added to, and at the last count there were 234 000. This includes information on 1778 companies, 95 sports, over 1000 UK towns and villages, 173 countries, 156 types of job, 125 Government Departments and all 635 MPs. It also covers 64 exchange rates, 713 share prices and the prices of 63 commodities some of which are updated every five minutes. Buying and booking are also represented with over 48 different wines, 184 hotels world wide, 55 holiday companies and 25 airlines. Entertainment is also featured on the system with 68 games, 52 quizzes, 13 stories, 3 mazes, 8 personality tests, 8

Figure 27.6 *Getting a bank statement in your home at the press of a button*

competing horoscopes and hundreds of jokes and limericks.

Figures 27.4, 5 and 6 show some of the uses of Prestel.

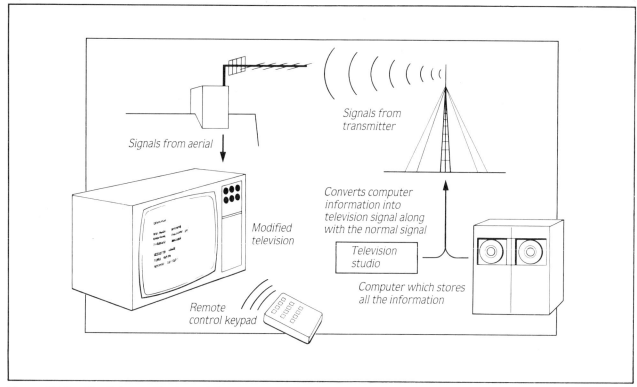

Figure 27.7   *The Teletext (Ceefax and Oracle) network system*

Ceefax and Oracle (teletext)

Ceefax and Oracle are known together as **teletext**. Unlike the more sophisticated Prestel system, Ceefax and Oracle do not operate through the telephone network. Instead they use spare space in television transmission. Ceefax is the system operated by the BBC and Oracle is the system operated by the IBA. In order to receive Ceefax or Oracle you need a slightly modified television set. To pick a particular page you press a few buttons on a keypad, like in the Prestel system (Figure 27.7).

The sort of information you can obtain using the teletext system includes pages of news, finance, hobbies, weather, food prices, recipes, cinema etc. Generally, the teletext system is of more interest to domestic users than business users.

The Ceefax and Oracle systems are now available at a little extra cost on a variety of television sets.

Prestel and the future

The Prestel system is an interactive system because it allows information to flow in two directions. Because of this two-way flow of information, there have been

Figure 27.8   *Using Gateway to book an airline ticket*

many plans to expand the system. Oracle and Ceefax are one-way only systems. They are really just electronic magazines. However, the Prestel system has a lot of potential.

Already, the Prestel system has been extended to send mail electronically through the telephone network. Using the Prestel system called Gateway it is possible to book flights directly on airline computers or with tour operators (Figure 27.8).

In the near future, we may be able to get the computer to work out problems which a lot of people have, such as income tax problems and social security payment problems. The Prestel system could be used as an electronic citizens' advice bureau.

Other uses include advertising in much the same way as the yellow pages or Thompsons Directory. Here, businesses or people who want to advertise their services could use the Prestel system to do this. We are not far away from 'armchair shopping' where you could order goods direct from a company using the keypad and the Prestel network. This is happening to some extent now.

In the next few years the Prestel system will expand greatly. It will soon provide the user with the quickest and most effective form of communication.

Electronic mail

Electronic mail is an extension of the Prestel system and wordprocessing. In this system, instead of producing a letter or document on a wordprocessor

Figure 27.9 *Displaying a message using electronic mail*

and then sending it through the post, the letter is sent via the telephone lines and comes up on a visual display unit, (VDU), at the other end. If the person at the other end is not able to look at the screen immediately, then the message is stored by the computer until the person is ready to recall it. In this way, information can be passed from one place to

another almost instantaneously.

Altogether, this system increases efficiency tremendously and the process of sending out a letter and receiving a reply can take minutes rather than about a week. You could argue that we can still do this by picking up the telephone, telephoning and dictating the letter. This is fine, but most business transactions require written documents for legal reasons. Also, if you try to contact someone during office hours, it can be very difficult.

Due to high cost and low productivity of our existing postal service, electronic mail will eventually become as much a part of our lives as the telephone is today (Figure 27.9). Already, British Telecom have an electronic mail system which they are selling. It is called Telecom Gold and already has 70 customers and nearly 1300 mailboxes.

Test yourself

Using the words in the list below, copy out and complete sentences A to G. Underline the words you put in. The words in the list can be used more than once.

wordprocessor   telephone   Oracle
electronic   Prestel   business
interactive   teletext   domestic

A _____ is an information service provided by British Telecom.
B A specially converted television set is connected to the _____ line.
C The _____ system is an interactive system because the information flows both ways.
D Ceefax and _____ are information services which are known together as _____.
E At present, Prestel is more suited to the _____ user while the less expensive _____ is more suited to the _____ user.
F It is now possible to transmit letters electronically using the Prestel system. This is called _____ mail.
G Using a _____ and the _____ system, it is possible to send letters much more efficiently.

Things to do

1   Which one of the following is an example of viewdata?
    a   Teletext
    b   Ceefax
    c   Oracle
    d   Prestel

2   Which of the following provides the Prestel service?
    a   The BBC
    b   The IBA
    c   Teletext
    d   British Telecom

3   Name two teletext services.

4   Prestel is which of the following?
    a   A telephone system
    b   An information service
    c   A television programme
    d   A device that speaks
    e   A foreign language translation device

5   Which of the following is not a television based information system?
    a   Ernie
    b   Oracle
    c   Prestel
    d   Ceefax
    e   Teletext

6   a   A friend of yours is interested in having an information system in his home. Write an explanation of the teletext and Prestel systems. Outline the advantages and disadvantages of each of the systems.
    b   Which system do you think he should buy? Give reasons.
    c   If your friend were a stockbroker and wanted a system for work, which system would he now choose?

7   Teletext and Viewdata are both information retrieval systems.
    a   Give an example of a teletext system.
    b   Explain how teletext is broadcast and received.
    c   What is the name of British Telecom's Viewdata system?
    d   Give **two** possible uses of viewdata:
        i   in the home
        ii   in a business

8   Teletext is really only an electronic magazine. Do you think that magazines and newspapers will be replaced by computerized information systems? Explain your answer.

9   a   Write a list of the steps involved in the writing of a letter by hand.
    b   Assume that you are the manager of a large company. Now, write a list of the steps taken to produce a letter, bearing in mind that you would have a secretary to type the letter for you.
    c   From your answer in part b write down the steps which you would not need if you were using electronic mail.

10 Explain what 'electronic mail' is and why its use is likely to escalate in the future.
    Do you see its introduction replacing the postman? Give reasons for your answer.

11 'The laborious process of moving a letter from one part of the world to another shows the limitations of traditional methods of coding and transmitting information.' (The Mighty Micro, Dr C Evans)
    a   Describe the traditional methods referred to by Dr Evans.
        Give **four** different limitations of these methods.
    b   The traditional methods may be replaced by 'electronic mail'.
        Show how this might operate.
        Explain **two** advantages and **one** disadvantage it would have over the traditional methods for a large company.

12 Write down the meaning of serial access and random access. The Prestel system uses a disk pack means of storage. Why would magnetic tape be an unsuitable storage medium for the Prestel system?

28
Social implications

The impact on society of computers

The impact of computers on society, has been as far reaching as any other development in the history of mankind. Twenty years ago, computers were on the fringes of our lives, but now they are a central and integral part of them. How we cope with the changes that the new technology brings us is up to us. Our past record of coping with technological changes, has not been very good. Figures 28.1 and 28.2 show some of the advantages and disadvantages of computers.

The speed of change

One of the problems that introducing information technology (IT) can bring is that the change can be extremely rapid. It was only in 1951 that the first computer was introduced into commerce. Now it would be rare to find any medium-sized business without one. The speed of change brings many problems. For example, engineers need to be trained quickly to be able to maintain these new machines. Operators, programmers and systems analysts need to keep up with the constantly changing systems. Peoples' working conditions change. The hours of work and type of work change drastically. Clearly, peoples' attitudes need to change at the same speed in order to cope.

Some people think that the introduction of this new technology has got out of hand and there is no control over its introduction. There is some truth in this. Some people say that a few people employed by the computer manufacturers in areas such as research and development are responsible for changing the lives of nearly everyone in the world. These people think that there should be some policy by the Government to monitor and control the introduction of the new technology.

The Japanese have adapted well to change. They have been fairly successful at implementing IT. One thing that helped quick introduction of computers without any resistance from the workforce was a life-time employment guarantee given to the workers by their employers. To be able to pay for this companies have had to expand and staff have had to be more flexible.

Like it or not, information technology is here to stay. It is reckoned that by 1990 around £400 million per day will be spent on information technology products. In a few year's time the computer industry will be the largest industry in the world.

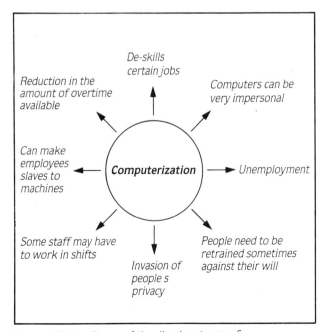

Figure 28.1 *Some of the disadvantages of computerization*

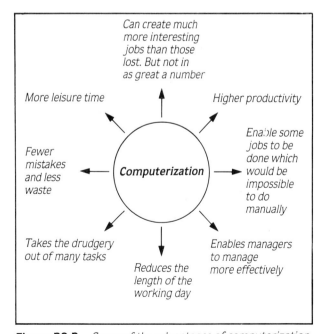

Figure 28.2 *Some of the advantages of computerization*

Unemployment and computers

When computers were first introduced into the business world, it was thought that this would lead to mass unemployment. This did not happen. Instead, the jobs that were lost were replaced by new jobs such as computer operators, systems analysts, computer engineers, programmers and data preparation staff. The first computers needed lots of people to make them work efficiently.

But the situation has changed greatly. Because modern computer systems are so simple, not as many people are needed and computers can now be used in areas where it would not have been possible to use them previously. Data preparation is one area in which great advances have been made. Modern computers need very little data preparation. Also, the computers are much more reliable due to the introduction of the silicon chip and integrated circuitry.

The advert shown in Figure 28.3 is a recent advert by the largest computer manufacturer in the world called IBM (International Business Machines). It shows quite clearly how the statement 'If we did not have computers, there would be more jobs' could be answered. How far, though, are we prepared to go before someone says 'no more replacement of people by machines'? How many jobs need to be lost before someone says 'no more new technology'?

As more and more microprocessors are used, unemployment will probably increase. Our society will have to accept this and cope with it. What must not happen is for a small part of the population to be employed at extremely high salaries while the rest of the population is unemployed. Different work patterns will be needed. Shorter hours of work, job sharing, lowering the retirement age and raising the school leaving age are some things that could lessen the problem.

In the future it will not be uncommon to find huge factories with only a few people employed. Most of the work will be done by microprocessor-controlled robots and computers. These robots can perform the same mechanical motions performed by machine operators. The robots work 365 days a year, don't go on strike, don't require people to administer them and don't need much maintenance. Now it is possible to produce an assembly line that is completely automated. This means that the raw products go in, are assembled, and the final finished product, for example, a refrigerator, comes out without any humans being involved. Ten years ago, this would have been science fiction, but now with new low cost technology it has become fact in a lot of factories.

It may well be that in the future most people will not be working in manufacturing industries because this type of work can be performed by computers and robots. In the last industrial revolution, people's muscles were extended by using machines which could do the same job quicker and more efficiently. In the computer revolution, people's brains have been extended. In the future, people will be able to use their brains for original thought, which is impossible for the computer to do, rather than repetitive mundane tasks. Some people talk of a 'post industrial society' where the people are no longer dependent on manufactured goods for wealth. Instead, skills and knowledge become more important for wealth.

Two men were watching a mechanical excavator on a building site. "If it wasn't for that machine," said one, "twelve men with shovels could be doing that job."

"Yes," replied the other, "and if it wasn't for your twelve shovels, two hundred men with teaspoons could be doing that job."

There are two ways to regard technological development. As a threat. Or as a promise. Every invention from the wheel to the steam engine created the same dilemma.

But it's only by exploiting the promise of each that man has managed to improve his lot. Information technology has given man more time to create, and released him from the day-to-day tasks that limit his self-fulfilment.

We ourselves are very heavy users of this technology, ranging from golf-ball typewriters to ink-jet printers to small and large computers, so we're more aware than most of that age-old dilemma: threat or promise.

Yet during 30 years in the UK our workforce has increased from six to 15,000. And during 30 years not a single person has been laid off, not a single day has been lost through strikes.

Throughout Britain, information technology has shortened queues. Streamlined efficiency. Boosted exports. And kept British products competitive in an international market.

To treat technology as a threat would halt progress. As a promise, it makes tomorrow look a lot brighter.

IBM

IBM United Kingdom Limited P.O. Box 41, North Harbour, Portsmouth PO6 3AU

Figure 28.3

Improvement in working conditions

The jobs that are replaced by computers are often the more mundane repetitive jobs. Quite often, the people doing these jobs are retrained to do something to do with the computer. Sometimes they are not replaced when they leave, which avoids redundancies.

Although there are disadvantages in using computers, there are some advantages too. For example, computers can do some complex jobs which would be impossible for people to do. These tasks include weather forecasting, censuses, clearing bank cheques, sending up rockets and satellites and the use of credit cards.

Some industrial processes are very hazardous. Computer controlled robots could be used to control these and prevent some terrible diseases that people have contracted in the past from materials such as asbestos, lead, nuclear waste and dangerous chemicals. Computers can also work in dirty, noisy environments.

There are computer controlled traffic lights in nearly all of our major cities. They prevent the build-up of traffic that causes traffic jams. Computers also help us book our holidays, air tickets and rail tickets more easily than in the past. Hazard warning lights on motorways are controlled by computers and have helped to save many lives. Computers are also being used in schools as an aid to learning languages, maths and spelling.

Although computers have led to job losses, they have also led to the creation of many interesting jobs such as systems analysis, programming and maintenance. Jobs in the computing industry are generally well paid and interesting. Working conditions are usually very good too because computers need clean places to operate effectively.

Trade union reactions to computers

Any reduction in the workforce is automatically opposed by the trade union movement. Some unions accept change more readily than others. Many trade unionists are worried that they are the only people who are taking any notice of the rapid use of new technology. They feel that there is no government policy for its introduction.

Most trade unionists are realistic and realize that the introduction of IT is inevitable. For example, the leader of one union said 'Trade unions know that a future without microelectronics is no future at all'.

One industry which had the new technology at a very early stage is the telephone industry. Years ago this industry was very labour intensive because switching was done mechanically. There were 33 000 job losses in this industry when it went over to electronic switching. The new System X system needs very few people (Figure 28.4). We could say that

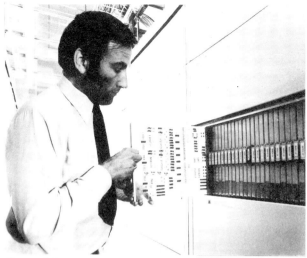

Figure 28.4 *The System X computer-controlled telephone exchange replaced an older system. This meant loss of jobs*

these job losses were intolerable and any machines or technology that cause this problem should not be used. The trouble with this argument is that if we do not react to the changes, the Japanese or the West Germans or some other nation will. This would mean we would lose our share of the market and there would be more job losses. This has happened before in the television manufacturing industry. Britain was in front in the initial development, but could not apply the new technology quickly enough. As a result of this, we rapidly lost our share of the TV market, which led to large job losses.

At the moment we are on the verge of the electronic office, where a lot of routine secretarial and clerical jobs will be done by an integrated computer system. The sort of jobs that people will do will combine wordprocessing, electronic mail and automatic filing and retrieval. Some people say that, in the future, the electronic office will be paperless – all the work will be done on visual display units (VDUs).

Wordprocessors are one type of machine that the office workers' unions are very concerned about. Wordprocessors are extremely productive and quickly cover their initial cost. To give you some idea how effective they are, here are some figures to help you make up your own mind about them.

An average copy typist produces about 250 lines of text per day. An audio typist can produce a greater amount – about 350 lines. Both these typists will be able to type 50 words per minute. So in any average day, these typists should be able to produce 1800 lines. So what are they doing, and why can't they produce this larger amount? The answer is that people are not machines. They need to rest, take time off and talk and they are occasionally sick. The wordprocessor would have little problem in producing 1800 lines per day with an experienced operator.

It is reckoned that a wordprocessor can do the work of 2½-5 typists. The best wordprocessors cost about £4000 to £7000. An average typist costs a company £5000 a year, so the initial cost for a wordprocessor is rapidly recovered. Less skilled people can use these wordprocessors. It is not as important to avoid typing mistakes as they can be easily corrected later. Also, the setting out of letters is done by the machine.

Unions are fairly united in their opposition to wordprocessors. The machines certainly lead to unemployment and make the typists who operate them almost slaves of the wordprocessors. The machines actually monitor the performance of the operators. A lot of typists find no satisfaction in using wordprocessors. There is no variation in the types of job the typist does – there is no longer any shorthand, filing or setting out. It may soon be possible to dictate letters straight into a computer.

Some of the biggest opposition to new technology being introduced came from the printing unions in the newspaper industry. For example, the management of *The Times* and *Sunday Times* newspapers wanted to do away with an old method of producing print for newspapers. The new technology would have done away with between 40% and 45% of the workforce in the composing room. The job was previously done in very bad working conditions. Working temperatures were intolerable, ink used to get all over the people who worked in the room, and the noise could be bad at times. If new technology were introduced the same job could be done in clean working conditions, using a VDU. The introduction of this technology really hinged on the loss of jobs and the workforce was on strike for many months and nearly caused the end of the two newspapers.

Computers and privacy

Recently, people have been concerned that computers may be eroding people's privacy. Until recently, information on people was held on computers by various Government and private bodies, but there was no cross flow of information from one department to another. Now, because it is easier to pass data between terminals, it is possible to link together a number of different computers containing information about a private individual. This has very sinister implications, and certain people are worried about the invasion of computers into people's privacy.

Britain is behind the rest of the world in laws about personal information contained on computers. In America, for example, the private citizen has the right to view any information kept about him.

From the day a baby is born until the day she dies, information will be built up about her by various sources and stored on a computer. If she is born in a hospital, the first computer with information about her will belong to the local area health authority. Then, information will be stored on the computer in the General Register offices which contain records of births and deaths. Throughout her life, information about her will be built up inside various computer memories (Figure 28.5).

Look at Figure 28.6. If a bank's customer receives more than £150 in interest a year then the Inland Revenue is automatically informed. This means that the person cannot hide money earning interest without paying tax on it. The Inland Revenue also swaps information with the Department of Health and Social Security and the VAT authority. The Police National Computer obtains information about the drivers of cars from the Driver and Vehicle Licensing Centre in Swansea.

It would be possible for computers to be used in what most people would describe as sinister ways.

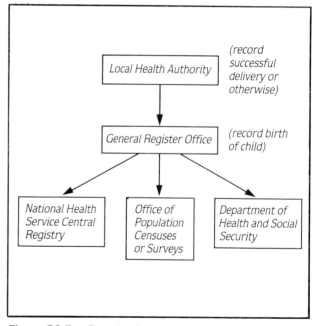

Figure 28.5 *Organizations that would keep details about a baby in the first few weeks of her life*

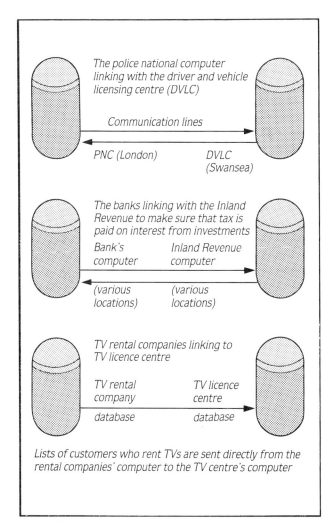

Figure 28.6 *Some database linkings that exist already*

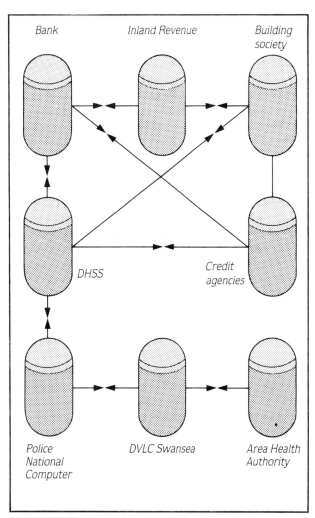

Figure 28.7 *Some database linkings that would cause loss of privacy*

For example, local Health Authorities could disclose the names of people who have bad eyesight to the police. The police could then look at lists of people who have had accidents but have told the police they had perfect eyesight. It would also be possible for the Government to build up a complete picture of a person's life regarding personal details, income and how he spends it. There are endless possibilities for the exchange of information.

Not only Government bodies exchange information about people. Private companies exchange information too. The most well known of these are the credit referral agencies who make a living out of selling information about people and companies. This information includes credit worthiness or an assessment of how much a person is worth. Lists of people under certain categories are very useful to companies, and it is possible to obtain a list of directors and even millionaires. Figure 28.7 shows some linkings of databases that would result in loss of privacy.

Wrong information

The problem with storing information on computers is that the information must be right. Quite often, wrong information goes into the computer, for example it may be typed wrongly. This can have severe consequences for the person concerned.

Often, people are blacklisted by the credit referral agencies incorrectly. Then they find it impossible to buy any goods on credit. It is also impossible for them to get a mortgage.

There are safeguards against wrong information. The Consumer Credit Act requires all credit referral agencies to check and correct their records if someone has been blacklisted incorrectly.

Should data be private?

A lot of people argue that if information is not passed on a lot of jobs are made harder. For instance, crimes can go undetected.

While looking for the Yorkshire Ripper, the Yorkshire Police, wanted a list of men who were self-employed from the Department of Health and Social Security. They were not allowed to have this list and, as a result, finding the Yorkshire Ripper took much longer.

Another police force were looking for a rapist. If one of the London police forces had informed them that a man had been released from Broadmoor and was living in their area, they would have caught him much sooner.

Government recommendations are that information obtained for one purpose should not be used for another. But the two examples show that this recommendation does not always work for the public's good.

Jury vetting has been going on for many years. It involves actually selecting certain people to sit on the jury rather that just picking them randomly. The police can obtain information about the members from computers, so they can select certain members of the public who are sure to convict the defendant. Whether you think this is right, or fair to the defendant, is a matter of opinion.

As it becomes easier to link up computers the question of privacy of information needs to be looked into very carefully. Do you think there should be stricter laws on passing on information?

Computers and crime

Some computers such as the Police National Computer (PNC) and the Driving and Vehicle Licensing Centre (DVLC) computer, are used to help the police catch criminals.

However, computers can cause problems and have invented new crimes. Computer fraud is on the increase and some ingenious ways of committing it have been thought up by clever criminals. One of the problems of computer crime is that it is extremely hard to detect. For example small amounts of money can be taken from lots of accounts without anyone noticing them, as they are often disguised in a mass of data. Quite often, the crimes are discovered merely by accident. Most of the crimes are detected by something the thief does afterwards, for example, gambling heavily.

One worrying point is that society in general takes a different view of computer thieves, because they do not injure anyone, and people think that the large organizations can afford to lose the odd million pounds. Some people even admire computer thieves.

In America, computer crime probably costs about 300 million dollars. The average amount stolen in each fraud is about half a million dollars. In Britain the average fraud is much lower. It is probably about £30 000.

A lot of companies take many precautions to keep their goods secure but leave their computers unprotected. The staff are often trusted completely. Checking the computer is the last thing anyone thinks of.

The types of computer crimes are ingenious. For example, one employee programmed a computer to pay vast sums of money into a fictitious bank account. He also programmed it to return the money to its owners every time there was an audit (account check). All he stole was the interest. He was eventually caught because he put £15 000 on the horses every day. Some thieves in banks steal money held in dormant accounts. This is where someone has died and the account still has some money in it. There is no customer around to complain and people have got away with millions of pounds with the help of the computer.

Quite often, the person who is caught is only dismissed and those who are prosecuted only receive comparatively light sentences. Some companies do not prosecute computer criminals because they would then have to admit to losing a lot of money. This would be highly embarrassing to the large companies.

Test yourself

Using the words in the list below, copy out and complete sentences A to E underlining the words you have inserted. The words may be used more than once.

automated	privacy	DVLC
robots	unemployment	wrong

A When computers were first introduced people thought that they would lead to _____.

B More and more factories are now using _____ on their assembly lines. These factories are _____.

C Many people worry that a lot of personal information is held by computers. They worry that their _____ may be invaded.

D Quite often the information stored on a computer

is _____ and this can have severe consequences to the person involved.

E Two computers frequently used to catch criminals are the _____ and the PNC.

Things to do

1 a 'Making the computer the villain in the invasion of privacy simply diverts attention from the real dangers.'
      Briefly explain what you understand by this statement, including in your answer what is meant by 'invasion of privacy'.
      Give **two** examples and indicate why they are invasions of privacy. What are the real dangers?
   b 'Computers are continually being blamed for taking over jobs'
      Briefly explain why you agree/disagree.

2 In a few years from now, a large computer will have lots of details about our private lives stored on it. This computer will be used by the Government for a variety of things. No longer will people be able to avoid paying National **Insurance contributions and tax. They will know** every detail about us. As in the book Nineteen Eighty Four, Big Brother is watching you. They will even be able to find out if you own a dog by information obtained from the Supermarket's main computer. Dog licence avoidance will no longer be possible if you want to buy dog food from the supermarket.
   The above statement represents a rather pesimistic Nineteen Eighty Four type view of the future. How far is this statement true? Give any instances where information used for one purpose is used for other purposes. Discuss whether you think the above statement is justified. Give some situations where the transfer of information is a good thing.

3 'With the development and widespread use of computers many new jobs have appeared and many older jobs have disappeared.'
   a i Discuss briefly this statement, giving **four** reasons why this has happened.
      ii Give **two** examples of new jobs that have appeared and two examples of jobs that have disappeared as a result of this development.

   b i How is the computer likely to affect the job situation in the next ten years?
      ii Give an example of a job where you expect computers to play a more important part.
      iii Give an example of a job where the impact of computers is not so great.

4 Imagine you are the owner of an engineering company which employs about 30 people. You are thinking of buying a computer to improve your company's efficiency. The union is opposed to its introduction.
   a Write down and explain fully why the unions would be opposed to its introduction. Give **three** reasons.
   b Write a short speech which could be read to the staff to try to dispel their concern. Try to emphasize how the computer will improve the business and their working conditions.

5 a All large companies will keep files on employees, sometimes for long periods, so they can write references. Write down **two** departments in the company which would have access to these files. Other than name, address and telephone number, list three items of information that each department would have on the file.
   b Do you think it is right for the employee to be able to see the file? Explain your answer.
   c What guarantees should the company give to the employee regarding the privacy of this confidential information?

6 a It is generally accepted that personal data (data about people) which is stored in a computer system should be **accurate**, **secure** and **private**. With the help of examples, briefly explain the meanings of these three terms.
   b Computer systems used by government, local authorities and commercial organizations all store personal data. Describe **three** computer systems which use personal data and indicate any dangers which would arise if the data were not accurate, secure and private.

Full name	Address
Tel. no.	Years at above address
Single/married/divorced/widowed	
Religion	Politics
Any union membership?	If yes, which one?
Are they an active member of the above union if applicable?	
If yes, give any details on any danger to company.	
Do they own their own house?	
If yes, how much mortgage outstanding?	
Bank account number	
Have they ever been bankrupt?	
Salary	Tax code
Mother's and Father's occupations	

7   The above shows some of the items of
     information that could be held on a computer
     file by the personnel department.
     a Write down any of the questions which you
        feel would be an infringement of your
        privacy. Explain why you object and give
        reasons why you might not want the
        company to know the details.
     b Imagine you were the owner of the company
        and you were responsible for the design of
        the form. Write down some reasons for the
        inclusion of some of the more intrusive
        questions in the above form.

8   Mr Smith, a professional engineer, and his wife
     own their own home and have a teenage son
     who attends the 6th form of the local
     comprehensive school. Mrs Smith has had to
     take a part-time job as a shop assistant in order
     to meet the hire-purchase demand on their
     second car.
     a A number of computer files will refer to Mr
        Smith. Write down:

     i   **one** held by a government department;
     ii   **four** financial files (excluding gas and
          electricity);
     iii **one** of interest to the police;
     iv   **one** held by the local authority;
     v   **one** held by his employer.

9   It has been suggested that all persons over the
     age of 16 should be fingerprinted and the
     records kept on computer files. Whilst this
     would be very helpful to the police it is felt by
     some people that it is not a good idea.
     a Give **one** way in which this would help the
        police;
     b Do you consider it a good idea? Give **two**
        reasons for your answer.

10   A politician, in a speech, said the following:
     'In order fully to prepare pupils for life in a
     modern world, every pupil should be taught
     'Computer Studies'.'
     a Explain why you **either** agree or disagree
        with this statement.

b How are peoples' lives being affected by computers in:
  i   recreation,
  ii everyday life,
  iii employment?

11 The 'Computer Revolution' is frequently referred to as a problem which is imminent. Well meaning and authoritative articles are to be found warning of the social problems which will occur. The reality is that the revolution has been successful. Many businesses could not now function without their computers. Microcomputer automation in engineering has been found to be essential if firms are to remain competitive. Computer based information systems are available on everybody's television.

  a Name a business that is committed to the extent suggested in the above passage and explain why it would not be able to manage without computers.

  b Give an example of microcomputer automation and explain why it is more efficient than the system it replaced.

  c Name a system that provides computer based information via home television. State **two** advantages for people obtaining information in this way.

12 Distinguish between the privacy of information and the security of information giving one example of how each may be achieved.

13 Computer snooping
   The modern computer using control data banks is capable of storing vast amounts of information about individuals. The fear has arisen that this would be used for anti-social ends. The greatest alarm has been caused by the feeling that the computer will strengthen bureaucracy, enabling it to increase enormously the information it gathers about individuals, and to use that information in new ways.

By interrogating the central computer store, information on any citizen could be immediately retrieved and pointed out. There would be nothing new about the information stored; most of it was available to the diligent searcher before the use of data banks.

Bureaucracy criticized for so long because of its inefficiency is now coming under attack because it is about to become too efficient.

  a What is meant by a 'central data bank'?

  b Give **three** examples of information concerning the 'Average Citizen' which is stored, and can be used by a computer.

  c How can the information be used in 'new ways' to the
   i   advantage or
   ii disadvantage
   of the individual?

  d Give **one** advantage and **one** disadvantage of having information in a central data bank.

  e How could information be protected from unauthorized access?

  f Suggest conditions that both private and government users of data banks should be obliged to fulfil whenever personal files are created or updated.

14 The Metropolitan Police (London based police force) alone has access to computer files on more than 23 million of us, both in its 'C' computer and the Police National Computer. In the criminal computer there are 1.25 million Special Branch files on people who are not necessarily criminals nor even suspected of a crime.
   Comment on the above passage saying whether you consider it is a good or a bad thing that so much information is held about us, bearing in mind that the population of Great Britain is approximately 55 million.
   Why do they need this quantity of information? Give reasons.

29
The history of computers

Like many modern inventions, computers were not invented by an individual person, but by a series of different people. The developments in computers have been extremely rapid over the last ten years, but before then, they were a lot slower. It is hard actually to decide who made a significant contribution to the computer's development. Rather than go through all the people, we will just look at the people who made clear and significant contributions.

In the early days of computing, computers were really only calculating machines: they could only add or subtract. Quite often, they were mechanical rather than electronic devices, consisting of cogs and wheels which were very cumbersome and prone to breaking down. It is hard to believe that the sleek machines of today had such beginnings as these.

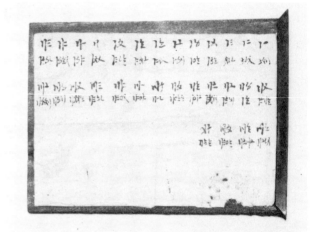

The early calculator machines: cogs and levers

There are many inventions which could be thought of as simple calculators, for example, Napier's Bones (or Rods), the Abacus and Logarithms (Figure 29.1). But these can't really be traced back from computers so we will start by looking at the earliest mechanical calculators which used cogs and levers for their operation.

Figure 29.1 *The Abacus and Napier's rods were the earliest calculating devices*

1647: Pascal's Arithmetic Machine

This was the first proper calculating machine and was invented by the French mathematician Blaise Pascal in 1647 (Figure 29.2). It consisted of a series of toothed wheels which were numbered 0 to 9 (Figure 29.3). When the wheel on the right hand side had been turned through one revolution, the wheel directly to the left advanced one number. This process was repeated for the other wheels. The machine was used for tax calculations but it was limited because it could only add or subtract.

1671: Leibniz's calculating machine

This machine was similar to Pascal's except that it was more complicated (Figures 29.4 and 29.5). As well as addition and subtraction, it could perform multiplication and division. In Leibniz's time the engineering skills needed to make the machine weren't available, but the mechanism still forms the basis of many of the earlier tills and calculating machines which are still used today.

Figure 29.2 *Blaise Pascal*

Figure 29.4 *G.W. Leibniz*

Figure 29.3 *Pascal's Arithmetic Machine*

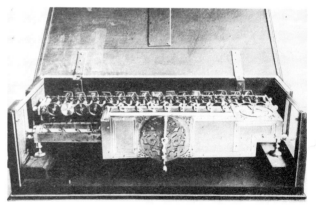

Figure 29.5 *Leibniz's calculating machine*

The beginning of data processing

The machines we have just looked at bore little resemblance to the modern day computer. Now we will look at some of the machines that were invented and developed to do more complicated tasks than just pure calculation. These machines were capable of performing a variety of tasks without human intervention. The trend moved away from

calculations to data processing. What was needed were machines capable of performing, automatically, a set of instructions. This is how the concept of a stored set of instructions started. These machines were the first truly automatic machines and could do many different tasks — much like the computers of today. Some of the machines resembled our present day computer controlled robots, except they were much cruder.

1804: Jacquard's Card-controlled Loom

Joseph Jacquard, a French textile manufacturer, developed a system which used punch cards for controlling a weaving loom (Figure 29.6). The punched cards were used to control the loom and also to determine the pattern to be woven. If the patterns had to be altered, new cards could be made.

Jacquard used the following bistable system for the following instructions: hole present meant that a warp thread had to be raised and no hole meant that it didn't need to be raised. By using Jacquard's Loom, more complicated patterns could be woven automatically.

Jacquard's idea of controlling a process was later put to use in the steam organ. The steam organ played tunes at fairgrounds and was controlled by a series of cards containing holes all joined together.

1822: Babbage's Difference Engine

Charles Babbage, an Englishman, was a controversial professor of mathematics at Cambridge University (Figure 29.7). He was a brilliant man. His first machine was the Difference Engine (Figure 29.8). This was used to make up various mathematical and astronomical tables. Up until then, these tables were unreliable. But Babbage's machine worked by the principle of differences which produced very accurate values. He did manage to build a small version of the difference engine, but the full size version was never built because his grant ran out.

1834: Babbage's Analytical Engine

Babbage's second machine, the Analytical Engine, was an ambitious affair, and was so complicated that it could not be built. It was the first machine that resembled the modern day computer because it had input devices, a processing unit and output devices. Babbage designed his machine so that it could be programmed to do a variety of tasks. He used Jacquard's idea, from card controlled looms, of using punched cards to instruct the machine (Figure 29.9).

Babbage's Analytical Engine was very much a 'Heath Robinson' contraption and it consisted of cogs, wheels, rods and levers. Although in theory, Babbage knew the machine would work, it could not be built at the time because it was so complicated and the engineers lacked the necessary skills.

When Babbage's funds from the government ran out, he had to finance his machine himself. The Countess of Lovelace, who was Lord Byron the poet's daughter, helped Charles Babbage in the programming of the Analytical Engine (Figure 29.10). But, since the machine couldn't be built at the

Figure 29.6 *Jacquard's Loom. The pattern woven into the cloth could be controlled automatically using punched cards*

Figure 29.8 *Babbage's Difference Engine*

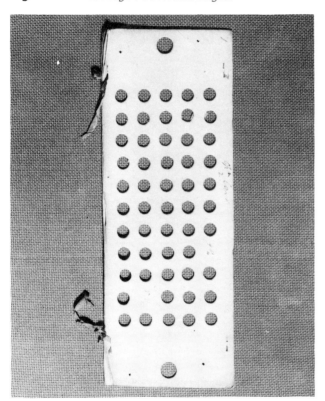

Figure 29.9 *The punched cards used by Babbage's Analytical Engine*

Figure 29.10 *The Countess of Lovelace*

Figure 29.11 *Babbage's Analytical Engine*

time, her programs could not be tested. Nevertheless, the Countess of Lovelace is considered as the first computer programmer.

Babbage worked on the Analytical Engine until his death and the machine was never made. However, seventy years later, at Harvard University in America,

Howard Aitken used electronics rather than mechanics to produce a machine which resembled the Analytical Engine in organization and processes (Figure 29.11). It was called the Automatic Sequence Controlled Calculator (ASCC), and it consisted of an extremely large number of parts. It was this machine that paved the way for the development of electronic calculating machines.

Although Babbage failed with his computing machines, he is still remembered for some inventions which we see today, such as the cowcatcher seen on some American trains and the black box recorder which records information which can be used to find the cause of a train crash.

Further developments in data processing with punched cards

1890: Hermann Hollerith's Pantograph Punch and Electrical Tabulator

Hollerith was a statistician who worked at the US Census Bureau (Figure 29.12). One of the problems

Figure 29.12 *Hermann Hollerith*

that the Census Bureau faced was that the 1890 Census was upon them and they hadn't finished working out the results of the previous census which took place in 1880. It was obvious to Hollerith that a new, quicker and more accurate method of obtaining the results needed to be found. A machine needed to be developed to perform this task.

Like his predecessors, Hollerith decided to use

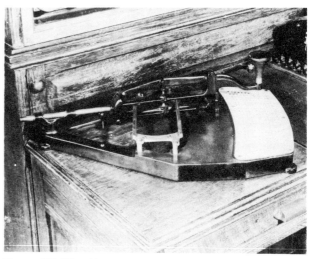

Figure 29.13 *Hollerith's Pantograph Punch*

punched cards to input the information. He developed a punch which could produce these punched cards (Figure 29.13). The information obtained from printed census forms was transferred onto punched cards using his punch. The cards were then placed through a device called a tabulator which sorted and processed the information as quickly as possible. Using Hollerith's machine, the results of the census were available in about half the time (Figure 29.14).

Date	Population	Time taken to complete census
1880	50 million	7 years
1890	63 million	3 years

Figure 29.14 *Hollerith's machine meant that the US census of 1890 took less than half the time taken to do the census of 1880*

The Hollerith tabulator was an electro-mechanical device and was very efficient and reasonably reliable. The success of Hollerith's machine led him to explore more uses for the machine. Automatic data processing became a reality, and later on, Hollerith became one of the founders of the largest computer manufacturers in the world, namely IBM. His assistant started the British company ICL.

Tabulators were used up until the 1960s when advances in electronics enabled electronic machines to be built which were smaller, cheaper and more reliable.

Some machines still use punched cards as a method of inputting information to the computer.

The development of electronics

Two of the problems with electro-mechanical devices is that they are very slow and, due to the vast number of moving parts, they are very unreliable. What was needed was a device which could act like a switch, but contained no moving parts and could work thousands of times faster. The thermonic valve was the answer (Figure 29.15). In 1946 the first electronic computers were developed. These early computers were extremely large. Because of the large quantities of electricity they used, they produced huge quantities of heat and needed to be kept in air conditioned rooms.

Much of the work on thermonic valves took place during World War II where they were used for breaking codes and calculating ballistic tables for shells and rockets. The development of the thermonic valve paved the way for the development of many electronic machines. Here are some of them.

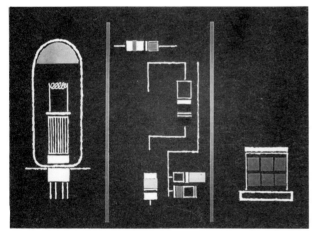

Figure 29.15 *The developments of electronics. First there were valves (left), then transistors (centre) and then the chip (right)*

1943: Colossus

Colossus was a machine used to break secret German codes during World War II. It was used to break the top secret German ENIGMA code. Colossus had 15 000 valves and used paper tape for the program.

1946: Electronic Numerical Integrator and Calculator (ENIAC)

This was a machine used to calculate the paths that bombs or rockets would take. Again, valves were used.

Figure 29.16 *EDSAC 1 at Cambridge University*

1949: Electronic Delay Storage Automatic Computer (ESDAC)

This machine was the first computer to use a stored program (Figure 29.16).

Many other machines followed these – here are a few of the more famous ones.

1946: The Von Neumann Report

Because the designing of computers seemed to be going off in all directions, Von Neumann decided that certain criteria should be met by all computers:

1   Data and instructions should always be represented as binary codes. They should be treated identically and stored together and should occupy the same storage space.
2   The computer should be able to process both the data and the instructions.

1951: LYONS ELECTRONIC OFFICE (LEO)

LEO was the world's first commercial computer. It was made for the commercial food company, Lyons. Quite a few of these models were built. Cards or paper tape were used as input.

1951: UNIVAC

UNIVAC stands for Universal Accounting Machine. The first UNIVAC machine was used for working out the USA census. Later machines were used for accounting purposes.

All the computers we have just looked at can be classified under the heading of 'The first generation of computers'.

The second generation of computers

The first generation of computers were unreliable, bulky and slow. It must have come as a great relief to the computer designers, when the transistor was invented in 1948 at the Bell laboratories. The transistor replaced the earlier valves which were very inefficient.

Transistors work in an identical way to valves, and they have the advantage that they are cheaper, much smaller, more reliable and they consume much less power. Transistors are bistable devices; they only have two stable states. This means that they operate in much the same way as an ordinary switch.

Another development which improved computers was the development of **core storage**. **Core stores** contained rows of small ring magnets that could be magnetized in an anticlockwise or a clockwise direction (Figure 29.17). Core stores were used inside the central processing unit to store the information.

As more storage was needed, ways of storing information outside the CPU were looked into. **Backing storage** was the answer. This consisted of magnetic disks, drum cards and tape, which could store the additional information. Before this, paper tape or cards were used for the input or output of information. This was slow and bulky, so the new methods of storage greatly improved computer efficiency.

During the second generation of computers there were more business users. Computers were no longer just used by universities or research establishments. The second generation computers were much more flexible than their predecessors. The computer manufacturers decided that they would build computers in **modular** form. This was called **modular construction**. Each module would have a specific purpose. Then they could be combined together to form a computer system which would satisfy the computer users' needs. There were modules available for processing, storage, input and output. The advantage of modular construction is that the system can be expanded if necessary. Also, modules from different computer manufacturers can be put together. It is possible to use the best CPU with the best VDU, and so on.

Figure 29.17 *A section of core store*

Computer language development

While advances in computer hardware were happening computer languages were being developed to run on the machines. The earlier computers had to be programmed using a long series of binary codes (called **machine code**). This was a very difficult and laborious task. What was needed was an easy to understand computer language which used words and symbols similar to the ones used in mathematics and English. These easy to understand languages were called **high level languages**. They included FORTRAN, COBOL, RPG II and ALGOL.

1964 onwards: The third generation of computers

The third generation computers used integrated circuitry. Transistors and all the other electronic components needed could be produced in a single crystal. Then large scale integrated (LSI) circuits were developed which could contain over 1000 components. These circuits were all contained on a very small piece of silicon called a **chip**.

The development of integrated circuits meant that computers became much smaller, cheaper and reliable. Computers that previously would have occupied a room the size of a classroom, could now be placed inside a briefcase.

The development of the chip

The development of the silicon chip has led to a huge increase in the use of computers. It is hard now to imagine life without computers. Because chips can be produced cheaply, in vast quantities, they are now in all sorts of devices. Cars, televisions, washing machines, record players, toys and many more can all work more efficiently if chips are used to control them.

Computers in the future

It has always been difficult to predict the future of any invention. Computers are no exception. One thing is certain, as computers become smaller and cheaper their applications will increase. One area in which there has been rapid growth recently, is in telecommunications. This is probably an area which will change greatly. In the future every home will probably have a computer linked to the television set and linked to a telephone line. This system will operate in much the same way as the PRESTEL system. From this computer, we will be able to order goods, contact the bank etc. We may not even have to go to work; it may be possible to do all our work at home!

As the growth of computers and robots increases, the social problems will also increase. Ways of dealing with the unemployment problem will have to be looked at. Our society in the future is likely to be greatly different from today's.

Test yourself

Using the words in the list below, copy out and complete sentences A to J underlining the words you have inserted.

transistors   Hollerith   punched cards
Analytical   Von Neumann   modules
Arithmetic Machine   divide   chips
modular construction   Lovelace   IBM
Babbage   ENIAC   Jacquard   cogs
Pascal   Leibnitz's

A   The first calculating machine was invented by _____. It was called the _____ _____ and consisted of many _____ and wheels.
B   _____ Calculating Machine could multiply and _____ as well as add and subtract.
C   A French textile manufacturer called _____ used _____ _____ to control his looms.
D   In 1822, Charles _____ invented the Difference Engine. His _____ Engine designed in 1834 was so complicated that it could not be built.
E   Babbage was helped by the Countess of

_____ who became the first computer programmer.
F   Hermann _____ invented a tabulator which could process the American Census results very quickly. He went on to form the American computer company, _____ which is the largest computer company in the world.
G   Colussus, _____ and ESDAC were computers which made use of electronics rather than mechanics.
H   The _____ _____ report laid down criteria for computer design.
I   _____ were used by the second generation of computers. They were built in _____ and this was called _____ _____.
J   The third generation of computers had _____ which made them fast, reliable, cheap and compact.

Things to do

1   Which of the following men helped in the development of computers?
   a   Pythagoras
   b   Babbage
   c   Erasmus
   d   Rousseau

2   a   Describe the developments, since 1946, which have made computers both easier to use and more reliable. Your answer should cover aspects of both hardware and software, indicating broadly the order in which these developments occurred.
   b   The use of punchcards and paper tape as input media is diminishing. Outline **two** of the developments that are causing this to happen.

3   Which of the following designed the Analytical Engine?
   a   Lovelace
   b   Babbage
   c   Hollerith
   d   Jacquard
   e   Stephenson

4   What electronic components distinguish the first three generations of computers?

5   Who invented the weaving loom with punched cards?

6 Copy and complete this crossword on the history of computers using the clues below.

Across

1 The first counting frame.
5 Inventor of the Difference Engine.
6 The name of the German secret code broken by the Colossus computer.
7 A programming language used for business purposes.
8 University in the USA where Aitken invented the automatic sequence control calculator.
12 Name of a table used as a calculating aid.
13 Inventor of an arithmetic machine consisting of toothed wheels.
15 The man who invented logarithms and a series of rods to help in multiplication.
18 The material Napier used for his rods.
19 The World's largest computer company.
20 _____ circuit. Another name for a chip.
21 First computer to use a stored program.
22 Abbreviation for large scale integration.

Down

1 One of Babbage's engines.
2 Hollerith invented his machine to cope with this immense task.
3 This man built a card controlled loom.
4 Abbreviation for first electronic office.
5 Type of algebra invented by George Boole.
7 A small integrated circuit etched onto a slice of silicon.
9 The early computers contained lots of these.
10 A programming language.
11 Aitken's machine.
14 Last four letters of the surname of the first computer programmer.
16 The computer used to calculate paths of shells fired by a gun.
17 A Napier _____.
18 Name of the laboratories where the first transistor was invented.

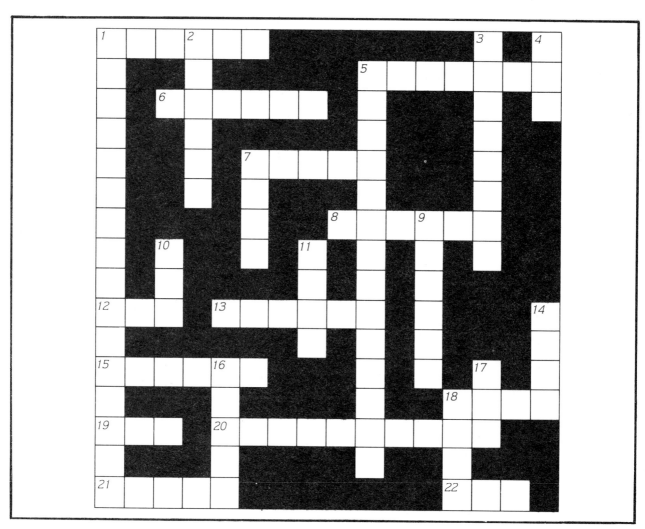

7 State the main contribution of each of the following people in the development of computing:
   a Pascal
   b Babbage
   c Jacquard
   d Hollerith

8 Early electronic computers were used for which of these?
   a Stock control
   b Payroll analysis
   c Solving mathematical problems
   d Controlling traffic lights
   e Aircraft seat booking

9 a State the name of the first known calculating aid.
   b Name the main component which characterized second generation computers.

10 Why was the introduction of punched cards in the late 19th century so important to the subsequent development of information processing?

11 The worlds's first commercial computer called LEO, was used in England by which company?

12 What is the name of the electronic components used in the logic circuits of first generation computers?

13 Charles Babbage designed two computing machines. One was called the 'Difference Engine'. What was the name of the other, which could be programmed using punched cards?

14 a Why were the computers of the late 1940s unreliable?
    b Why have computers become smaller and more powerful since the 1940s?
    c Explain briefly what contribution the following made to the development of computers:
       i   Jacquard
       ii   Countess Lovelace
       iii LEO (Lyons Electronic Office)
       iv   ENIAC

15 a i   State **one** characteristic of a first generation computer.
       ii   State **two** characteristics of a second generation computer.
       iii State **two** characterisitics of a third generation computer.
    b There have been several major developments in computing since 1945. Choose **three** of the following areas and for each describe how it has changed since 1945:
       i   Computer languages
       ii   Operating systems
       iii Memory devices
       iv   Peripherals

16 Since the first generation of computers was developed in the late 1940s, progress in computer technology has been rapid. For each generation of computer, outline the main technological developments and explain how the needs of commerce and industry led to the changes.
    With the aid of examples show how these developments have extended the range of computer applications.

17 Read the following passage written in the early 1950s and answer the questions given below.
    'If a computer is made very small it becomes increasingly difficult both to build and service it, except in certain special cases, there is little to be gained by reducing the bulk of a machine beyond a certain point; nevertheless, once ninety per cent of the valves in a machine can be replaced by other components which are both smaller and cooler, we can well imagine that the computer of the future will be smaller, more reliable, more compact, and that it will use less power that we shall come to regard as the rather primitive and temperamental devices of today.' (Faster than thought, p. 99).
    a Describe the developments in technology that have enabled the valves in the early computer 'to be replaced by other components which are both smaller and cooler'.
    b Do you think that the predictions made above have been fulfilled. Discuss, with examples the reasons for your answer.
    c Give an example of an application of computers which have been made possible **only** because computers have become 'more reliable and more compact'.

18 You have been asked to write an article for the school magazine describing the development of the computer since 1945. You decide to split your article into two equal parts:
a the development of computer hardware, and
b the development of computer software.
Write a description of the main points you would include in your article.

19 'The advent of chip technology and microprocessor systems has brought the world of computers nearer to the man in the street'. Discuss this statement with reference to size, availability and cost of computers, their usage and other relevant information.

20 'Because of their cheapness and versatility, microprocessors and microcomputers are being used in an increasing number and variety of applications. It is likely that by the end of the 1980s, the large mainframe computer will have become extinct.'
a Describe **four** ways in which microprocessors/microcomputers are being used. Indicate the effect, if any, which each of these applications is having on the use of large mainframe computers.
b Comment on the suggestion, made in the quotation above, that by the end of the 1980s no large mainframe computers will be in use.

30
Computer applications

Computers and the police force

Crime has become very sophisticated and, as a result of this, harder to detect. To handle this, the police now have very sophisticated methods of crime detection. 'Information' is the key word in crime detection and this information must be accurate and obtained quickly.

To obtain immediate access to up-to-date information about crime and criminals, computers are used. The old manual systems were far too slow and, in 1968, the Police National Computer Unit was set up in Hendon to provide all the various police forces throughout the country with fast, up-to-date information.

The Police National Computer (PNC) and its background

The Police National computer (PNC) now provides quick access, day and night, information of national as well as local significance to all the police forces in England, Scotland and Wales. The Police National Computer is situated at Hendon. It is linked to terminals in police stations all over the country. The linking is done via the telephone systems, using modems. There is a large number of terminals attached to the main computer so there is a fairly complex switching mechanism which allows each terminal to obtain information from the main computer in as short a time as possible.

The information held on the PNC is separated into indexes. Each deals with a particular subject. It is possible for some crossreferencing between these indexes. By looking at a particular index, a policeman can obtain any relevant information and also find out where to get further information. We will now look at some of these indexes.

Stolen and Suspect Vehicle Index
One crime which has increased tremendously over the last few years is car theft. Every day hundreds of cars are stolen. Some are only taken for joy rides and are recovered by the Police fairly quickly. Others are stolen permanently and are re-sold and some are stripped down for their parts. Often, cars are stolen and used in other crimes.

As soon as the owner reports that the car is missing information such as registration number, make and colour are keyed into the Police National Computer via one of the many terminals. Once this information has been obtained, it is transmitted via radio to the patrol cars who are then on the lookout.

The index is divided into two parts. Firstly, there is the index of registration numbers and, secondly, an index of engine and chassis numbers. The first index is used more often, but when cars are involved in a crime, they quite often have false plates and so the second index is used to identify them.

If only part of a registration number is known, it is possible for the computer to produce a list of possible vehicles. Stolen contractors' plant and marine engines are also contained in this index.

Vehicle Owner Index
The information for this index comes from the Driver and Vehicle Licensing Centre at Swansea (DVLC). The index contains all the names and addresses of the registered keepers of motor vehicles, together with descriptions of the vehicles.

If the registration number is known, then the owner can be contacted if the car is stolen without the owner knowing. Again, if the number is only partially known, it can still be traced.

It is possible for the Stolen and Suspect Vehicles Index and the Vehicle Owner Index to be searched together, using the registration number as the search key.

Fingerprints Index
The Fingerprints Index is a coded version of the National Fingerprint Collection which is held by the police at New Scotland Yard.

Any person who has been convicted of a crime will have his fingerprints held on this index. It is used to check the identity of prints found at the scene of a crime with prints of people who have been convicted before.

Names Indexes
The Police have records in these indexes of people who fall into any of the following categories:
1 Persons convicted of serious offences.
2 Persons wanted or sought by the Police for various reasons.

3   Persons missing or found.
4   Disqualified drivers.

As soon as the Police receive details about any person who falls into one or more of the above categories, they can obtain the information from the PNC. Once they have this information, they can then decide whether they need more information. These indexes also tell the user where to obtain further, more detailed information.

The computer can assist the Police greatly by informing them if a suspected person is likely to be armed or dangerous. It is also possible for the computer to search all the files simultaneously to find out anything known about a particular person.

Other uses of the PNC

Other than the indexes, the PNC is also used to help the Police in other ways.

Broadcast system

This is a system by which one Police Force can send urgent information to other Police Forces. The clever thing about this system is that the PNC can choose the particular Forces which should be told the information. If a car is stolen and used in a serious crime, then all the Police Forces along a certain stretch of motorway can be alerted. Ports and airports can also be alerted using this system to stop criminals escaping to another country.

Crossreference system

The PNC can also help to find information which is not on its files by telling the user, by a reference number, how they can obtain the details from a particular Police Station.

Other computers used by the Police

Most of the Police Forces now have their own computers in their Police Headquarters. These computers are used for administrative work but some are used to help to solve crimes.

At the moment the Essex Police are trying out a £600 000 system called MIRIAM (Major Incident Room Index and Action Management). This computer will be used to contain information from enquiries about serious crimes, so that senior officers can decide how to go about their investigations. (Figure 30.1). It is hoped that MIRIAM will enable criminals such as the Yorkshire Ripper, who evaded capture for

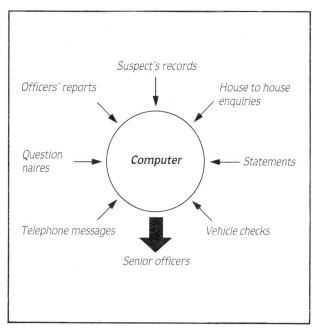

Figure 30.1   *How MIRIAM sorts out all the information from a large scale enquiry so that the senior officers can make decisions about how to solve the crime*

five years, to be caught much sooner.

If the Essex Police find MIRIAM effective then the Home Office will look into the possibility of every Police Force having one. Figure 30.2 shows a command control system used by one of Britain's Police Forces.

Computers and traffic control

Computers are also used by the Police for the control

Figure 30.2   *A command control system used by one of Britain's police forces*

of traffic. Junctions which have caused problems due to traffic jams often have computer controlled traffic light systems. The computer can control which lights should be given priority due to the build up of traffic. By quickly analysing the numbers of cars which are approaching the lights, it can decide how long the lights should stay red or green. Using this method prevents traffic building up at trouble spots.

In case accidents happen at these spots, it is possible for the computerized system to be overriden using a manual system. You have probably seen cameras at some of the large road junctions. The Police use these cameras to watch the position of the traffic so that if an accident happens, the lights can be altered manually.

Computers in medicine

Nearly all the hospitals in the National Health Service now have computers. Because of the diverse nature of the work that hospitals do, the computer has lots of quite different uses.

Records of patients

Computers can be used to provide a complete, accurate, up-to-date, and readily available source of information about patients' health. Records of patients are usually kept for the duration of their life, so in the past a large amount of space was taken up by paperwork. There were also problems in finding a particular patient's file.

Most hospitals now store patients' records on magnetic tapes or disks. The information can be found immediately by the computer. There are terminals at certain places in the hospital. The doctors or nurses can find details on a patient very quickly.

Inpatients' records are probably best kept on magnetic disk. This method allows quicker access because it is a random access storage medium. These records will be needed much more often than the outpatients' records. Outpatients' records contain a large quantity of information that may only be used a couple of times in a patient's lifetime. So these records can be stored on magnetic tape which the computer may take some minutes to find.

New information can be added to the patients' records by keying the information into the computer via a terminal. So the patient's record can be kept up-to-date with the latest information about his condition or circumstances.

Doctors and nurses used to spend about 30% of their time processing information in files, but now this has been vastly reduced because of the introduction of computers.

One problem with using a computer like this is that very confidential information is kept about the patient. Obviously, the patient would not like this information to be seen by anyone. One way round this problem is to introduce a code or a password which the user needs to type into the computer before she can gain access to the patients' files. Another way, used in some of the extremely complicated systems, is to only allow the terminals a certain amount of necessary information for different users. So, a nurse could obtain some information and a doctor would be able to get further details.

Figure 30.3 shows how a computer system could be used in a hospital laboratory.

Monitoring instruments

In Intensive Care Units, computers are used to monitor instruments which record important data about the patient. If the data moves outside a certain limit, an alarm is sounded so that immediate medical help can be sought.

The measurements constantly taken by the computer would include blood pressure, pulse rate, heart waveshape from an ECG, respiration rate and volume, and electrical signals from the brain. Previously, this information needed to be taken so regularly that a nurse was needed for each patient. Now many more patients can be looked after by one nurse.

Computers are also used to monitor vital measurements during surgery in the operating theatre.

Diagnosis

Computers can be used to locate tumours at an early stage when they can be detected most easily. Body scanners are used which send rays into the human body (Figure 30.4).

After passing into the human body the rays are picked up by a detector. Signals from the detector are analysed by the computer and are connected to a digital form which can then be displayed as a picture on a television screen (Figure 30.5). On the screen the tumour appears as a dark patch.

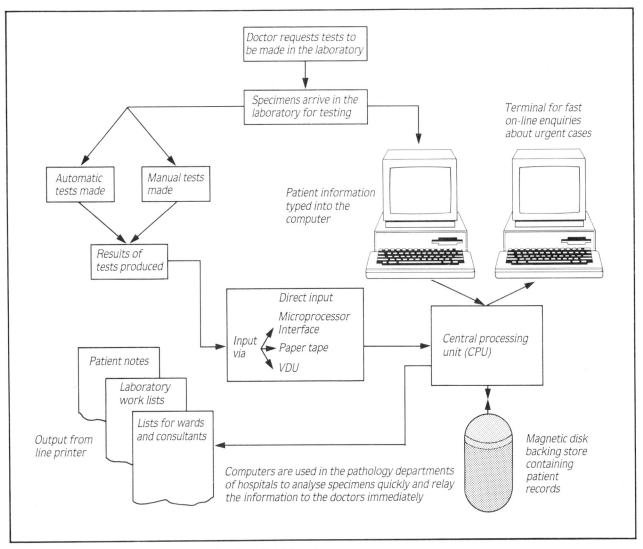

Figure 30.3 *Using a computer system in a hospital laboratory*

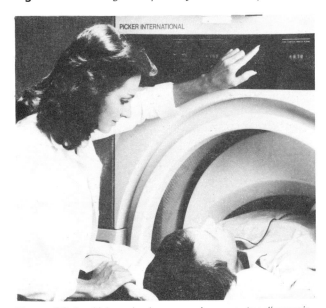

Figure 30.4 *Using a body scanner in computer diagnosis*

Figure 30.5 *Information from the scanner is used to build up a picture of a section of the human brain. If there are any tumours these can then be detected*

Computers and the family doctor

A doctor's diagnosis of what is wrong with a patient depends a great deal on how good the doctor's memory is, in other words how much information he can remember. Computers can help doctors make a better diagnosis because they contain more information than a doctor's short term memory.

An average doctor diagnoses correctly for about 50 – 60% of the time. Using a computer diagnosis is 70 – 90% accurate. So when computers are used in doctors' surgeries they help give more accurate diagnoses. This means that consultants (specialist doctors) are needed less.

Starting to use a computer in a doctor's surgery is not an easy task. In an average practice with four doctors there will be about 10 000 patients. To begin with, all the notes of the patients will have to be typed into the computer. An average record for a patient has about 1500 characters. So for 10 000 patients the computer will need 15 megabytes of storage. This means removable disk packs or fixed disk packs will have to be used for storage. The system will cost more than £10 000, so it is not cheap.

Figure 30.6 shows a family doctor using a computer to keep his patients' records.

Use in the Supplies Office

Most hospital supply departments contain terminals which are linked to a central computer usually situated at the Regional Health Authorities Headquarters.

Figure 30.6 *A family doctor using a computer to keep his patients' records*

All data about orders needed by the hospital and the deliveries received, are entered into the terminal where they are transferred to the headquarters via telephone lines. Once the hospital stocks fall below a certain level, they are automatically re-ordered by the computer. This prevents the possibility of running out of a certain drug, which could prove fatal.

Computers in dentistry

Britain has 15 000 dentists and these dentists have to cope with the nation's dental care. Vast quantities of records are kept about each patient. A lot of the information is about individual teeth. If you consider that every person can have a mouthful of up to 32 teeth, you will see that the problem of storing the information manually, is vast!

One of the main headaches for the dentist is keeping track of their appointments. Computers are now being used by several dental practices to keep computerized diaries.

After a course of treatment the dentist has the job of working out how much the National Health owes him. To do this, the dentist fills in a form which he sends to the NHS. What the dentist would like to do is to send the information direct to the National Health Service computer via telephone cables, and then receive payment.

Computers in dental practices are rare at the moment, but the Government is introducing a scheme which will partly finance computers for dentistry. When this scheme goes ahead most practices will have computers.

Computers in farming

You probably think that a farm is the last place where you will find a computer. You are wrong! Computers on farms are not new. They have been used to control sophisticated machinery for cutting and spraying crops. In one farm, the first call of the day is not the cowshed for milking, but the computer.

One of the main aims of modern farming is to achieve the maximum amount of produce from the smallest amount of land. In order to do this, much use needs to be made of fertilizers and insecticides. The computer is used to help make decisions about amounts of fertilizers used etc. Already 1000 farmers use computers to help run their farms more

Figure 30.7 *Computers in farming*

efficiently. The computer software allows the computer to ask the farmer certain questions, and it then uses the answers to these questions to make decisions. These questions include 'has he checked the rainfall?', 'has he checked the growth rate of wheat?' and 'has he found the number of slugs per square metre?' etc. (Figure 30.7). One user of a computer managed to get himself into the *Guinness Book of Records* by producing the largest crop of winter wheat from a certain area of land.

More and more farmers are using computers and, in the future, a computer will be as common as a tractor on the farm.

Weather forecasting

Modern weather forecasting is very sophisticated and more accurate than it was in the past. To produce accurate weather forecasts, a great amount of data needs to be collected and assimilated. The data is collected from weather stations, weather ships, aircraft, airports and satellites that are situated all around the world. This data is usually in the form of figures such as air pressure, humidity, temperature, wind speed and cloud cover. All this data is used to produce an accurate weather forecast. Some of the data will have calculations performed on it. Because of the complexity of some of the calculations and the speed at which they need to be performed, a very powerful computer is needed. The Meteorological Office at Bracknell, Berkshire, produces weather forecasts for this country and other countries. They use an IBM computer 24 hours per day. It can perform one million instructions per second.

Weather records are also stored on the computer. This means it is possible to find out whether the weather situation was the same in previous years. This information can be used to predict weather trends.

The computer can also produce weather charts using a graph plotter connected to the computer.

Computers have helped to change weather forecasting from a hit or miss affair into a precise science.

Local Authorities

Local Authorities handle huge amounts of money and have many responsibilities. They are responsible for administration, and spending money on housing, fire brigades, police services, child welfare and town planning. In order to run these various departments economically and efficiently, computers are used to handle and process the large amounts of data required. Nearly all Local Authorities in Britain now have their own computers.

Computers and banking

Banking was one of the first industries to use computers. A lot of the banking services we now take for granted, such as credit cards, would be impossible without computers.

Recently banks have put tills into their outside walls. This means that now we can get money from these automatic cash dispensers at any time of the day and at weekends (Figure 30.8).

Banking is a very competitive business. Banks are constantly looking for new ways of providing more customer service and increasing staff productivity. At the moment some of the banks are looking at ways of providing loans and savings facilities using computers. This would mean smaller buildings could be used and less staff would be needed.

In the future banks will probably be self-service, like shops. The work will not be done by the bank staff but by the customer.

In Germany, a bank is carrying out an experiment that allows customers to check their bank balances, move money from one account to another and order cash to be sent through the post. The customers do this at home, using a system similar to Prestel that links a terminal in the home to a central computer at the bank. Two New York banks are also looking at this system.

Computer systems in Lloyds Bank

Lloyds handle customers' transactions through approximately 4000 terminals which use 6 CPUs. This system cost well over £50 million to buy. These terminals include the 1000 Cashpoint cash dispensers. This is the largest network of cash dispensers in the world.

Automated teller machine systems (ATMS)

Automated teller machine systems (ATMS) can be seen outside a lot of banks (Figure 30.9). They are currently called Cash Dispensers. They are linked to a central computer. Although they do give out cash, they can also perform other tasks. You can use these machines to obtain bank statements on current accounts and some of them allow you to order a new cheque book.

Soon it will be possible to obtain information on deposit and loan accounts. In the future the ATMS will also be able to allow the customer to move money from one account to another.

To get money from an ATMS you put a plastic card into the machine. Then you type your secret customer identity number, then you type in what service you require and tell the machine how much money you require. If you have the money in your account, the machine will dispense it. If you are overdrawn and do not have the money to cover the amount, the machine will keep your card and not give you the money.

Electronic fund transfer

Electronic fund transfer (EFT) is a modern banking system that transfers money from one place to another. It works instantly so it saves time in clearing

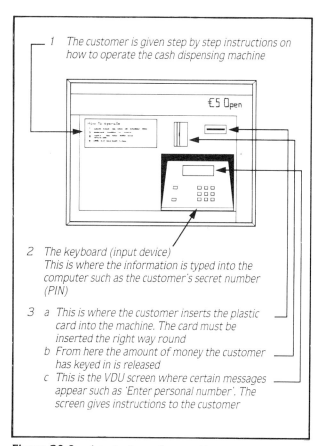

1 The customer is given step by step instructions on how to operate the cash dispensing machine

£5 Open

2 The keyboard (input device)
This is where the information is typed into the computer such as the customer's secret number (PIN)

3 a This is where the customer inserts the plastic card into the machine. The card must be inserted the right way round
b From here the amount of money the customer has keyed in is released
c This is the VDU screen where certain messages appear such as 'Enter personal number'. The screen gives instructions to the customer

Figure 30.8 *Automatic cash dispensers provide customers with banking services 24 hours a day and 7 days a week*

Figure 30.9 *A cash dispensing machine*

Figure 30.10 *This disk at the top of the Post Office Tower in London sends and receives messages to and from satellites. This means that computer information can be sent anywhere in the world at the speed of light*

Figure 30.11 *Using the Homelink service. Information is keyed in using the remote control keypad. The modem on top of the TV set connects up to the Homelink computer via the telephone lines*

Figure 30.12 *Electronic Funds Transfer from home. The Homelink service provided by the Nottingham Building Society and the Bank of Scotland allows customers to transfer money from the building society to the bank and vice versa*

cheques and doing paperwork.

EFT is used extensively by the international banks. It means that they can immediately transfer funds to a country where it will earn the best rate of interest. Because of electronic fund transfer, money can now be passed around the world by satellites, at the speed of light (Figure 30.10).

In America, electronic fund transfer is used in supermarkets and petrol stations. The customer puts his card into a special till and the money is automatically, and instantly, transferred from the customer's account. This avoids the necessary paperwork involved with the normal credit card.

The Nottingham Building Society and the Bank of Scotland have a system which allows EFT from home (Figure 30.11). Customers can transfer money from their building society to the bank and vice versa (Figure 30.12).

EFT will eventually replace the need for a vast and expensive network of bank branches. Very little paperwork needs to be done with this system so more time can be taken up with customer problems and the more important work.

The electronic fund transfer system is extremely expensive but can obtain its savings very quickly.

The main clearing banks are working together to develop a system called a **point of sale** system. This will allow customers to walk into a supermarket and pay for groceries with a plastic debit card linked to the customer's current account.

The Society for Worldwide Inter-bank Financial Telecommunications (SWIFT)

SWIFT is an organization owned by 900 banks. It is based in Brussels.

At the moment, 39 countries use this system. The system can handle 290 000 transactions per day. The

Figure 30.13 *Many millions of pounds of foreign currencies are bought and sold by Williams and Glyn's Bank each day using sophisticated computers and telecommunications equipment*

system connects all the member banks' computer systems together using telephone lines and satellites (Figure 30.13).

It is extremely expensive to be a member of SWIFT so only the larger banks can afford to use it.

One of the problems of passing information through telephone lines is security. It is fairly easy to intercept a telephone message and also information from the computer can be gained in the same way. The way around this problem is to **scramble** (mix up) the information whilst it is going through the telephone lines and then convert it back again at the other end. This is called **encoding**. It is done by a machine similar to a modem.

The main computers of the SWIFT system are situated in several places and are duplicated in case any break down. They are not all in the same place for security reasons; if there is a fire, not all the computers will be affected.

The future – a cashless society

In spite of credit cards, we still make about 95% of our total payments for goods or services in cash. A future without the use of any form of cash is unlikely, but in the next few years we will probably see more payments being made without using cash.

Machines have now been developed which can read and understand handwriting. This will make document handling much easier. These machines are not in use at the moment but machines are being used that can understand printed characters optically rather than magnetically. These machines use **OCR** (**optical character recognition**) rather than the method used for reading cheques: (**MICR**) **magnetic ink character recognition**.

Advantages

One of the main advantages of looking towards a cashless society is that it will not be necessary to draw large sums of money out of the bank to make large purchases. This leads to less risk of being robbed. It also avoids the inconvenience of having to draw out money from the bank all the time, after waiting in queues. Credit cards allow people to buy goods and then to decide whether to pay for them at the end of the month or to obtain them on credit paying a portion each month.

Disadvantages

One of the main disadvantages that a cashless society could bring is that it would be very easy to spend more than you can really afford. Most transactions would be done by credit card and since this money is 'money on paper' people might spend more on purchases than they would if they were using cash.

Another disadvantage is fraud. In America, the New York police arrested a number of people who were running a school for credit card fraud. The school instructed pupils in how to steal credit cards, read the codes for the credit limits and how to alter the card by ironing down the existing number and embossing it with a new one. Fraud with credit cards has become more widespread recently because credit cards can now be used to obtain money from some cash dispensers if the thief has the person's personal identification number (PIN).

At the moment, a lot of research is being done into ways of overcoming the problems of fraud using credit cards. Some machines that can detect mistakes in signatures have been introduced but they can be unreliable because people's handwriting can vary slightly. Other machines can detect voice patterns to identify a person. When all these problems have been ironed out, we should see a large increase in the use of these cards.

Computers in libraries

You may be lucky enough to have a computer in your local library. Libraries use computers for many different tasks.

Recording details when books are loaned and returned

Borrowing books

The most popular method for recording details about borrowings is the system which uses bar codes on the books and on the borrower's ticket. The black and white stripes correspond to a code which the computer can understand. The numbers and letters of the code can be seen above the bar code in Figure 30.14. They are there in case the bar codes get damaged. If this happens the code could be typed into the computer using a small keyboard.

The last two digits on the bar code are check digits. When the wand reader is passed across the bar code, the computer automatically does a small calculation with all the other numbers. The result should give the last two numbers. If it doesn't then a light will flash. Usually when the bar code reader is passed along the bar code there is a sound. There is one type of sound which tells the librarian that the code has been read correctly and another which tells her that it hasn't (Figure 30.15).

Once both bar codes have been read then the details are passed to a transaction file at the computer centre which may be in one of the libraries (Figure 30.16).

Returning the books

Returning books is more simple because the borrower's ticket is not needed as the computer already knows that the borrower has the book. When the book is returned another wand reader is passed across the bar code and this automatically tells the computer that the book has been returned. If the book has been reserved by someone else then a light will flash. This tells the librarian that she must put the book to one side.

Books can be renewed by phone if a person hasn't finished reading them. When this happens the librarian types in the bar code via a terminal and then the computer extends the length of the loan.

Reserving books

Reserving books is easy. The book code is typed into

Figure 30.14 *The bar code on a library ticket. The last two digits of the borrower's code number are used as check digits*

Figure 30.15 *Taking a book out of the library*

the terminal and the computer will then automatically alert the librarian when the book is returned so that she won't loan out the book to someone else. Figure 30.17 shows a librarian using a terminal.

Sending out reminders on overdue books

Information about books out on loan is contained in the Loans Master File. Before sending out reminders the computer needs to consult the Borrowers' Master File. This contains information about the borrowers e.g. names and addresses. Reminders are usually sent out once a week using a computerized system.

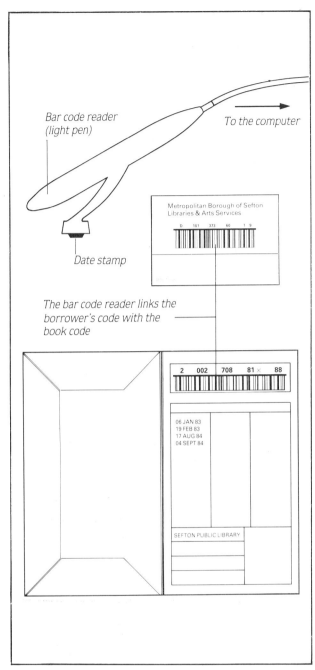

Figure 30.16 *Recording the details when a book is borrowed*

Figure 30.17 *Using a terminal in a library. These terminals can be used for enquiries about books and also for reserving books*

If the library doesn't have the book, then another library in the area may have it. The librarian can check this at the library's terminal too.

Recording details about new members

Libraries keep library cards with bar codes on them. Each new member is given one of these after his name and address has been filled in on the card.

Before joining a library you will be asked to fill in a form. This form is used as a source document for input to the computer. Normally the form will have these fields:
Name
Address
Some indication as to whether the borrower is a child
The borrower's library code (this is above the barcode)

All the details about members are held on the Members' Master File. Information about new members is added to a Members' Transaction File which is sorted into order and then used to update the Members' Master File at the end of the week. Some computers give details about members who have not used their tickets for a few years so that they can be deleted so as not to take up valuable computer space.

Cataloguing of books

All libraries have catalogues of their books. Sometimes the catalogue consists of cards with information about each book which are kept in lots of drawers. Computers can make cataloguing a lot easier.

Locating books

Suppose someone wants to look at or borrow a particular book. First the librarian will access the library's Book Master File. If the library has the book it may be out on loan. Instead of going to the shelf to see if the book is out, the librarian can check the Loans Master File. This is done at the library's terminal.

New books are constantly coming in and these have to be recorded. Also old and tatty books will be taken out of service. When each new book arrives it is given a bar code. These bar codes are prepared in advance just like borrowers' bar codes. Additions and deletions of books are recorded by the librarian onto a Book Transaction File. At the end of each week the Book Transaction File is sorted into book code number order and used to update the Book Master File. This is shown in Figure 30.18. Notice in the diagram that after the information about the book is entered via the keyboard and VDU that it is validated to make sure that it is correct. All the files are sorted into book number order. The reason for this is that in this system magnetic tape is used. If the details are not in order then the tape will have to be continually rewound when the file is being updated.

Microfilm and microfiche

Catalogues of all the books a library have are usually contained on microfilm or microfiche. This is because large quantities of information can be kept in a very small space. The film is updated every month when new additions and deletions of books are made.

Privacy

Libraries could keep records about what books a particular person reads. This would be very time consuming. This information could be interesting to a potential employer.

Borrower's names and addresses are on the Borrowers' Master File. This could be sold to an outside organization e.g. a book club which could send unwanted mail.

It is also possible to sort borrowers into groups according to what sort of books they borrow. So it would be possible for this information to be passed on to a manufacturer. This could mean that, for example, a manufacturer of greenhouses would send out information to everyone who borrowed gardening books.

It is very unlikely that any of these things actually happen. But, they are possible. The councils who control the libraries need to make sure that this doesn't happen.

Computers in supermarkets

Supermarkets can keep their prices low by high productivity. In other words they must have the

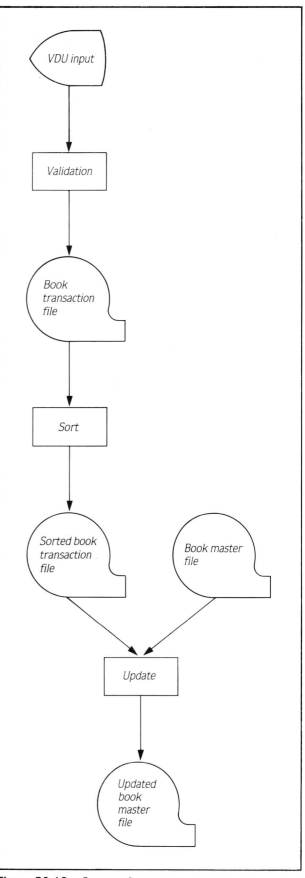

Figure 30.18 *Systems flowchart for updating the Book Master File*

correct goods on their shelves and must never run out of fast selling items. Also they must keep costs down by employing as few staff as possible. It is not surprising that they use computers to help them.

When you reach the check-out counter of a supermarket you are given a sales slip (receipt) which records your purchases. Some systems in British supermarkets allow the assistant at the check-out point (till) to calculate and record a customer's purchases very quickly. Each item on the shelves is marked with a special bar code. This is used to give information about the product including the price. The check-out assistant passes each item over a scanner unit. This reads the bar code and transmits the information to the store's computer. Some systems use a light pen which is passed over the bar code but the other method is used more because it is quicker (Figure 30.19).

The store computer is programmed to use the information from the scanner to do a number of different supermarket jobs. A few seconds after a customer's last purchase has been read in at the check-out point, the computer can define each item bought, total the prices, print out a detailed sales slip for the customer and use the same information to update the warehouse stock list (Figure 30.20).

Point of sales terminals

A point of sale terminal is a computer terminal placed on the counter where the goods are sold. These are expensive, so only larger supermarket chains such as Tesco, Sainsbury and Co-op stores use them. Point of sale terminals are input devices, consisting of a drawer to contain the money, a light pen or a light sensitive screen on the counter, a visual display unit and a printer which prints out a receipt for the customer.

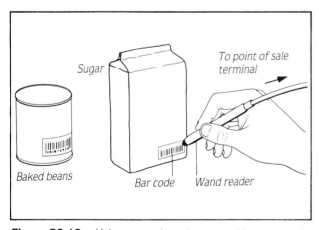

Figure 30.19 *Using a wand reader to read bar codes of goods*

```
       ***        VICTOR VALUE        ***

               CARRIER BAG              .03
               PLAIN CRISPS             .27½
               SLOT    4741             .47
               WHTE BAP 4PK             .24
               COOK-IN-SCE              .44
               STWBY YOGURT             .14½
               STWBY YOGURT             .14½
               QTR POUNDER              .76
               DUSTBIN LINE             .14½
               DUSTERS                  .22
               RITZ                     .27½
               TOM KETCHUP              .41½
               FUDGE BROWNI             .56
               DISINFECTANT             .59
               TINY TIM.                .35
               CRNISH PASTY             .36
               SAVOURY RICE             .39
               BALANCE DUE             5.81

               CASH                   10.00

               CHANGE DUE              4.19

       11/08/84 13:41 9184 0001   1       1009
          **  THANK YOU - COME AGAIN  **
```

Figure 30.20 *An itemized receipt from a point of sale terminal*

The POS terminal is connected to the computer inside a store by a cable. Because the computer will often have to deal with large numbers of these terminals, a hardware device called a multiplexer is used to share the time allocated to each terminal by the CPU. Some of the bigger stores have one central computer, usually in their Head Office. Information gets to this computer along telephone lines.

Bar codes

Bar codes are the thick and thin lines you see on most goods. A bar code reader or a light pen is used to read the code contained in these lines into the computer. The computer has already been told what this code means. Using the product code the computer can link this code with the price of the article. The price is not contained in the code itself because if the store wanted to change the price it would mean giving the product a new bar code. Some goods do not have bar codes on them. For these a code could be keyed in using the keyboard. The information which the computer can obtain by reading a bar code is shown in Figure 30.21. The stripes represent a 13 digit code number. No information about price or sell by date is contained in the code itself.

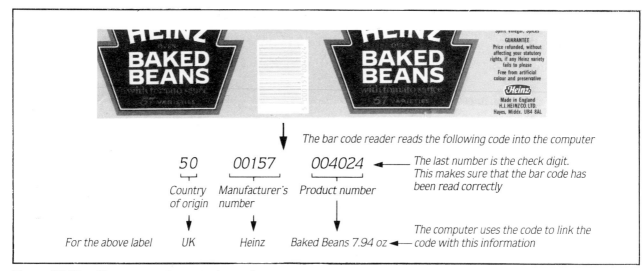

Figure 30.21 *How a computer uses a bar code*

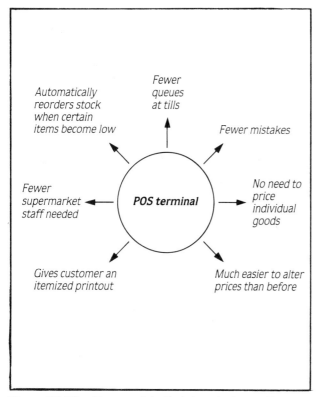

Figure 30.22 *How a point of sale terminal saves time and money*

*Some uses of point of sale terminals*_____

Buying stock
After an item has been bought at the POS terminal the computer automatically deducts it from stock. When the stock reaches a certain level the computer can automatically order more stock from the manufacturers.

The media (e.g. TV and radio) are responsible for large fluctuations in demand for certain items.

Fashions are constantly changing, rumours of shortage cause panic buying, and some items are in demand only at certain times (e.g. Easter eggs). Supermarkets have to respond to these things very quickly. The computer can provide quick up-to-date information on what's selling. Things that aren't selling well can be spotted and items can be chosen for sales promotions. The effect of all this on the shop is an increase in the amount of profit the shop makes.

Tracking productivity
The computer can produce reports on the productivity of the sales staff. This could include a list of the total value of sales and returns for each of the sales staff over a period of time. This can be used to compare departments or members of staff. Some stores might use this information to pay staff a commission.

Accounts
The computer can also be used to produce the accounts of the store.

Figure 30.22 shows how a point of sale terminal saves time and money.

*Bar codes and the shopper*_____

Advantages
1 Due to an increase in speed there will be fewer queues at the tills. This means that the shopper won't have to wait so long.
2 With an increase in productivity it may be possible to lower the prices.

3 The supermarket can offer a greater variety of items and they are less likely to run out of things because their stocktaking is more efficient.
4 The shopper gets an itemized receipt showing the items and the prices.
5 The POS terminal makes fewer mistakes because information doesn't need to be typed in.

Disadvantages

1 It is easier for the shops to alter prices. Before POS terminals they would have to alter the price tags on every item. With the new system they only have to key a few numbers into the computer.
2 As there is no need to price individual articles it is harder for shoppers to keep track of how much they have spent.
3 Some customers, particularly older ones, may not like the system because they don't understand it.

Other methods of data capture used in shops

Kimball tags
Kimball tags are mainly used by shops that sell clothing. When you buy an item the assistant removes the Kimball tag. These are collected and at the end of the week they are batched together and sent to the computer for processing. A Kimball tag is a small punched card with information about the product e.g. size and colour. They are used for stock control.

Magnetic tags
These are labels which have magnetic stripes on them. The magnetic stripe contains the same information that would be held on a Kimball tag. The information is read using a special wand reader.

Test yourself

Using the words in the lists below copy out and complete the sentences. The words may be used more than once.

Police

owner   indexes   traffic   MIRIAM
modems   fingerprints   DVLC

A   The Police National Computer based at Hendon is connected to terminals in police stations throughout the British Isles via telephone lines using _____.
B   The PNC is separated into _____.
C   The vehicle _____ index comes from the _____ at Swansea.
D   A new police system called _____ is used by Essex police to help solve serious crimes.
E   Computers can also be used to control _____ in large cities.
F   The national _____ collection is also held on computer at New Scotland Yard.

Medicine, farming and weather forecasting

control   fertilizers   tape   code
disk   diagnosis   graphplotter   calculations

A   Hospitals use computers to keep information about patients. Inpatients' records are held on magnetic _____ whereas outpatients' records can be held on magnetic _____ because they are only needed now and again.
B   So that only certain people can look at confidential patient files a _____ has to be keyed in before the computer can be used.
C   Computers can be used to _____ instruments in intensive care units.
D   Computer _____ is used to detect illness at an early stage.
E   Computers are used on farms to give information about amounts of _____ to use on their land.
F   Computers are used for weather forecasting because they can do lots of complicated _____ in a small time.
G   Weather charts can be produced using a _____ connected to the computer.

Banks and libraries

plastic   secret   check   cash dispensers
code   keyboard   magnetic   ATMS   EFT
terminals   microfilm   book   bar code

A Banks now use _____ _____ which allow customers to obtain money at any time including weekends.

B Cash dispensers or _____ are also used for obtaining bank statements and ordering cheque books.

C To use one of these machines a _____ card is inserted into the machine. The card has a _____ stripe on it. A _____ number is typed in along with how much money you need. The machine then gives you your money and returns the card.

D _____ is a modern banking system which can transfer money from one place to another without any paperwork.

E The most up-to-date library system uses a _____ _____ system.

F A series of black and white lines represent a _____.

G If the bar code gets damaged then the code can be input via a _____.

H The last two numbers in the code are _____ digits.

I The computer links the _____ code with the borrower's code.

J _____ are used for enquiries about books as well as reserving books.

K Catalogues of the books are often kept on _____ or microfiche.

Supermarkets

desk   re-order   bar code   Kimball
point of sale   productivity   checking
thirteen   relationship   light pen   priced
deducts   magnetic   CPU   productivity
accounts   itemized   check   increase

A Supermarkets can keep prices low by high _____ .

B Most items in a supermarket now have series of lines on their labels. This is called a _____ _____ .

C A bar code reader is usually set into the _____ and the goods are passed across it. Sometimes a _____ _____ is used instead.

D The terminal at the check-out point is called a _____ _____ _____ terminal.

E The POS terminals are connected to a central _____ .

F The lines that make up a bar code are used to represent a _____ digit code.

G The last number on the right of the code is the _____ digit. It bears a numerical _____ to the other numbers in the code.

H Using a POS terminal, when an item is sold the computer automatically _____ it from stock.

I When an item of stock becomes low the computer will automatically _____ it.

J The computer along with the POS terminal can also be used for _____ productivity of the staff and preparing the store's _____ .

K An advantage of using a POS terminal is that the customer gets an _____ receipt.

L Prices should be lower because of the greater _____ of the store.

M A possible disadvantage for the customer is that the individual article may not be _____ so it is harder for customers to keep track of their spending.

N Also, it is easier for the shops to _____ prices.

O Other data methods used in shops include _____ tags and _____ tags.

Things to do

1 Explain what the following abbreviations mean with reference to computers used in banking. For each one, explain how banking efficiency is improved using them:
  a MICR
  b OCR
  c SWIFT
  d EFT

2 Name **two** 'real time' applications of a computer.

3 a Name an application which would use COM.
  b Name an application which would use an OCR.

4 Describe a banking application which you have studied. Include in your answer:
  a The reasons for having a computerized banking system.
  b A description of the methods used for inputting data.

c Reference to the file storage media used.

d A sample description of a customer record.

e A description of a method used to reduce the risk of error when an enquiry is made by a branch of a bank for the balance of a customer's account.

5 Small computers now find more frequent application in places such as medical centres.

a Why should such a place find it helpful to use a computer?

b What type of backing storage would be used and why should this type be chosen?

c What changes would there be to the job of the receptionist?

d Write a list of the sort of information which the centre would keep on file about the patients.

6 Describe how **four** of the following people might come into contact with computers in their jobs:

a A person operating a supermarket checkout.

b A travel agent.

c A company director.

d A policeman.

e A British Leyland car worker.

f A secretary.

7 You will have seen banking machines operating through the walls of the banks in our high streets.

a Explain what these machines do.

b What do the initials ATMS mean?

c In addition to dispensing cash what other banking jobs can they do?

d Do you think people prefer to use these machines? Explain your answer.

e Outline the advantages and any disadvantages which these machines have over the normal banking services offered inside a bank.

8 **a** Describe **three** ways in which computer systems have been used in the Health Service. (You should include details of hardware used and how people, doctors and nurses make use of the system.)

b What are the benefits gained by doctors, nurses and patients in using the system you have described?

9 Computers are affecting more and more aspects of everyday life. Select **two** applications from the following list. Briefly describe what each does giving its benefits and its drawbacks:

a A wordprocessor system

b A credit card system

c 'Instant cash' machines outside banks

d Traffic control (for example, road signs/traffic lights)

10 Choose **two** of the following and explain one way in which their work could be assisted by the use of a computer:

a A civil engineer designing a motorway bridge

b A weather forecaster

c A bank cashier

d Police attending an accident involving a lorry carrying a poisonous substance

11 Draw a diagram of a cheque. Label on the cheque the following things:

a The individual account number

b The name and address of the bank (make up an address)

c The serial number of the cheque

d The sorting code number of the branch

e The space where the magnetic ink characters are placed

Why aren't the magnetic ink characters placed on the cheque like the rest of the other numbers? What information is contained within these numbers?

12 Some computer experts believe that because computer systems are so successful in dealing with money transfers that it would be possible for society to completely do away with cash (coins and notes).

a Name **three** different ways, other than cash, of paying for goods or services.

b Describe what part the computer system plays in making the money transfer in one of the ways you have named.

c It is certainly possible to design computer systems which would enable society to do away with cash but it is very unlikely that a 'cashless society' will occur in the near future. Give **two** reasons why this is so.

13 **a** Describe an application of computers in each of the following:

a *Local government* b *Education*
c *Hospitals*
Your descriptions should include how the computer is used in this application, what input/output devices and backing stores might be found. In each case, you should give **one** *reason why the use of a computer is better than a manual system. Name* **one** *other field in which computers have been applied.*

14 *Name and briefly describe* **two** *examples of large data banks (or data bases) where personal details of many individuals are kept. Using these two examples, state the advantage of such data banks to:*
a *The organization using the data bank*
b *An individual*
Describe what steps might be taken to ensure the accuracy of the data in these data banks.

15 *The use of computers has affected many people. Choose* **two** *from the following list pf people and describe how the increased use of computers has affected their lives:*
a *A patient in a hospital*
b *A housewife*
c *A criminal*

16 *Describe how a computerized library system would record details of:*
a *Books in stock*
b *Borrowers*
c *Loans and returns*

17 *A lending library uses a computer to hold details of its books and of its users. It keeps two files, the book file and the user file. The book file has details of every book in the library, and the user file has details of every user.*
The system:
allows users to reserve library books which are on loan to someone else
checks when books are returned, to see if they have been reserved by someone else
sends out reminders on overdue books
checks that a borrower is not trying to take more books than he is allowed
Answer the following questions about this system:
a *What kind of backing store would be most suitable for this application?*

b *Name* **two** *other peripherals which would be needed.*
c *Apart from the name of each book and its author and publisher, give* **four** *other items of information which would be kept in each record of the book file.*
d *Apart from the name and address and other personal details, give* **two** *other items of information which would be kept in each record of the user file.*
e *How would each file be updated when a user borrowed a book?*
f *How would each file be updated when a user returned a book?*
g *What would happen when a user wanted to reserve a book?*
h *How would reminders about overdue books be prepared?*

18 *A local County Library Service has decided to install a computer system. It decides on an in-line real-time system with terminals in each of the 15 branch libraries linked to the main-frame at Library Headquarters. The* **system is designed to control lending and** *borrowing as well as book re-ordering and receiving.*
a *State what hardware would be suitable in each branch library and say why.*
b *Explain suitable methods of collecting data in the following situations:*
  i *When a customer borrows a book*
  ii *When a book is returned*
  iii *When a new book is introduced to a branch library*
c *State* **three** *files that would be needed at headquarters indicating their contents and the purpose they serve.*
d *Give* **two** *advantages of this system over a manual system for:*
  i *Customers using the library*
  ii *Running the County Library Service*

19 *Hitworth Public Library uses a computer in the administration of its book lending service. The computer files used for this include a file of data about borrowers and a file of data about books in the library.*
a *A record for a borrower includes five fields:*
  the name of the borrower
  the address of the borrower
  a field to indicate whether the borrower is a

child
the borrower's library number
the number of books which may be
borrowed at any one time

  i These details are written on a
pre-printed form which is then used for
entering the data in the computer, via a
visual display unit which has a screen of
20 lines, each of 40 characters. Design a
suitable form for this.

  ii Other fields in a borrower's record relate
to the books currently held by the
borrower. Each book is known by its
number, which is assigned by the library.
The file of data about the borrower is
updated regularly. Describe the various
types of transaction which will be part of
the updating process.

b i If the system is used in real-time mode,
state what checks should be made before
a book is issued to a borrower.

  ii State, with reasons, the file medium the
library would use in the real-time system.

20 Many supermarkets are now using
computerized tills, called point of sale terminals.
Each point of sale terminal has a wand reader
connected to it which is used to read the bar
codes on the goods. The terminals are able to
produce an itemized receipt for the customer.
The terminals are connected to a main
computer and when an item is sold the
computer automatically deducts it from stock.
The computer is able to produce important
management information on which lines are
selling well etc. Some systems automatically
re-order goods from the suppliers when stocks
are low.

a Explain why point of sale terminals will help
the shop to improve efficiency.

b Explain **two** advantages it will have for the
customer.

c What is a bar code and how is it used?

d The bar code reader (wand reader) is a direct
form of data capture. What does this mean
and what advantage does it have over
indirect data capture?

e Although the computer can tell the manager
of the shop when items of stock are low,
periodic stocktaking may still be required due
to losses due to shop lifting and pilfering by
staff. Explain why the computer is unable to
take account of these losses.

f Some customers are worried that it is far too
easy to alter prices using this system. Explain
why their fears will be justified.

g Give **two** jobs that the supermarket staff will
not have to do that the computer will do
automatically.

21 **a** Where in a supermarket would you find a
point of sale device sometimes called a POS
device?

b Other than a keyboard, what kind of input
device might it use?

c What sort of information is read by the input
device?

d How is the information represented?

e List **three** things that the point of sale device
prints out for the customer.

f What additional information does the point
of sale device give specially to help the person
who operates it?

g How does the point of sale device help to
maintain the correct level of stock?

h Describe briefly how the stock control system
would work.

22 Shoppers in the North West have reacted with
hostility to the use of bar codes in
supermarkets.

a Describe briefly **three** practical
disadvantages to the shoppers.

b List **three** advantages to management, and
three advantages to shoppers in the use of
bar codes.

c List **three** items of information which are
contained within a bar code.

23 Read the following passage:

'In a shop, a microprocessor is incorporated into a cash till which is used as a point of sale terminal and is connected on-line to a central mainframe computer. Details of each sale are validated by the terminal before transmission to the mainframe where the data is used immediately to update the master stock file and calculate statistical information. The central computer is connected in this way to approximately 100 shops. After the shops close for the day, the central computer processes the updated stock file to produce new stock reports and other management information.'

Answer the following questions:

a State, giving a reason, the type of file access which would be suitable for the master stock file.

b Name and describe **two** possible reports produced by the central computer which would be of use to management.

c Describe **two** security methods that could be used, one for each of the following cases:
  i in case of corruption of the master stock file;
  ii in case of a breakdown in the telecommunications network.

d In the context of this application, why is it necessary to validate the sales data?

24 A food and drink wholesale warehouse uses a computer stock control system. The goods have labels on them and a cashier types in data from the labels at a terminal. A bill like the one below is produced by the computer, for each registered customer.

a State **two** data items on the bill below that the cashier types in from reading a label on the goods themselves.

b Why would those items be on labels on the goods?

c Give **two** different items of information that would be printed onto the bill direct from the computer.

d Explain what the numbers 464 and 1357 indicate and suggest information that the company obtains by including them on the bill.

e Give **two** separate benefits this system has for the customer.

f Give **two** different benefits this system has for the wholesale warehouse.

g Explain how the collection of data could be automated.

```
   ALLIANCE CASH & CARRY     BRANCH 464
      WILSON ROAD, HUYTON, LIVERPOOL
   TEL 051 489 4421    VAT  222 3640 04


 INVOICE NO.  00954               3/ 8/81
          CUSTOMER.NO.     1357



  1 ð  0.96    064  A    BACON      0.96
  1 ð  1.15    151  B    SHERRY     1.15
  2 ð  0.85    129  A    CHEESE     1.70
  1 ð  2.59    086  B    SHERRY     2.59
  1 ð  0.99    076  B    LEMONADE   0.99
  1 ð  2.47    099  A    MEAT       2.47

                        GOODS TOTAL 9.86

     GDS A  5.13 ð  0.00%   0.00
     GDS B  4.73 ð 15.00%   0.71
                      TAX TOTAL   0.71


                      SALES TOTAL 10.57
                        =====
```

31
Revision

Revising

Most people think of revision as just reading notes and trying to remember them. This is true to some extent but there are some ways of revising more effectively. We will look at some ways of revising and some of the likely questions you would want to ask about revision.

Where should you revise?

Choose a room where there will be no distractions. Work at a table or desk, make sure that there is a bright light on the table and that the room is warm. Some students like to work in a local library. This is quite a good idea but there can be distractions, such as people moving around. However, there won't be the other distractions that you have at home such as brothers, sisters, radios and TVs. Try to work in silence. Your revision will be a lot more effective and you will not need to revise for as long (Figure 31.1).

You should make a timetable and decide how long to revise for, then you will have earned your free time. Planned breaks in revision increase the amount of information you retain.

Figure 31.2 *Revision should be a constant process throughout the course*

How often to revise

Revision should be a constant process throughout the two years of your course (Figure 31.2). Try not to leave your revision to the few weeks before the exam. Divide your work into topics and then revise a topic at a time. Don't move on to a new topic until you have mastered the old one. It is better to have a thorough knowledge of a few topics than a skimpy knowledge of the whole syllabus.

When is the best time to revise?

Most people are at their peak early in the morning. Near exam time try to get up earlier. If you are on holiday then early morning is an ideal time because you will have fewer distractions from other people in the house. Early evening is a good time, before you get tired.

Figure 31.1 *It is important to revise in the right surroundings*

What shall I revise?

Ideally it would be best if you could revise the whole syllabus. If you have difficulty with certain topics then it is possible to leave them out, but if you do this you have to make sure that you understand the other topics really well because you will be relying on them.

Make a revision checklist like the one in Figure 31.3 and tick off the topics as you master them.

The syllabus and past papers

It will help a lot if you can get your own copy of the examination syllabus (Figure 31.4). Ask your teacher for a copy or write to the examination board for a list of their publications. Your teacher will be able to tell you what board and syllabus you are doing, and their address. Then you can buy your own copy and, at the same time, some recent examination papers. You may

---

Revision checklist

Input and output devices
○ Punched cards and tape and their devices
○ Magnetic ink character reader
○ Mark sense reader
○ Line printers
○ VDU
○ Graphic display unit and light pen
○ Point of sale terminal

Backing storage
○ Magnetic disk
○ Magnetic tape
○ Serial (sequential) or direct (random) access

Data and source errors
○ Transcription and transposition errors
○ Verification and validation
○ Error checks (hash, field, check digits, etc)

Operating systems
○ Batch, multiprogramming, multi-access
○ Real time, timesharing

Output formats
○ Standard forms, microfiche, microfilm
○ Digital/analogue converter

The CPU
○ Three parts
○ LSI and chips
○ ROM and RAM
○ PROM and EPROM
○ The microprocessor

Computer arithmetic
○ Base 2 (binary)
○ Base 8 (octal)
○ Base 16 (hexadecimal)
○ Conversion from base 16 to base 2
○ Conversion from base 8 to base 2

○ Conversion from base 2 to base 8
○ Conversion from base 16 to base 2
○ Conversion from base 2 to base 16
○ Binary arithmetic
○ Sign and magnitude coding
○ Twos complement coding
○ Subtraction with twos complement coding

Bits, bytes and words
○ Parity checks
○ Accumulators, registers and buffers
○ Half and full adders

Computer logic
○ Gates and operation tables
○ Boolean expressions

Organization of data
○ Bits, characters, fields, records
○ Files, keyfields
○ Sorting and merging
○ Master files and transaction files
○ Grandfather/father/son principle

Computer languages
○ High and low level languages
○ Machine code

Systems software
○ Translation software
○ Compilers, assemblers and interpreters
○ Executive or supervisor program

Applications software
○ Software houses
○ Documentation
○ Software costs
○ Program libraries

People who work with computers
○ Systems analysts
○ Programmers
○ Computer operators
○ Data preparation officers
○ File librarian
○ Other staff

Adopting a computer system
○ Systems analysis and project approval
○ Design, training, writing manuals
○ Implementation
○ Parallel and pilot running
○ Monitoring the live system

Security of the system
○ Tapping of phone lines
○ Alteration of data by staff
○ Damage by staff or other people
○ Ways of making files secure
○ Accidental erasure

Computer applications
○ Police
○ Medicine
○ Dentistry
○ Farming
○ Weatherforecasting

○ Local authorities
○ Banking
○ Libraries
○ Shops

Wordprocessing
○ Advantages and disadvantages
○ Hardware needed
○ Software

Communication networks
○ Prestel
○ Ceefax and Oracle
○ Differences between Teletext and Prestel
○ Electronic mail

The social implications of computers
○ Effects on employment
○ Privacy
○ Exchange of information
○ Computers and crime

History of computers
○ First generation computers
○ Second generation computers
○ Third generation computers
○ The chip

Figure 31.3 *A revision checklist*

find that your local library will have copies of these publications. If you can't find them, ask the librarian in the reference section.

Near the time of the exam check to see how much of the syllabus you have covered. Sometimes your teacher may not have time to cover the whole syllabus. If this happens, look at your syllabus to see which parts have been left out. You could then study the missing parts on your own. Having a set of past papers will enable you to see the way the exam is set out. You can familiarize yourself with the structure of the paper (i.e. the form of the questions and the number you have to do) (Figure 31.5).

You can use the exam papers as an aid to your revision. Give yourself mock exams to see how your revision is going. Check your answers using this book or ask your teacher to have a look at them. Once you can answer most of the questions from the past papers, you will have nothing to fear about the actual exam.

CERTIFICATE OF SECONDARY EDUCATION
Syllabuses
FOR THE
1984 and 1985 Examinations

PRICE
30p
postage free

F | COMPUTER STUDIES

THE WEST MIDLANDS EXAMINATIONS BOARD
Norfolk House, Smallbrook Queensway, Birmingham B5 4NJ

Figure 31.4 *A syllabus is helpful*

```
Joint Matriculation Board
_____

General Certificate of Education
_____


Computer Studies Ordinary
_____


Thursday 9 June 1983   1-30—4


Surname ..............................................

Other names .........................................

Centre number .......................................

Name of centre ......................................





Careless work and untidy work will be penalised.

Answer all the questions in Section A and three questions from Section B.

Details of work, including rough work, must be shown where appropriate.
```

Tie loosely any supplementary sheets you use to the back of this answer book before handing it to the Supervisor

	Do not write in this column
A	
B 9	
B 10	
B 11	
B 12	
Total	

Figure 31.5 *The front of the exam paper will look like this*

Preparing for the exam

Using the glossary

At the back of this book you will find a **glossary**. This is a sort of dictionary of computer words, with their meanings. Whenever you meet a word that you don't understand, look it up in the glossary. This is good revision and will reinforce your knowledge of the subject. You will find that several of the smaller questions will ask you what is meant by certain computer terms. It is a good idea to try to learn all the words in the glossary. You will then be able to use them in the larger, essay style questions as well as being able to answer the smaller questions.

Learning the glossary

Find some paper or cardboard and cut it into rectangular pieces about the size of a playing card. Take two cards at once. Write a computer term on one card and its meaning on the other (Figure 31.6). Shuffle all the cards and then try to match the terms with their meanings. Check them using the glossary.

Program	A set of instructions that the computer can understand

Figure 31.6 *Make up revision cards like this*

Overlapping areas

You might find that you do number bases in maths as well as in this subject. You can kill two birds with one stone if you revise this section thoroughly.

Planning an essay style answer

Some examination questions (usually in section B) require a larger, essay style answer. It is important when answering this sort of question not to lose track of what the original question was about. A lot of students lose marks because they stray off the subject. To avoid this, it is a very good idea to use a plan before you start your essay. Generally, all the best essays are based on some sort of plan. Without a plan it becomes very difficult to include all the facts. The examiners will have a list of facts which should have been covered in the essay. They cannot give you marks unless your essay includes these facts, no matter how much you write.

So, what is a plan and how do you do one? The best way to answer this is to look at a particular question and then devise a plan for it. The question we shall use to illustrate this is one on *The Social Implications of Computers*. Most students will tend to waffle when they do an essay on this topic. To keep to the question and include all the relevant facts it is essential to use a plan.

Question

Write an essay on the problems that have been caused by the introduction of computers and state their effect on our society. How might some of these problems be solved or turned into advantages?

Plan

A plan for this question could be set out like Figure 31.7. Once the plan has been written you can elaborate on it and join it together to form the final essay. You will then have a very good essay which contains all the relevant facts without too much unnecessary padding.

There are parts of the syllabus for which you will never be asked to write an essay style answer.

You might find it useful when you revise to write brief notes in plan form. They help you to remember all the important facts. Once you have remembered the headings then it becomes a lot easier to remember the other parts.

Figure 31.7 *An essay plan*

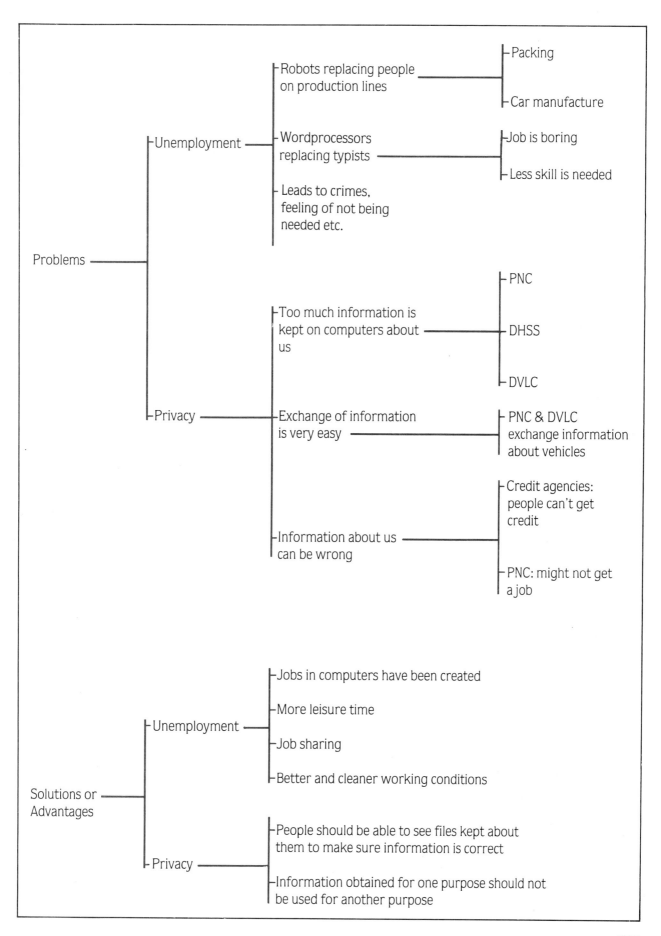

Problems

- Unemployment
  - Robots replacing people on production lines
    - Packing
    - Car manufacture
  - Wordprocessors replacing typists
    - Job is boring
    - Less skill is needed
  - Leads to crimes, feeling of not being needed etc.
- Privacy
  - Too much information is kept on computers about us
    - PNC
    - DHSS
    - DVLC
  - Exchange of information is very easy
    - PNC & DVLC exchange information about vehicles
  - Information about us can be wrong
    - Credit agencies: people can't get credit
    - PNC: might not get a job

Solutions or Advantages

- Unemployment
  - Jobs in computers have been created
  - More leisure time
  - Job sharing
  - Better and cleaner working conditions
- Privacy
  - People should be able to see files kept about them to make sure information is correct
  - Information obtained for one purpose should not be used for another purpose

Things to check just before the exam

1 Collect the necessary equipment: two pens, in case one dries up; two pencils; a sharpener; a rubber and a ruler. You may be allowed to use a flowchart template but check first. You probably won't be allowed to use one with the names of the boxes on it.
2 Always take a watch into the exam. There will be a clock in the exam room but if you are at the back of the room you might not be able to see it.
3 Go to the toilet before the exam; this avoids the embarrassment of having to leave the room under supervision.
4 Check to see if you have to wear school uniform (Figure 31.8).

Figure 31.8 *Find out if you should wear school uniform*

Things to check in the exam room

1 Check that you have the correct exam paper in front of you. Several exams might be going on at the same time.
2 Check that there are not any pages missing from the paper. It is not unknown for some of the pages to be blank. If there is anything wrong with the paper, such as your not being able to read the print, then you should ask for a new paper.

The actual exam

The following list gives some hints on things you should do when actually taking the exam.

1 Always read the instructions on the front of the paper carefully. Check the number of questions that you need to answer from each section and the time that you should spend on each section.
2 Answer the correct number of questions from each section. If the paper says answer 3 questions from Section B and you answer 5 then you will have wasted your time. The first 3 questions will probably be marked and these may not necessarily be your best questions.
3 Have a good look at all the questions before you start and, where you have a choice, choose the questions carefully.
4 When you have made your choice of questions, read the whole of each question, not just part of it. It may be that there is part of the question that you cannot answer and you could answer another one much better.
5 Time yourself. Don't spend too much time on a question that you are good at, at the expense of other questions.
6 Try to write neatly. The examiners have hundreds of scripts to mark and it is not worth risking annoying an examiner by making him waste his time deciphering an untidy script.
7 Number your questions carefully and correctly, including all the relevant subsections.
8 Only do what the question asks. If it asks for two reasons, make sure that you give two; not three or one. Always check that in an answer to a question that has two parts, you have not written similar answers to both parts. If you do, you will only be marked on one of them.
9 After you have answered a question, read it through again to make sure that you have not missed part of it out.
10 Plan your essays in the way suggested in this chapter.

Project work

All the examinations in computer studies require some sort of project to be done. Sometimes the marks for the project can make up as much as 50% of the total exam mark. More usually it is about 25 – 30%. In most cases the project will be marked by your teacher and then marked again at a moderators' meeting where the moderator checks that the projects have been marked to a similar standard.

To find out about the number of marks for the project and the type of project you have to do, check your syllabus or ask your teacher.

Most of the exam boards require that a project involving programming should be done. Normally you will have to write fully documented programs which illustrate a variety of programming techniques.

Sometimes the exam board allows non-programming projects which are usually of the following type. Sometimes coursework is a combination, involving some programming. We will now look at the non-programming coursework.

Essays

Some boards require a number of coursework essays. Usually you have to write about a particular computer installation you have seen or read about. Other topics can include the social implications of computers. Each essay usually needs to be about 1000 words long. You might have to write an essay on a particular application in the actual exam. You are told which application has been chosen a short while before the exam. The advice about the longer type of project might help you in planning your essay. This sort of project is fairly common and we will look at it in detail.

Advice about project work

Most examination boards require a project to be done about an application of computing. Since the marks can represent a large part of the examination marks, it can be worth spending some time on it.

What project do I choose?

This is the first problem you will encounter (Figure 31.9). Generally, it is best to choose a topic which you are most interested in. Also, the particular application you choose must be one that you can find a lot of information about. This is often quite difficult to

Figure 31.9 *Choose your project carefully*

```
The use of computers in banking
The social effects of computers
The microprocessor revolution
Computers and disabled people
The military uses of computers
Information from your armchair
(Prestel, Ceefax and Oracle)
Wordprocessing
Computer dating
Computers in libraries
Careers in computing
The growth of home computers
A comparison of home computers
Computers in medicine
The cashless society
The electronic office
Computers in the manufacturing industry
Computers and crime
The use of computers in supermarkets
Theatre and concert booking systems
The Electricity Board and computers
Computers in the future
New hardware developments
Computers in education
(computer assisted learning)
Computers in the police
Computerized robots
The history of computers
Computers in the retail trade
Computers in local government
Computer aided design
Travel agents and computers
Airlines and computers
Computers: unemployment or employment?
Computers and privacy
Computers in the Third World
Computers in insurance companies
Artificial intelligence
The silicon chip
Electronic mail
Computers in a sales office
```

Figure 31.10 *Suggestions for projects*

obtain. If you find that you cannot find sufficient material for one topic, then you should devise another without wasting too much time.

Some of the best topics are based on particular companies and how they use their computers. Obviously, printed material on this topic would be difficult to obtain, but you could use the help of a relative or friend who works with computers at a company, to explain to you how the computer system works and what it does. If you decide on such a topic, you should try to arrange to go to see the computer installation, and take a tape recorder, sketch pad and camera.

When doing your project try to get all the information together before you start, and divide your project into chapters. Once you have done this, you can then divide the chapters into sub-headings. Try to make the title of your topic as broad as possible (Figure 31.10).

How the marks are allocated

A general marking scheme is shown in Figure 31.11. Most marking schemes give marks under these headings. When you are doing your project, you should keep referring back to the marking scheme to make sure that you have included in your project all the points that you get marks for. If, for instance, there is a mark for an index, then if you don't include one you can't expect any marks in this column.

Where do I get the information from?

This is your first problem. You must use all the sources of information that you can think of. The first obvious place to look is the school and local libraries. Then you can look at the larger city libraries. In the libraries, you will find text books on computer studies which can be very useful. You can also send for information from various companies or organizations.

Now we will look at some of the places you can look for the information in more detail.

Public and school libraries

You will find the public library more use because it has a much wider range of periodicals, newspapers and books. Don't forget that the librarians are there

INDEX	Chapter numbers. Page numbers.	Small summary of headings in each chapter.
LAYOUT	The way in which all the information is put together. The use of headings, sub-headings and diagrams.	A logical approach to the chapters is required and not just a string of unrelated facts joined together.
LEGIBILITY	Neatness. Clarity.	How neatly and clearly it has been written.
SOURCE REFERENCES	Publications. Correspondence. Important note: The project should be written in your own words, not just copied from lots of different articles. Styles of writing differ and the examiner would realize that you had copied it.	Always say where you gained your information. You could enclose a list of magazines, papers, TV programmes, articles etc. that you've used. You could also enclose copies of any letters you sent asking for information and the replies to them.
DIAGRAMS	Photographs Line drawings Cartoons Flowcharts Systems flowcharts	Plenty of diagrams help to break up the writing and can often say a lot more than words alone.
INTRODUCTION	Content. Approach.	This is a brief description of what the project is about and how you have approached it. It's often best to leave this until last.
INDIVIDUALITY	Originality.	If you do a project about a particular company then it is much more likely to be original than if you did one on, say, the Police. This is because the people doing projects on the Police are likely to use exactly the same information. You must make your project your own original work. Don't copy chunks out of books.
METHOD OF SOLUTION	Overall coverage.	This is the way that you have approached the whole project and whether you have have included all the important points. A lot of marks are usually given in this section, since it gives an overall impression of the project.
USE OF RESOURCES	Research. Correspondence.	This is a measure of how well you have researched the project. If you have sent lots of letters, have lots of source references and diagrams, then you will get a good mark in this section.
DIFFICULTY	Use of information available.	Some projects are much more difficult to do than others. The hardest projects take a lot more research and understanding. Topics about individual companies tend to be difficult. Topics about the police, supermarkets and banks are more straightforward.
SEQUENCE OF IDEAS	Logic. Development.	Your topic should consist of a series of chapters in a logical order. If you plan your project before starting then you will find it much easier to build up the sequence of ideas
CONCLUSION	Inferences. Problems.	Here you should write about what you learnt from the project and any difficulties you encountered.

Figure 31.11

to help you find things out, so don't be afraid to go and tell them what you are looking for.

Here are some of the places to look in your local library (Figure 31.12).

Newspapers and periodicals section

Newspapers do contain sections about computers regularly. The trouble is that you would need to look at them all every day. It is better to approach friends and relatives and tell them what you are doing and ask them to look out for any relevant information and to cut it out for you.

The following newspapers and magazines could be more useful:

Financial Times	often has a complete section on computer applications.
Computer Weekly	is a newspaper specifically for the computer industry.
Office Equipment News	is very good for addresses for getting literature on small business computers and wordprocessors.
New Scientist and *Scientific American*	both occasionally have very good articles on computer applications.

More and more computer magazines are coming on the market. Have a look at all of them to see if they are any use.

N.B. Some of the periodicals are monthly and the newspapers are daily. Libraries do not always throw these out and you can often obtain them going back over a considerable period of time. It would be worth ploughing through them. You will probably need to ask at the reference library for them.

Figure 31.12 *You may find the information you need in the library*

Books

The trouble with some computer books that you find in the library is that they can be out of date. Because of the popularity of computers, it is likely that the most up-to-date books will be out on loan. Have a look at the index (or ask the librarian) to find out what books they have, and try to order them.

Television and radio programmes

Tommorow's World and *Horizon* are two popular television programmes that are worth watching for information. Keep a note pad handy and jot down any points. If you look at the outline of *Horizon* and find it is on a topic such as robots, try to get someone to record it for you.

There are many computer programmes and Open University programmes which will be of use. Unfortunately, it is not always possible to find out the programme contents beforehand. Try to have a look at the *Radio* or *TV Times* each week since they give much more detailed outlines of the programmes than the newspapers do.

Relatives, neighbours and friends

If you know anyone who works in the computer department of a company then it would be a good idea to do a project about how that company uses computers. Try to arrange to visit the company to see the computer system. Go with a tape recorder, notepad and, if possible, a camera. Record conversations with people, sketch any important diagrams and take photographs of the computer systems. You may need to make several visits before you have enough information. Although the work involved in a project of this type is much greater than for others, you will gain more marks. The highest marks are usually awarded to projects of this type.

If you do not intend doing a project about an individual company or organization, you can still ask relatives, neighbours and friends to help you. Since people all read different magazines and newspapers you could ask them to look out for any information on the topic you have chosen.

Writing letters to companies and organizations

One very good way of obtaining further information on computing applications is to write to the companies and organizations which manufacture or use the computers. Stick to the larger companies that are more publicity conscious. If you are interested in smaller computer systems, then you will find the names and addresses of companies who manufacture them in the popular computing magazines. If you decide to contact a smaller organization to ask how their computer systems work, enclose a stamped, addressed envelope.

Don't forget to include copies of the letters you have sent and the replies received in your project. It shows the examiner the work that you have put in.

When writing letters for information, always mention the school that you attend, what project you are doing and the sort of information that you are looking for.

Figure 31.13 shows a typical letter asking for information.

```
                                        J Smith,
                                        25 Any Lane,
                                        Anytown,
                                        ANY 1OQ

                                        12 November 1985


Dear Sir,

I am a pupil at Anytown Comprehensive School and will
be taking my O level (or CSE) examinations next year.
One of the subjects I am taking is Computer Studies.
Part of the examination mark comes from a project on an
application of computing.

My chosen project is on Wordprocessors. As your company
is involved in the manufacture of these machines, I
thought that I would approach you for any brochures,
leaflets, etc. which could help me in my project. I
would be most grateful if you could send me as much
information as you can spare on Wordprocessors.

Thanking you in anticipation.

Yours faithfully,


John Smith


John Smith
```

Figure 31.13   *A letter to a manufacturer can be useful*

32
Careers in computing

After taking computer studies, you may decide that you would like to work with computers when you leave school. If you have a qualification in computer studies then this will help you but the main qualifications, as in most jobs, are English and Maths. Companies look for people with a good, all round education rather than people who are just good at computer studies. Large companies and organizations have large computer departments where a variety of specialist staff work. Smaller companies do not employ specialist staff. They might just have a secretary who uses a wordprocessor.

Let's now look at some of the jobs and the relevant qualifications you would need.

Data control clerk

This is the person who sorts out all the data before it is put into the computer. He liases between the clerical workers and the people who actually type in the data.

Data preparation operators

These people operate the input devices. Usually the system will use key-to-disk and this will involve typing information via the keyboard onto a VDU to be stored eventually on disk. In small organizations they can also be involved in data control as well as computer operating.

Computer operators

Computer operators work with the computer hardware and software in the computer room. They load tapes and disks and check to see that the correct jobs are being processed. In large companies or organizations, the operators may work in shifts.

Qualifications for data control, preparation and operating staff

To do these jobs you need basic qualifications such as 16+, CSEs or O levels. Computer studies qualifications should help you but qualifications in English and Maths are more important. Above all, you must have an aptitude for working with computers. Usually, when you apply for a job you will be asked to take an aptitude test. This tests your ability to solve problems logically. You will be working as a team with others, so the ability to get on with other people is important. To operate a VDU and keyboard, which would be on a computer or wordprocessor, typing skills would be important.

Promotion prospects

Once you have done these jobs for a few years you might want to progress further. Two higher jobs are Shift Supervisor and Operations Manager. These jobs require managerial skills as well as clerical skills.

It is possible for computer operators to move into programming or systems analysis by gaining extra qualifications. It is much harder for control and preparation staff to move into these areas because their qualifications are not usually as good as the operators'.

Programmers and systems analysts

Very good educational qualifications are needed for these positions. A levels or a qualification from a technical college such as BTEC are usually needed along with the usual range of O level, CSE, or 16+ subjects. Lots of programmers and systems analysts are graduates. These are quite highly paid jobs and if you want to do them your aim should be to get as many high grade qualifications as you can.

Designing, making and installing computers

These jobs require qualifications in electronics. Again they are well paid jobs and you will need good qualifications from school as well as technical qualifications obtained from colleges, polytechnics or universities.

Courses in computer studies

Competition for vacancies in computing is intense. There are not many jobs for school leavers. You may decide that you would like to gain more qualifications to improve your chances. Colleges offer all sorts of courses in computing such as City and Guilds, BTEC, A levels and British Computer Society exams. Try to find out about these courses from your local careers office. Sometimes your local library will have details. If your qualifications are not too good you may prefer to do a practical course. Again, ask at your careers office or see your careers teacher at school.

Glossary

A

Access   To obtain data from the computer. This may be stored inside the CPU or on a backing store.

Access time   Time taken to get the required data after being given the instructions.

Accumulator   Special location used to store the answer to a calculation when doing some arithmetic.

Acoustic coupler   Device that allows data to be transmitted over telephone circuits without making an electrical connection to the line.

Address   Number for the place where something is stored in a computer's memory.

ALGOL   High-level programming language. It stands for ALGOrithmic Language.

Alphanumeric   Letters of the alphabet A to Z and the numbers 0 to 9.

Analogue computer   Computer that works on data represented by some continuous physical quantity such as current.

Analogue to digital converter   Converts analogue signals into digital ones in a hybrid computer.

AND gate   Logic gate whose output is 1 when all of its inputs are 1.

Application   What a computer can be used to do.

Arithmetic and logic unit (ALU)   Part of the central processing unit. It performs all the arithmetic and logic operations.

Assembler   Program which converts assembly language into machine code.

Assembly language   Low level language where one programming instruction corresponds to one machine code instruction.

B

Backing store   Memory storage outside the CPU. It is non-volatile. This means it does not disappear when the computer is switched off.

Bar code   Code of lines on the side of goods.

BASIC   High-level programming language. Abbreviation for Beginners All-purpose Symbolic Instruction Code.

Baud   Rate data is transferred along a communication line. Usually 1 bit per second.

Batch processing   Programs are run in batches and data is processed in batches. The operator only needs to load the computer once.

Binary arithmetic   Arithmetic involving base 2 numbers 0 and 1.

Binary coded decimal (BCD)   Coding which uses four binary digits to represent a base 10 number.

Bistable device   Device with only two stable states. A lamp is a bistable device because it can only be either on or off.

Bit   Binary digit 0 or 1.

Block   Set of records, figures or words stored together on backing store which can be transferred as a single unit of data.

Branch   A path from one part of a program to another away from the normal path.

Bubble memory   Type of memory where data is stored by magnetic bubbles in a silicon chip.

Bubble sort   Way of sorting numbers into order with the smallest at the top.

Buffer   Temporary storage location for data as it is transferred from one device to another. It is needed to compensate for the difference in speeds of the various units.

Bug   Mistake or error in a program.

Bureau   Company which does data processing for other companies.

Byte   Set of bits (usually eight) which is used to represent one character.

C

Card reader/punch   The punch punches holes in the cards and the reader reads the data on the cards into the computer.

Ceefax   BBC information service. Ceefax and IBA's version Oracle are known together as Teletext.

Central processing unit (CPU)   The computer's brain. It stores and processes data. It has three parts; the ALU, control unit and memory.

Character   Letters, numbers or symbols that can be used to communicate with the computer. They can be seen on the keys of the computer.

Character code   The binary (base 2) code used to represent characters.

Check digit   Number placed after a string of numbers to check that they have all been correctly input into the computer.

Chip   An integrated circuit etched onto a thin slice of silicon.

COBOL   It is a high-level programming language used mainly for business situations because of its good file handling ability. Abbreviation for COmmon Business Oriented Language.

Compiler   Language which converts a high-level language into a low-level language or machine code.

Computer   Machine used to store and process information.

Computer output on microfilm (COM)   The output from a computer screen is photographed and placed on microfilm. This allows a large amount of information to be held in a small space.

Configuration   The pieces of hardware that are needed to make up a complete computer system.

Continuous stationery   Stationery that is all joined up. It can be pre-printed and is used by a line printer.

Core store   Storage inside the central processing unit. The word 'core' goes back to the days when layers of ferrite core were used for internal storage.

Counter   The step in a program used to count how many times a process is carried out.

Cursor   A square or letter which appears on the VDU to show the position of the display. When you press a character key the cursor moves to where it is on the screen.

D

Data   Information in a form the computer can understand.

Data base   Series of files stored in a computer which can be accessed in a variety of different ways.

Data capture   How the computer gets information for processing.

Data preparation   The series of processes that information goes through before it is in a form that the computer can understand.

Data processing   Operations such as collecting, storing, processing and transmitting information.

Debugging   Removing all the errors in a program.

Denary   Base 10 i.e. the numbers we normally use.

Device   Piece of equipment that is part of a computer system.

Digital computer   Computer which works on data represented by numbers. Most ordinary computers are digital.

Direct access memory   *see* RAM

Disk   Storage medium used to hold data. It is a flat circular disk coated with a magnetic material. It can either be flexible (floppy) or hard.

Disk unit   Machine which reads data off disks and transfers it to the computer.

Documentation   The paperwork that accompanies a computer program. It consists of all the instruction manuals and how to detect errors. It also explains how the program works.

Document reader   Input device used to read information in documents. It can read shaded areas in documents and ticks in yes/no boxes.

DOS (Disk Operating System)   Program which controls the operation of the disk drive.

Dot matrix printer   Line printer which produces characters made up of a series of very small dots.

Dry run   Writing down the results of each step of a program manually to check that the program is correct.

E

Edit   Changing and improving a computer program

Electronic Fund Transfer (EFT)   Transferring booking details along telephone wires and via satellites around the world to transfer money very quickly.

Electronic mail   Process in which letters are sent by a computer along telephone lines to come up on a VDU at their destination.

Electrostatic printer   This type of printer electrically charges the paper and then forms dust particles in the air, to the areas to form the print.

Even parity   When the total number of 1s in a byte or a word is 1.

Exchangeable disk pack   Pack containing a magnetic disk which can be removed from the disk drive.

Executive program   Program which organizes the running of the CPU.

F

Feasibility study   Study carried out by experts before a computer is bought to see what type of computer system is needed.

Ferrite core   Used to store information in the memory of the older type of computers. They have now been replaced by the silicon chip.

Field checks   Checks performed by the computer to see if the data is the right type. The checks would detect numbers where letters should be and vice versa.

File   Collection of related data. It is in a certain order so that a particular item can be found quickly.

File librarian   Person who looks after all the magnetic tapes and disks in a computer department.

Floppy disk   Flexible piece of plastic coated with a magnetic material which is used to store data.

Flow charts (diagrams)   Diagram used to break down a task into smaller parts.

FORTRAN   High-level language used mainly in scientific applications. Abbreviation for FORmula TRANslation.

Full adder   Logic circuit which adds together two input bits and a carry bit to produce a sum and a carry output.

G

Gate   Logic element which acts a bit like a switch.

Generation of files   Every time a file is updated, a new generation of the file is produced.

GIGO   Abbreviation for Garbage In Garbage Out. It means that if you put rubbish into the computer then you get rubbish out.

Graphical display unit   This is a VDU on which graphs or drawings can be displayed, sometimes in colour.

Graph plotter   Printer which enables pictures and graphs drawn on a graphical display unit to be output onto paper.

H

Half adder   Set of gates used to add two binary digits to give the sum and carry digit.

Hard copy   Printed output from a computer which can be taken away and studied.

Hardware   The components that make up a computer system.

Hash total   The computer adds all the numbers in a code together so that if the number is input again into the computer it can check the total.

Hexadecimal   Base 16.

High-level language   Programming language where each instruction corresponds to several machine-code instructions.

High-resolution graphics   Computers which can produce lots of small dots of light (pixels) can produce very detailed graphs and drawings. This is high-resolution graphics.

Housekeeping program   Program that deals with the internal workings of the CPU.

Hybrid computer   Computer in which digital and analogue devices are connected together and the data is passed between them.

I

Immediate access store   Storage in the memory of the CPU.

Information   What we get from a set of data.

Ink-jet printer   Printer that works by spraying ink onto the paper to make up the shapes of characters.

Input device   Device which allows the computer to understand the data it has to process.

Integrated circuit   Solid state circuit in which all the components such as transistors, resistors etc. are formed out of a single piece of semiconductor.

Interpreter   Program that converts a high-level language into machine code. The interpreter is different to a compiler because it translates and instructs and then carries it out. The compiler translates all the instructions before carrying them out.

Invoice   A bill.

K

K   Unit of memory size, 1 K = 1000 bytes

Keyboard   A computer keyboard consists of the standard typewriter keys plus calculator keys and some special keys.

Key-to-disk   A way of inputting data directly into the computer and onto disk using the keyboard.

Kimball tag   Piece of card with holes punched in it which represents a code. When something is bought, the card is removed and can be input into a computer.

L

Language   A computer language is a language that the computer can understand.

Large-scale integration   Integrated circuit with more than 1000 logic elements.

Light pen   Pen which can draw, move and change pictures on a graphical display unit.

Line printer   Printer which can print an entire line in one go.

Log   Record kept manually or by the computer of all the work done in the computer.

Logic circuit   Electronic circuits which can perform logic operations.

Loop   A loop is used when a process needs to be done more than once. It takes the last instruction of a process back to the beginning.

Low-level language   A programming language very similar to the machine language of the computer. Each low-level instruction can be easily converted into a machine-code instruction.

M

Machine code   Language the computer can understand without it being translated. It consists of a series of binary digits.

Magnetic ink character recognition (MICR)   Input device process of reading magnetic ink characters on certain documents such as cheques.

Main frame   CPU of a large computer which has many terminals.

Main store   Memory inside the CPU. It is volatile so the data disappears when the computer is switched off.

Mark sense documents   Documents with spaces for marking in by a pencil. The document reader can transmit the information in these shaded areas into the computer.

Matrix printer   Printer which produces characters made up from a series of dots of ink.

Medium   Name given to the material on which data can be stored, such as magnetic tape, disk etc.

Megabyte   A million bytes.

Merge   When data from two different sources is joined together.

Microfiche   Piece of film about the size of a postcard that contains about 250 pages of microfilm.

Microfilm   Piece of film like a transparency which can contain lots of information. It has to be magnified to be read.

Microprocessor   Chip which represents the complete central processing unit.

Mini computer   Computer in between a mainframe (very large) and a micro computer (very small).

Modem   MODulator/DEModulator. It converts data from the computer into tones which can be passed along a telephone line.

Monitor   Special type of television which produces a clearer, defined picture when used with a computer.

Multi-access system   System which allows many different users to gain access to the computer. Each user appears to have sole access because of the speed of the CPU although in actual fact the time is being shared amongst the users.

Multiplexer   Device which switches the computer between the various users to allow them a share of the CPU time.

Multiprogramming   Sharing the time and memory of a CPU amongst several programs.

N

NAND gate   Logic gate which consists of an AND joined to a NOT gate.

NOR gate   A NOT and an OR gate joined together.

NOT gate   This gate has only one input and output. The output is always the opposite of the input.

Numeric   This refers to the denary (base 10) numbers.

O

Object program   Program in machine language that is produced by a compiler or assembler from a source program in a high-level or assembly language.

Octal   Base 8.

On/off-line   When a device is connected to the CPU, it is said to be on-line. Off-line means that the device is not in direct communication with the CPU.

Operating system   Program or a series of programs supervising the running of other programs. It co-ordinates the running of all the peripheral units.

Optical character reader   Peripheral input device which can read characters written on a specially designed form.

Optical mark reader   Reader that can detect marks on a piece of paper. Shaded areas are detected and the computer can understand the information contained in them.

Oracle   IBA's information service. With Ceefax it makes up the Teletext service.

OR gate   An OR gate is a logic gate with two or more inputs and only one output. As long as one or more of the inputs are 1, then the output will be 1.

Output   The result of data processing.

P

Packing density   The number of characters that you can store on a magnetic tape or disk.

Paper tape   An old type of input medium. Data was coded by punching holes in the tape.

Parity bit   Bit placed at the end of a byte for checking purposes.

Password   Word that needs to be typed into the computer to gain access to the data.

Peripheral   Device connected to the CPU outside the computer.

Point of sale (POS)   Computerized till placed where the usual check out till can be found in supermarkets.

Prestel   British Telecoms' viewdata service. It is a two-way system and people can communicate with the **Prestel** computer via a keypad and a telephone.

Process   What is done to the data by the computer after it has been input.

Program   Series of instructions written in a form that the computer can understand.

Programmable read only memory (PROM)   Chip with a non-volatile memory. Using a special hardware device the PROM can be programmed.

Programmer   Person who writes computer programs.

R

Random access memory (RAM)   Memory where you don't have to go through other records to find the one you want.

Range check   Data validation technique which checks that the data input into the computer is within a certain range.

Read only memory (ROM) Part of the memory inside the CPU which can be accessed but not altered.

Real time A real-time system accepts data and processes it immediately and reads back its results immediately. The results have a direct affect on the next set of available data.

Remote access Access gained to the computer from a terminal at a remote site away from the CPU.

S

Scramble Mix up information before passing it down telephone lines to stop people interfering with the data.

Sector Portion of a magnetic disk or drum.

Semi-conductor Material such as silicon or germanium which has peculiar electrical properties. Transistors and chips are made from semi-conductor materials.

Sequential file File where records are kept in order.

Serial access Accessing data in sequence. The time it takes to locate an item depends on its position.

Sign bit Bit placed at the end of a binary number to show what sign the number is. 0 is positive and 1 is negative.

Software Programs that enable the hardware to do a useful job.

Sort Arranging data into some sort of order for example, alphabetic or numeric.

Source documents Original documents where the data comes from.

Source language Language in which the programmer writes his program. The computer can't understand it without first changing it to machine code.

Standard form How the computer stores very large and very small numbers.

Systems Hardware and software working together to do a job.

Systems analyst Person who decides what the computer should be used for and how it should be done.

T

Teleprinter Printer connected to a telephone line which can be used to send and receive messages.

Teletext Information service offered by IBA and BBC. They are referred to together as Teletext.

Telex System in which people can communicate with each other using a teleprinter and the telephone lines.

Terminal Device which provides a link between the person using the computer and the CPU. It allows the input and output of data.

Time share Where two or more users use the computer at the same time. They appear to have sole use of the computer but in fact the computer is sharing its time between them but, because it works so quickly they don't notice it.

Track Circular printer used for storing data on a magnetic disk or drum. It can also be a row of holes on a punched paper tape.

Transaction A piece of business being performed e.g. payments of a cheque, receiving an order etc.

Transaction file File on which all the transactions in a certain period of time are kept. It is used to update a master file.

Truth table Table which shows the input and output of a logic circuit.

Two's complement A way of holding negative numbers using binary notation. The most significant bit is made negative.

U

Unit A device.

Update Change the details on a master file which have become out of date because a transaction has been made. The transaction file is used to update the master file.

User Person who uses the computer.

Utility program Program stored permanently by the computer to be accessed by other programs when needed.

V

Validate This is a check written into the computer program to see if the data input is valid i.e. allowed.

Verifier Machine used to check punched words to see if they are correct. The data is retyped and then checked with the data on the card before being put into the computer. With key-to-disk systems the information is keyed in twice.

Verify Check that the puched cards or tape have been punched correctly.

Visual display unit (VDU) Screen like a television set used to display the output from the computer.

Volatile memory Memory such as RAM which disappears when the computer is switched off.

W

Wafer Thin slice of silicon which can be used to make an integrated circuit or chip.

Word Group of bits which the CPU treats as a single unit.

Wordprocessor Computer which can store, correct, and read written information.

Work station This is a bit like the old desk and filing cabinet except it is a VDU and a keyboard which can do all the office jobs electronically.

Write permit ring This is a ring attached to a magnetic tape. When it is removed it is impossible to erase the information contained on the tape.

Index

A

Abacus **172**
Accessing a record **117**
Accidental erasure **151**
Accumulator **77**
Acoustic coupler **51, 52**
Adders **77**
ALGOL (algorithmic language) **125**
Alphanumeric **27**
Analogue **28**
Analogue control **21**
Analogue to digital converter (ADC) **21, 57**
Analytical engine **174**
Ancestral file system **152**
AND gate **80**
Application packages **131**
Applications programmer **135**
Applications packages **131**
Arithmetic and logic unit (ALU) **59**
ASCC (automatic sequence controlled calculator) **175**
Assemblers **128**
Assembly language **128**
Automated teller machine systems (ATMS) **189**
Automatic machines **18, 19**
Automatic processing **18**
Automaton **23**

B

Babbage, Charles **174**
Backing store **107, 178**
Backing store, comparison of **111**
Banking **188**
Bar code reader **99**
Bar codes **39, 99, 195**
BASIC (beginners all purpose instruction code) **125**
Batch processing **49**
Batch totals **46**
Binary addition **70**
Binary arithmetic **70**
Binary numbers **65**
Binary subtraction **70**
Bistable systems **63**
Bits **64, 116**
Body scanner **186**
Boolean expression **91**
Boole, George **91**
Bubble memory **112**
Buffer **59, 77**
Byte **76**

C

Card reader **97**
Careers in computing **213**

C (continued)

Car manufacture **25**
Cash card **40**
Cash dispensers **189**
Cashless society **191**
Cassettes **110**
Ceefax **160**
Census (US) **176**
Central processing unit (CPU) **59**
Chain printer **100**
Character codes **76**
Character printer **99, 100**
Character reader **97**
Characters **76, 116**
Check digits **45**
Cheque clearing **38, 49**
Chip **79, 178**
COBOL (common business orientated language) **125**
Coded information **27**
Codes **150**
Coding negative numbers **71**
Colossus **177**
Compilers **128**
Complete control systems **19**
Computer **10**
Computer aided design **102**
Computer control **28**
Computer design **138**
Computer engineers **140**
Computer languages **125**
Computer logic **79**
Computer operator **135**
Computer output on microfilm/microfiche (COM) **56**
Computers in dentistry **187**
Computers in farming **187**
Computers in libraries **192**
Computers in medicine **185**
Computers in supermarkets **194**
Computer system design **145**
Console **136**
Control programs **128**
Construction of computers **138**
Continuous stationery **55**
Control unit **59**
Core storage **178**
Credit cards **191**
Crime **168**

D

Daisy wheel printer **100**
Damage (deliberate and accidental) **150**
Data capture **38**
Data, division of **116**
Data errors **44**
Data preparation operator **136**
Data processing manager **136**
Data sources **26**
Data type (field) check **45**
Debugging **134**
Denary numbers **64**
Dentistry, computers in **187**

Difference Engine **174**
Digital **28**
Digital control **20**
Digital control systems **20**
Direct access **108**
Direct data capture **38**
Directory **109**
Diskettes **108, 109**
Disk operating system **109**
Disk packs **109**
Documentation **132, 134, 146**
Document reader **97**
Dot matrix printer **100**
Drum plotter **102**
Drum printer **99**
Dry run **33**
DVLC (driver and vehicle licensing centre) **183**

E
EDSAC (electronic delay storage automatic computer) **177**
Electronic fund transfer (EFT) **189**
Electronic mail **161**
Encoding **191**
ENIAC (electronic numerical integrator and calculator) **177**
Erasable programmable read only memory (EPROM) **60**
Erasure **151**
Exam, preparing for **206**
Exchangeable disk packs **109**
Exchange of information **167**
Executive (supervisor) program **49, 128**

F
Farming, computers in **187**
Feasibility study **145**
Feedback loop **28, 57**
Field checks **45**
Fields **116**
Files **116, 146**
Fixed disks **109**
Flat-bed plotter **102**
Floppy disk drive **110**
Floppy disks **108, 109**
Flowcharts **30**
Form design **27**
FORTRAN (formula translation) **125**

G
Gates **79**
Gateway **160**
Generations of computers **178**
Generations of files **119**
GIGO (garbage in, garbage out) **11**
Going live **147**
Grandfather-father-son principle **119**
Graphical display unit **102**
Graph plotter **102**

H
Half adder **77**
Hard copy **54**
Hard disk **110**
Hardware **10**
Hash totals **46**
Hexadecimal numbers **66**
High level languages **125, 178**
Hollerith, Hermann **176**
Homelink **159**

I
Implementation **147**
Indirect data capture **38**
Information **10**
Ink jet printer **101**
Input, process and output **12**
Instruction manuals **146**
Integrated circuit **59, 80**
Interpreters **128**
ISBN (international standard book number) **46**

J
Jacquard, Joseph **174**

K
Keyboard **96**
Key fields **116**
Key-to-disk **38**
Kimball tags **197**

L
Large scale integrated circuit (LSI) **60**
Laser printer **101**
Laser scanner **195**
Leibniz's calculating machine **172**
Librarian **136**
Light pen **102, 195**
Line printer **99**
Logarithms **172**
Logic diagrams **80**
Logic element **80**
Loom (card controlled) **174**
Lovelace, Countess of **175**
Low level languages **125**
Lyons Electronic Office (LEO) **177**

M
Machine code **126**
Machine orientated **125**
Magnetic cartridges **111**
Magnetic disk **107**
Magnetic disk drive unit **109**
Magnetic encoding **40**
Magnetic ink character recognition (MICR) **38, 191**
Magnetic tags **197**

Magnetic tape 107
Main memory 59
Main store 107
Manual processing 15
Mark reader 97
Mark sensing 39, 97
Master file 118
Medical applications 185
Medium 107
Memory 12
Merging 118
Meter reading sheets 26
MICR 38, 191
Microfiche 55, 112
Microfilm 55, 112
Microprocessor 8, 61, 80
MIRIAM 184
Modem 51, 52, 158
Modular construction 178
Module 135
Monitoring the live system 148
Multi-access 50
Multiple choice answer sheets 39
Multiplexer 50
Multiprogramming 49
Multitasking 50

N
NAND gate 82
Napier's Bones 172
NOR gate 83
NOT gate 82
Numeric 27

O
Object program 128
OCR 39, 98
Octal 65
Operating systems 49
Operations manager 137
Operation table 80
Operators console 136
Optical character recognition (OCR) 39, 98
Optical mark recognition (OMR) 97
Oracle 160
Organization of data 115
OR gate 81
Overflow bit 72

P
Pantograph punch 176
Paper tape reader 97
Parallel running 147
Parity check 77
Pascal, Blaise 172
Passwords 150
Patient records 185
Payroll 15, 16

Peripheral devices 96
Pilot running 148
PIN (personal identification number) 191
Place values 64
Point of sale terminal (POS) 195
Police National Computer (PNC) 183
Port 20
Pre-printed stationery 54
Prestel 158
Printers 99
Privacy 166, 194
Problem oriented 125
Procedures 146
Program libraries 132
Programmable read only memory (PROM) 60
Programmer 134
Project approval 145
Project work 208
Pulse train 79
Punched tape reader 97

Q
Questionnaires 27

R
Random access medium 108
Random access memory (RAM) 60
Range checks 45
Read only memory (ROM) 60
Read/write heads 109
Real time 50
Records 116
Registers 77
Remote access 50
Remote job entry 50
Research 137
Revision checklist 204
Revision techniques 203
Robotics 23

S
Sales and marketing of computers 138
Sales master file 120
Sales transaction file 120
Scrambling of information 191
Second generation of computers 178
Sectors 108
Security 150
Semiconductors 59
Sensors 28
Sequential access 107
Serial access 107
Sign and magnitude coding 71
Sign bit 71
Social implications 163
Software 10
Software development by user 132
Software house 132

Sorting **117**
Source documents **26**
Source program **128**
Standard forms **55**
Stock control **103, 196**
Storage location **77**
Stored program **18**
Supervisor (executive) program **49, 128**
SWIFT (society for worldwide inter-bank financial
telecommunications) **190**
Systems analyst **134**
Systems flowcharts **121**
Systems programmer **135**
Systems software **128**

T

Tape unit **107**
Telecom gold **161**
Teletext **160**
Theatre/concert booking system **121**
Third generation of computers **178**
Timesharing **50**
Trade unions **165**
Traffic control **185**
Training **146**
Transaction file **118**
Transcription errors **44**
Translation software **128**
Truth table **80**
Two's complement coding **71**

U

Unemployment and computers **23, 164**
UNIVAC **177**
Updating **119**
Users **134**
Utility programs **132**

V

Validation **45**
Valves **177**
Verification **45**
Viewdata (Prestel) **158**
Visual display unit (VDU) **57**
Volatile/non-volatile memory **60**
Von-Neumann Report **177**

W

Wand reader **41, 99**
Weather forecasting **188**
Weighted modules **46**
Word **79**
Word length **79**
Wordprocessing **154, 165**